The
Unwritten
Laws of Life

Unofficial Rules as Handed
Down by Murphy and Other Sages

by

Hugh Rawson

Published in Great Britain in 2008 by Carbolic Smoke Ball Co.

Carbolic Smoke Ball Co.
Silverbeck
Jumps Road
Churt
Farnham
GU10 2HL

Tel. +44 (0)1252 795951
www.lawsoflife.co.uk
www.carbolicsmokeball.com

British Library Cataloguing in Publication Data
A CIP record for this book can be obtained from the British Library.

ISBN 978-0-9556557-1-5

Printed by the MPG Books Group in the UK

Introduction

Our lives are circumscribed by edicts and enactments, rules and regulations, declarations and proclamations. Typically, they are printed in miniscule type and presented in seemingly endless sections and subsections, causing the eyes gradually to glaze over and the mind to become numb. Such is the rule of law – and of lawyers, bureaucrats, administrators, apparatchiks, and officialdom generally.

For all their wealth of detail, however, these written codes are of limited value in negotiating one's way through life. The most basic ones tend to be cast in negative terms: Thou shalt not kill; thou shalt not covet thy neighbour's wife (nor his maid, nor his ox, not his flashy new car); thou shalt not conspire to fix prices; thou shalt not publish blatant lies about anyone (unless he or she is a public figure, in which case you have a good chance of getting away with it). And so on.

Laws of this sort tell you what *not* to do, but they are not much help in telling you what *to do*. For positive guidance, for an understanding of how life really works, as opposed to how legislators and other officials say it should work, we must look to the realm of unwritten law. This realm consists of the adages, maxims, morals, observations, precepts, principles, proverbs, and other sayings that have been handed down over the years by humanity's unelected legislators, and which, taken together, constitute the collective wisdom of humankind.

Many of this book's some five hundred laws (plus many more amendments and corollaries) come from certifiably deep thinkers, such as Lord Acton ("Power tends to corrupt and absolute power corrupts absolutely"); Heraclitus ("You can't step twice into the same river, for other waters are forever flowing on to you"); George Santayana ("Those who cannot remember the past are condemned to repeat it"); and Ludwig Wittgenstein ("Of that which nothing is known, nothing can be said"). Others emanate from such lesser known savants as Lady Nancy Astor ("All women marry beneath them" – and she herself was married to a viscount); the nineteenth century humorist Josh Billings ("The wheel that squeaks the loudest is the one that gets the grease"); science fiction writer Theodore Sturgeon ("Ninety percent of everything is crud"); and the actor Peter Ustinov ("Those who rise to executive positions lack the qualifications for anything lower").

In conformance with Robert (*Anatomy of Melancholy*) Burton's Rule ("No rule is so general, which admits not some exception"), some laws from fictitious individuals also are included here. Among them: Anthony's Law of the Workshop ("Any tool, when dropped, will roll to the least accessible corner"); Finagle's Law ("If anything can go wrong with an experiment, it will"); Gunter's Laws of Air Travel (the first of which is "When you are served a meal aboard an aircraft, the aircraft will encounter turbulence"); and Zimmerman's Law of Complaints ("Nobody notices when things go right").

Gunter's Laws may possibly derive in some roundabout way from the name of the English mathematician and inventor Edmund Gunter, though he lived and worked about three hundred years before the Wright brothers got off the ground. The existence of Anthony, Finagle, and Zimmerman is more tenuous, however. Lacking complete names and without further details of their lives, it seems safe to assume that they are purely mythical figures, created by popular demand, so to speak, as pegs for hanging laws upon.

A number of other laws, though associated with the names of bona fide individuals, actually are distillations of essentially anonymous, proverbial wisdom. Thus, many of Aesop's Adages, such as "Don't count your chickens before they hatch" and "Familiarity breeds contempt," probably had been around for quite some time before Aesop composed his *Fables* in the sixth century B.C. The same applies to the rules attributed to such later lawgivers as the English author (and spy) Aphra Behn ("Here today, gone tomorrow"), the Dutch scholar Erasmus ("The grass is always greener on the other side of the fence"), and the German philosopher and socialist Karl Marx, who allowed, somewhat surprisingly for a non-religious person, that "The road to hell is paved with good intentions."

Unwritten laws come in two basic varieties: descriptive and prescriptive. The first category consists of those laws that have been devised in an effort to make sense out of the apparent contradictions, difficulties, and vicissitudes of life as we know it. Best known of these is Murphy's Law ("If anything can go wrong, it will"). But Murphy – Captain Edward A. Murphy Jr., with all flags flying – was by no means the first to sense the inevitability of mischance in human affairs. More than a hundred years before Captain Murphy's lament, occasioned by the ineptness of technicians at Edwards Air Force Base in California, Benjamin Disraeli, a successful novelist before becoming an even more successful politician, noted in the story of *Henrietta Temple* (1837), "What we anticipate seldom occurs; what we least expected generally happens." And in the eighteenth century, Robert Burns came close to the essence of Murphy's Law, observing in 'To a Mouse' (1785) that "The best-laid schemes of mice and men Gang aft agley" – "often go wrong," in English as opposed to Scottish dialect.

Other examples of descriptive laws include Woody Allen's Law ("Eighty percent of success is showing up"); Ettore's Law of Lines ("The other line moves faster"); Fetridge's Law ("Important things that are supposed to happen do not happen, especially when people are looking"); John F. Kennedy's Law ("Life is unfair"); Joseph de Maistre's Law ("Every nation has the government it deserves"); and the so-called Law of Buttered Toast, more properly known as Payn's Law, after James Payn, who described it in verse as far back as 1884:

> *I've never had a piece of toast*
> *Particularly long and wide*
> *But fell upon the sanded floor*
> *And always on the butter side*

Many descriptive laws have deep scientific and philosophical roots. Thus, economist Milton Friedman's observation that "There is no such thing as a free lunch" is the counterpart in his field of the physical laws of conservation of energy and matter, and of the equivalence of action and reaction. Or, as Ben Franklin put it in his *Almanack* for 1745: "There are no gains without pains."

Another profound statement of this sort is Spencer's Law (after Herbert Spencer, the nineteenth-century philosopher and social theorist): "Every cause has more than one effect." Translated into personal terms, this becomes, as posited by biologist Garrett Hardin's Law, "You can never do merely one thing." And when the chains of causes and their multiple effects are considered in all their unfathomable complexity, it is apparent, in the words of the naturalist John Muir, that "Whenever we try to pick out anything by itself, we find it hitched to everything else in the universe."

Laws of the second, prescriptive sort serve as guides for conduct in daily life. Examples of this type include Algren's Laws ("Never eat in a place called Mom's. Never play cards with a man named Doc. Never lie down with a woman who's got more troubles than you."); Boren's Guidelines for Bureaucrats ("When in charge, ponder; when in trouble, delegate; when in doubt, mumble"); Conran's Law of Cooking ("Life is too short to stuff a mushroom"); Hoyle's Rule ("When in doubt, take the trick"); Kerr's Law ("If you can keep your head when all about you are losing theirs, it's just possible that you haven't understood the situation"); and Saki's Second Law ("A little inaccuracy sometimes saves tons of explanation").

Many of the prescriptive laws, like the descriptive ones, also have profound philosophical roots. Thus, Bentham's Law holds that "The greatest happiness of the greatest number is the foundation of morals and principle." Kant's Categorical Imperative instructs us to "Act only on that maxim which you can at the same time wish should become a universal law," and Socrates's Law provides the stark admonition that "The life which is unexamined is not worth living."

The philosophical laws also are of practical help. Ockham's Razor ("Do not assume more causes for any phenomenon than are absolutely necessary to explain it") remains as useful a tool for puzzling out today's problems as it was when William of Ockham devised it in the fourteenth century. Other guides of this type include Sherlock Holmes's First and Second Laws ("Eliminate all other factors, and the one which remains will be the truth" and "It is a capital mistake to theorise before one has data"); Papagiannis's Law ("The absence of evidence is not evidence of absence"); and Sagan's Standard ("Extraordinary claims require extraordinary proof").

Unofficial rules have proliferated especially in business and other bureaucratic settings, and often have far-reaching implications. Thus, Parkinson's Law ("Work expands so as to fill the time available for its completion") manifests itself most obviously in institutional settings but operates on a personal level, too. Professor Parkinson himself demonstrated both cases, citing in the first instance, among other examples, the

Royal Navy, whose complement of admiralty officials rose 78.45 percent from 1914 to 1928 while the number of capital ships declined 67.74 percent. At the same time, the professor pointed out, this law applies equally to the elderly lady of leisure who manages to kill an entire day in writing and sending a postcard – "an hour . . . in finding the postcard, another in hunting spectacles, half an hour in composition, and twenty minutes in deciding whether or not to take an umbrella when going to the mailbox in the next street."

On the other hand, Laurence J. Peter – one of the few modern lawgivers whose name can be mentioned in the same breath as that of Professor Parkinson and Captain Murphy – defined the Peter Principle exclusively in terms of bureaucratic situations ("In a hierarchy every employee tends to rise to his level of incompetence"). The same is true of Imhoff's Law ("The organization of any bureaucracy is very much like a septic tank. The really big chunks always rise to the top") and of the various laws of meetings, such as Hendrickson's Law ("If you have enough meetings over a long enough period of time, the meetings become more important than the problem the meetings were intended to solve") and Kirkland's Law ("The usefulness of any meeting is inversely proportional to the size of the group").

Other activities that have inspired rich collections of laws – again, frequently with applications extending far beyond the areas in which they arose – include economics, the law, philosophy, politics, psychology, and sports. This, the principle embodied in Gresham's Law ("Bad money drives out good") also applies to such diverse fields as language, where bad words tend to drive out good ones, as any moviegoer knows; the news business, where bad news about crimes and disasters, say, drives out good news; and television, where, as Marvin Kitman has pointed out, "Pure drivel tends to drive ordinary drivel off the TV screen."

By the same token, Senator George Aitken's advice to President Lyndon B. Johnson for getting out of Vietnam ("Claim victory and retreat") is a good solution for extricating oneself from quagmires of all sorts. Meanwhile, Simon Cameron's Rule of Etiquette ("You scratch my back and I'll scratch yours") applies to life generally, not just to the brand of corrupt politics in which he specialised; labor leader Walter Reuther's Law ("If it walks like a duck and quacks like a duck, then it must be a duck") makes a useful test for deciding many questions other than, as in its original context, whether or not someone in the union was an undercover Communist; and Thoreau's Ruling ("Some circumstantial evidence is very strong, as when you find a trout in the milk") is hardly limited to the common nineteenth-century fraud of watering down milk.

The unofficial rules of life differ in form as well as in kind, ranging from simply expressed insights to more complex statements.

Most basic are the straight declarative sentences – forceful pronouncements, issued ex cathedra, so to speak. Typical are Yogi Berra's Law ("The game isn't over until it's over"); Raymond Chandler's Law ("You can't win them all"); and – also from the world of sports, though phrased in all-encompassing terms – Branch Rickey's Law ("Luck is the residue of design").

Not all declarative laws are encapsulated in so few words, of course. Examples of longer ones include Russell Baker's Law of Inanimation ("Inanimate objects are divided scientifically into three major categories – those that don't work, those that break down, and those that get lost") and Aldo Leopold's prescription for land use ("A thing is right when it tends to preserve the integrity, stability, and beauty of the biotic community. It is wrong when it tends otherwise").

At the next level, the lawgiver casts what he or she perceives to be a general truth in the form of advice or a command. Examples here include Samuel Butler's Law ("Spare the rod and spoil the child"); Al Capone's Law ("You can get a lot more done with a kind word and a gun than you can with a kind word alone"); and, a White House parallel to Capone's streetwise wisdom, Teddy Roosevelt's Law ("Speak softly and carry a big stick; you will go far"). Rules of this sort do not necessarily involve an element of coercion, however, as the foregoing examples might suggest. Thus, John McNaughton's Rule gently urges clarity and concise expression: "Any argument worth making in a bureaucracy must be capable of being expressed in a simple declarative sentence that is obviously true once stated."

Another large group of positive laws highlight positive correlations, e.g. Niels Bohr's Law ("The crazier the theory, the more likely it is to be correct"); John Kenneth Galbraith's First Law ("The greater the wealth, the thicker will be the dirt"); Herblock's Law ("If its good, they'll stop making it"); and General Joseph 'Vinegar Joe' Stilwell's Observation, as true in social as in military circles, ("The higher a monkey climbs, the more you can see of its ass").

Exceptionally perceptive people often manage to discern inverse relationships, as in Saul Alinsky's Law ("Those who are most moral are farthest from the problem"); Eddington's Theory ("The number of different hypotheses erected to explain a given biological phenomenon is inversely proportional to available knowledge"); John Kenneth Galbraith's Second Law ("The more underdeveloped the country, the more overdeveloped the women"); and restaurant reviewer Bryan Miller's Law ("The quality of food in a restaurant is in inverse proportion to the number of signed celebrity photographs on the walls").

Finally, and inevitably, we have laws about laws. Some laws

of this sort apply to official statutes. e.g. suffragette Carrie Lane Chapman Catt's Law ("No written law has ever been more binding than unwritten custom supported by popular opinion"); Jean-Jacques Rousseau's Law ("Good laws lead to the making of better ones; bad ones bring about worse"); and New York City police inspector Alexander S. 'Clubber' Williams's Law ("There is more law in the end of a policeman's nightstick than in a decision of the Supreme Court").

Other unofficial laws cover their own kind, among them Harold Faber's First Law ("If there isn't a law, there will be"); Douglas Hofstadter's Law ("It always takes longer than you expect, even if you take into account Hofstadter's Law"); Thomas Babington, Lord Macaulay's Maxim ("Nothing is so useless as a general maxim"); and, a close parallel, Lady Mary Wortley Montagu's Motto ("General notions are generally wrong").

And unwritten laws, like written ones, are not always honoured, alas, even by the purest of heart. This we have on the authority of a certified saint, Augustine, whose Law to End All Laws provides the ultimate legal loophole:

Necessity knows no law.

A

Acton's Law

Power tends to corrupt, and absolute power corrupts absolutely.

Lord Acton (or, more formally, Sir John Emerich Edward Dalberg-Acton, 1st Baron Acton) enunciated this law on April 5th, 1887, in a letter to Bishop Mandell Creighton. A liberal Roman Catholic historian, Acton opposed nationalism and authoritarianism of all sorts. (When the pope declared that the opinions of Catholic writers were subject to the church's authority, he stopped publishing the Roman Catholic monthly that he had been editing while continuing to submit articles elsewhere.) The profound depth of Acton's distrust of authority becomes even clearer when the full text of his law is cited: "Power tends to corrupt and absolute power corrupts absolutely. Great men are almost always bad men, even when they exercise influence and not authority: still more when you superadd the tendency or the certainty of corruption by authority."

Acton was by no means the first to express the essential idea though his lapidary statement of it is the form in which it is best known today. Thus, William Pitt, Earl of Chatham, said in a speech in 1770 about the radical John Wilkes, who had been elected to Parliament but denied his seat: "Unlimited power is apt to corrupt the minds of those who possess it; and this I know, my lords, that where laws end, tyranny begins."

A year later, discussing the same affair, Edmund Burke put it this way: "The greater the power, the more dangerous the abuse." Poets also have chipped in: "Power, like a desolating pestilence, Pollutes whate'er it touches" (Percy Bysshe Shelley, *Queen Mab*, 1813).

In our own time, various amplifications of Acton's Law have been proposed. Among them:

The Stevenson Amendment

Power corrupts, but lack of power corrupts absolutely (Adlai Stevenson, speech, January 1963). Douglass Cater used slightly different wording – "If power corrupts, being out of power corrupts absolutely" – in *Dana: The Irrelevant Man*, 1970).

The Himmelfarb Corollary

Liberty too can corrupt, and absolute liberty can corrupt absolutely (Gertrude Himmelfarb, *On Liberty and Liberalism: The Case of John Stuart Mill*, 1974).

The Tuchman Rider

If power corrupts, weakness in the seat of power, with its constant necessity of deals and bribes and compromising arrangements, corrupts even more (Barbara Tuchman, *Atlantic Monthly*, September, 1970).

The Hitz Corollary to the Tuchman Rider

Absolute secrecy corrupts absolutely (Fred Hitz, interview, *New York Times*, July 30th, 1995). Mr. Hitz was Inspector General of the CIA at the time. 'Nuff said.

Meanwhile, those who have the power may well consider the dangers of corruption to be worth the risk. In the words of Henry Kissinger, when assistant to the present for national security, "Power is the great aphrodisiac" *(New York Times*, January 19th, 1971).

Addison's Law

He who hesitates is lost.

Actually, this is a common misquotation of Joseph Addison's line in *Cato* (1713): "The woman that deliberates is lost." In this context, Bertolt Brecht's corollary to Addison's Law takes some thinking about. From the prologue to *The Good Woman of Setzuan* (1938-40): "It is all right to hesitate if you then go ahead."

Other variations on this theme include "He who hesitates is bossed and usually lost," "He who hesitates is probably right," and "He who hesitates is last." The thought amounts to a touchstone for revealing the different approaches to life of different personalities. Thus, to the flamboyant Mae West is attributed the advice that "He who hesitates is a damn fool," while James Thurber observed more diffidently that "He who hesitates is sometimes saved" ('The Glass in the Field,' in *Fables for Our Time*, 1940). Thurber's thought has been further refined into what is known as the Coward's Creed: "When in doubt don't," a suggestion often made to people contemplating marriage ((Maureen Kim Sing, letter, May, 1991). The underlying idea is proverbial. "The cautious seldom err" is a saying attributed to Confucius (551-479 B.C.).

He (or even she) who hesitates for too long between two objectives or motives can be said to be riding Buridan's Ass. This is a hypothetical donkey which, positioned midway between two equally inviting bundles of hay, couldn't decide which to eat and so starved to death. The ass is named for a medieval French philosopher Jean Buridan. Mr. Long Ears does not actually appear in his writings, however. The creature may have been created by one of Buridan's scholarly opponents as a way of ridiculing his ideas of determinism vs. free will.

Addison's play, by the way, also was the source of the American patriot Nathan Hale's remark before being hanged as a spy by Addison's countrymen: "I only regret that I have but one life to lose for my country." The relevant line in the play, a popular one among colonials on account of its republican message, "What a pity is it that we can die but once to serve our country."

An elegant essayist as well as a government official, Addison also proposed a second law dealing with the female sex in the *Spectator*: "Men who cherish for women the highest respect are seldom popular with them." (See also **Ovid's Observation**.) In this connection, it is worth noting that the author, a shy man by all accounts, did not marry until he was aged forty-four. Three years later he died.

Ade's Law

Anybody can win, unless there happens to be a second entry.

This observation by the Indiana humorist and playwright George Ade is from one of the sketches that he wrote for the Chicago *Record*, then collected in book form as *Fables in Slang* (1899).

Aesop's Adages

Some of the oldest, as well as the wisest, rules for living come from the *Fables of Aesop* (ca 620-560 B.C.), a slave on the Greek island of Samos. Aesop is said to have come from Phrygia in west-central Asia Minor, though the inhabitants of Thrace, Athens, Sardis, and other places also have claimed him as a native son. Aristotle's statement that he conducted a public defence of a Samian demagogue indicates that he eventually was freed, since a slave would not have been permitted to speak in such a forum. Aesop probably didn't commit his tales to writing. We know them from the collections of later Greek and Roman authors, who included other ancient stories as well. Thus, some of 'Aesop's' fables have been traced to Oriental and Egyptian sources. Herewith a few examples of Aesop's wisdom, together with some amplifications and corrections of more recent vintage:

Be content with your lot; one cannot be first in everything ('Juno and the Peacock'). A half a millenium later, the Roman poet Virgil put it this way in his *Eclogues*: "We cannot all do all things."

Don't count your chickens before they are hatched ('The Milkmaid and Her Pail').

Familiarity breeds contempt ('The Fox and the Lion'). Later authorities on human nature also have amended this one. Thus, Mark Twain held that "Familiarity breeds contempt – and children" *(Notebooks),* while Goodman Ace noted that "Familiarity breeds attempt." See also **Bayly's Observation, Cornuel's Observation** and **Midas's Law.**

The gods help them that help themselves ('Hercules and the Waggoner'). This has been repeated with slight variations by others, including Aeschylus ("God loves to help him who strives to help himself") and Ben Franklin ("God helps those who help themselves").

It is thrifty to prepare today for the wants of tomorrow ('The Ant and the Grasshopper'). This message also appears in the Bible: "Go to the ant, thou sluggard; consider her ways, and be wise: Which having no guide, overseer, or ruler, Provideth her meat in the summer, and gathereth her food in the harvest" *(Proverbs 6:6-8).*

Slow and steady wins the race ('The Hare and the Tortoise'). Or as Samuel Johnson phrased it in *Rasselas*: "Great works are performed not by strength, but by endurance."

The smaller the mind, the greater the conceit ('The Gnat and the Bull').

United we stand, divided we fall ('The Four Oxen and the Lion'). Benjamin Franklin embellished this thought when he warned his colleagues at the signing of the Declaration of Independence: "We must, indeed, all hang together or, most assuredly, we shall all hang separately." (This was in reply to John Hancock's comment that "It is too late to pull different ways; the members of the Continental Congress must hang together.") Abraham Lincoln came closer to Aesop's original formulation with "A house divided against itself cannot stand" (speech, June 16th, 1858).

We would often be sorry if our wishes were gratified ('The Old Man and Death'). Oscar Wilde expressed the same thought in *An Ideal Husband:* "When the gods wish to punish us they answer our prayers."

See also **Publilius's Maxims** (no. 559) and **Wilde's First Law.**

Aiken's Solution

Claim victory and retreat.

This principle originally was proposed in a senate speech on October 19th, 1966, by George Aiken (R., Vt.) as a way of enabling the United States to save face while extricating itself from the war in Vietnam. Having become disillusioned with policies he had previously supported, Aiken urged that President Lyndon B. Johnson simply "declare the United States the winner and begin de-escalation." Johnson didn't take this advice, of course (The *New York Times* called the proposal "droll"), but after a great many more people were killed, LBJ's successor, Richard M. Nixon, negotiated a pull-out plan in 1973. Commenting on the 1973 settlement, which seemed likely to lead eventually to a Communist takeover in South Vietnam, Senator Aiken pointed out, "What we got was essentially what I recommended six years ago . . . we said we had won and we got out."

The utility of the Aiken Solution is not limited to military situations. For example: "Not so many days ago, it appeared that the Administration was ready to pursue an 'Aiken solution' to its energy policy problems . . . so little of the Carter energy policy had been enacted that it had become an embarrassment. Insiders and outside observers alike urged making the best of a retreat" *(New York Times,* May 25th, 1978). Then there was the Reverend Jerry Falwell, who officially dismantled his creation, the Moral Majority, in August 1989, saying "Our mission is accomplished." Skeptics thought that a 52 per cent drop in his TV ratings might also have had something to do with Reverend Falwell's decision to fold the Moral Majority's tent.

Nostalgia Department: TV ratings of many televangelists were in a slump at the time, and contributions were down, too. The difficulties of the broadcasting preachers stemmed mainly from scandals involving two of the most prominent ones, the Reverends Jim Bakker and Jimmy Swaggert.

First, Reverend Bakker's PTL ministry (a double abbreviation for Praise The Lord and People That Love) toppled into bankruptcy following the revelation that he had been paying blackmail to a former church secretary with whom he had enjoyed a liaison. Along with this came evidence that the Reverend and his wife Tammy had been shearing their flock rather closely, with their paychecks for the 1984-87 period totaling about $4.8 million.

Then, Reverend Swaggert, who had denounced Reverend Bakker as a "cancer on the body of Christ," was officially defrocked by the Assemblies of God after admitting to an unspecified sin – the admission being prompted by photographs of him at a motel frequented by prostitutes.

And down went the TV ratings.

Algren's Laws

Never eat at a place called Mom's. Never play cards with a man named Doc. And never lie down with a woman who's got more troubles than you.

Nelson Algren (1909-81), *née* Nelson Algren Abraham, tough-guy novelist from Chicago, repeated this credo with slight changes in wording in an essay 'What Every Young Man Should Know', in the novel *A Walk on the Wild Side,* and in many lectures. Mr. Algren did not live up to it, however. He led a complicated, sometimes self-destructive life, often gambling too much. He also had a long-running affair with Simone de Beauvoir. (He managed to confuse the FBI, which was keeping tabs on him because of his left-wing views, by changing his listing in the Chicago telephone directory in 1954 to 'de Beauvoir, Simon'.)

Nor did he invent the credo. H. E. F. Donohue reported in the foreword to *Conversations with Nelson Algren* (1964): "He shunts aside all rules, regulations, and dicta, except for three laws he says a nice old Negro lady once taught him: Never play cards with any man named 'Doc'. Never eat at any place called 'Mom's'. And never, ever, no matter what else you do in your whole life, never sleep with anyone whose troubles are worse than your own."

Even "the nice old Negro lady" may have been a fiction. A friend of Algren's from the 1930s, Dave Peltz, told Ralph Keyes, author of a book about misquotations, *Nice Guys Finish Seventh,* that he himself had devised the rules. Peltz said that he included them in a letter to Algren but attributed them to the black madam of a local whorehouse rather than to himself, knowing that the author would pay more attention to them if he thought they came from someone in the underclasses. "He always felt that people on the outside, people in the underground, were wiser than those of us in the mainstream, who belonged in the middle class," said Mr. Peltz.

A number of variants of Algren's Laws have been recorded, e.g. Steiner's Statements ("Never eat in a restaurant named Mom's, play poker with a man named Doc, or buy a car from a man named Frenchy") and Hartley's Second Law ("Never sleep with anyone crazier than yourself"), both of which were included by John Peers in his compilation of *1,001 Logical Laws, Accurate Axioms, Profound Principles, etc.* (1979). Meanwhile, John Winokur attributed "Never bet with a man named 'One-Iron'" to Tom Sharp in *Friendly Advice* (1990). The advice of Mr. Dooley (Finely Peter Dunn, 1867-1936) also is worth remembering in this connection: "Trust everybody, but cut the cards."

The rhythm of Algren's Laws recalls Shakespeare's advice in King Lear: "Keep thy foot out of brothels, thy hand out of plackets, thy pen from lenders' books, and defy the foul fiend." Here, 'lenders' books' are the account books in which debts are recorded and a 'placket' is the slit at the top of a skirt or petticoat, designed so that the garment could be easily put on and off but, obviously, opened occasionally for other, not-so-innocent purposes.

See also **Reagan's Rule** and **Runyon's Second Law**.

Alinsky's Law

Those who are most moral are farthest from the problem.

Saul David Alinsky spent most of his life (1909-72) on the firing line, confronting social and economic problems directly. He founded the Industrial Areas Foundation to train community organisers in 1939, worked with anti-communist unions in Italy in the 1950s, and promoted programs to enable African-Americans in inner-city ghettos to take charge of their own lives in the 1960s. This law is from his *Rules for Radicals* (1971).

Aesop's corollary. It is easy to be brave from a safe distance ('The Wolf and the Kid').

See also **Erasmus's Law** and **Simmons's Law**.

(Agnes) Allen's Law

Almost anything is easier to get into than out of.

This law, which applies to all aspects of human life, from corsets to Iraq, was formulated by Agnes Rogers Allen, author of *Metropolis, I Remember Distinctly,* and other works, and also the wife of historian Frederick Lewis Allen. She was inspired by her husband and one of his students, Louis Zahner. They had worked out versions of **Murphy's Law**, which they named for themselves. Frederick Lewis Allen's Law was "Everything is more complicated than it looks to most people." Professor Allen was the first to acknowledge the superiority of his wife's contribution, declaring that "at one stroke human wisdom had been advanced to an unprecedented degree" (Paul Dickson, *The Official Rules,* 1978). See also **Zahner's Law.**

Foreshadowing Agnes Allen by some twenty-five hundred years was Aesop, whose fable of 'The Lion, the Fox, and the Beasts' concluded with the moral, "While I see many hoof marks going in, I see none coming out. It is easier to get into the enemy's toils than out again." Allen's Law has two corollaries known as:

Eng's Principle. The easier it is to do, the harder it is to change.

Washlevsky's Rule. Anything is easier to take apart than it is to put together.

Ms. Allen herself also has been credited with the sage advice: "When all else fails, read the instructions" (*Omni,* May, 1979) This has been updated by computer users to 'RTFM,' which stands for "Read the fucking manual." Agnes

Allen also should be remembered for making the suggestion to the Ford Foundation that it provide funds for a special room for writers in the New York Public Library. Her role in establishing this workplace often is forgotten because the room is named after her husband.

See also **Kelly's Law** and **Gilbert's Law of Appearances.**

(Woody) Allen's Observation

Eighty percent of success is showing up.

The 'Allen' here is Allen Stewart Konigsberg, better known as Woody Allen, film maker extraordinaire. The quote was popularised by President George H. W. Bush, who amended it in speeches to "Ninety percent of life is showing up," and by Governor Mario Cuomo, of New York, who also used it frequently, but waffled on the exact percentage, declaring that "Most of life is just a matter of showing up."

Seeking to resolve the discrepancy, William Safire went to the source, whose reply was included in Safire's column in the *New York Times* of August 13th, 1989. Said Mr. Allen:

> The quote you refer to is a quote of mine which occurred during an interview while we were discussing advice to young writers, and more specifically young playwrights.
>
> My observation is that once a young person actually completed a play or a novel he was well on his way to getting it produced or published, as opposed to a vast majority of people who tell me their ambition is to write, but who strike out on the very first level and indeed never write the play or the book.
>
> In the midst of that conversation, as I'm now trying to recall it, I did say that eighty percent of success is showing up.

A somewhat similar 'ninety-percent' rule was proposed as far back as 1917 by Theodore Roosevelt, who in a speech on June 14th declared that "Nine-tenths of wisdom consists in being wise in time."

See also (**Robert F.**) **Kennedy's Law, Mencken's Second Law, Pareto's Law**, and **Sturgeon's Law**.

Anderson's Law

You can make a killing in the theatre, but not a living.

Robert Anderson made a killing with *Tea and Sympathy* (1953) and propounded this law in a newspaper article the following year. (He later tempered his law in lectures, saying that while you can't make a living in the theatre, it is possible "to make a life.") Anderson's Law sums up the difficulties of following a profession in which immense hits may never be repeated and, indeed, may be followed by a series of flops. Authors as well as playwrights enjoy repeating it for the same reason that a person gets pleasure out of pressing one's tongue against a sore tooth.

Anderson's Corollary to His Own Law. When you do make a killing, the taxman takes 90 percent.

Anthony's Law of Force

Don't force it, get a larger hammer.

Anthony may or may not be (have been?) a real person; his last name has not been preserved. If a real person, he probably was a young one, perhaps a toddler, at the time of the law's formulation, considering that the related Law of the Hammer is "When you give a child a hammer, everything becomes a nail" (Arnold Brown, *New York Times,* October 11th, 1989).

A variant of Anthony's Law, "When in doubt, use a bigger hammer," was credited to Joe Dobbin, a foreman in the model shop of Texas Instruments in Dallas, Texas, by Thomas L. Martin, Jr., in a satiric guide for bureaucrats, *Malice in Blunderland* (1973). The possibly mythical Anthony also has been credited with other great insights; see below.

Anthony's Law of the Workshop

Any tool, when dropped, will roll to the least accessible corner.

First Corollary to Anthony's Law of the Workshop. On its way to the corner, the dropped tool will always first strike your toes.

Second Corollary to Anthony's Law of the Workshop (also known as The Spare Parts Principle). The accessibility of the dropped part varies directly with its size and inversely with its importance to completing the task at hand.

The Law of the Workshop is essentially the same as Theodore Bernstein's First Law. See also **Lowery's Law, Murphy's Law,** and **Neely's Laws.**

Archimedes' Third Principle

When a body is immersed in water, the telephone will ring.

Archimedes, the great mathematician and physicist of the third century B.C., is better known for his first two principles, the Principle of the Lever ("Give me a firm spot on which to stand, and I will move the earth") and the Eureka Principle (a body immersed in fluid is buoyed up by a force equal to the weight of the fluid it displaces). Legend has it that he discovered the latter while getting into a tub in a public bath and named it immediately, shouting "Eureka" (meaning "I have found it" in Greek) as he ran home through the streets of Syracuse without benefit of clothes. Archimedes was excited because he had discovered a way of determining whether the new crown of Syracuse's King Hiero II was made of pure gold or adulterated with silver: the pure gold crown would have less volume and displace less water than an alloyed crown of the same weight. Fortunately for Archimedes and the incipient science of hydrostatics, his train of thought was not interrupted by the insistent ring of a telephone. The Third Principle – sometimes known as the Bell Theorem – was communicated to the author by a friend, Maureen Kim Sing, in the form of a letter, not a phone call.

Archilochus's Distinction

The fox knows many things, but the hedgehog knows one big thing.

Scholars have argued over the meaning of this line by the Greek poet (the first to write iambic verse), who lived in the seventh century B.C., but the simplest explanation probably is the best: The wily fox knows many ways of attacking but none are successful against the hedgehog's single defence of curling up, spines outward.

In our time, this line provided the title and theme for *The Hedgehog and the Fox* (1953), a brilliant essay by Sir Isaiah Berlin on Tolstoy as revealed through the novelist's philosophy of history. Applying Archilochus's Distinction to humans, Sir Isaiah wrote: "There exists a great chasm between those, on the one side, who relate everything to a single central vision, one system less or more coherent, in terms of which they understand, think and feel . . . and, on the other side, those who pursue many ends, often unrelated and even contradictory, connected, if at all, only in some de facto way . . . The first kind of intellectual and artistic personality belongs to the hedgehogs, the second to the foxes." Broadly speaking, using this rule, Dante, Plato, Hegel, Dostoevsky, Nietzsche, and Proust are hedgehogs, while Shakespeare, Herodotus, Montaigne, Goethe, Pushkin, and Balzac are foxes. As for Tolstoy, who demonstrated unsurpassed "powers of insight into the variety of life – the differences, the contrasts, the collisions of persons and things and situations, each apprehended in its absolute uniqueness," but who believed in the opposite, advocating "a single embracing vision" and preaching "not variety but simplicity, not many levels of consciousness but reduction to some single level – in *War and Peace* to the standard of the good man – as later to that of the peasants, or of a simple Christian ethic," Sir Isaiah revealed him to be a fox who yearned to be a hedgehog.

Robert Benchley (1889-1945), writer, critic, maker of some very funny film shorts, and grandfather to Peter *(Jaws)* Benchley, has been credited with a refinement of Archilochus's Distinction, i.e. "There may be said to be two classes of people in the world: those who constantly divide the people of the world into two classes and those who do not."

See also **Beerbohm's Second Law.**

Aristotle's Observation

The whole is greater than the sum of the parts (Metaphysics, 4th century B.C.).

In our modern age, where speed is of the essence, and information is conveyed in the smallest possible bites (as well as bytes), this observation has been reduced to a single catchword: *synergy.*

Arnold's Laws of Documentation

1. If it should exist, it doesn't.
2. If it does exist, it's out of date.
3. Only useless documentation transcends the first two laws.

(From the internet, and gleaned from an otherwise unidentified 'Arnold', January 8th, 1996).

See also **Beer's Law** and **Herblock's Law.**

Asimov's Three Rules of Robotics

1. A robot may not injure a human being, or, through inaction, allow a human being to come to harm.

2. A robot must obey the orders given it by human beings except where such orders would conflict with the First Law.

3. A robot must protect its own existence as long as such protection does not conflict with the First or Second Laws.

Isaac Asimov, who gave up teaching biochemistry to become a highly prolific science-fiction novelist and populariser of science, publishing well over 300 books, produced these three fundamental rules in the story 'Runaround' in *I, Robot* (1950). The word *robot* by the way, comes from the Czech *robota*, meaning 'hard work' or 'servitude'. It was popularised in the 1920s after Karl Capek's play, *R.U.R.*, featuring Rossum's Universal Robots, was produced in English.

Aspin's Axiom

If you give Congress a chance to vote on both sides of an issue, it will always do it.

When the House of Representatives voted against spending $988 million to build the first five MX missiles after having previously approved an appropriation of $2.5 billion for research and development of the four-stage, multiple-warhead, 'Peacekeeper' ICBM, Representative Les Aspin (D., Wisc.), a member of the House Armed Services Committee (and a future Secretary of Defense) told the *New York Times* (December 9th, 1982): "It was a significant vote, an important vote. But it doesn't mean the MX is dead. If you give Congress a chance to vote on both sides of an issue, it will always do it." And in 1985, after more than two years of additional backing and forthing, Congress eventually voted to proceed with the construction of twenty-one of the missiles. See also **O'Malley's Observation.**

Astor's Axiom

All women marry beneath them.

United States-born Nancy Witcher Langhorne Astor became the first woman member of the House of Commons in 1919, when she assumed the seat that her husband gave up when he inherited his father's viscountcy. And once she got it, she held on to it for a long time – until 1945. Her axiom was articulated in a speech given in 1951 in Oldham, in the form of an admission, "I married beneath me – all women do." The Viscount apparently took this in his stride. Winston Churchill was not so easygoing. When Lady Astor declared during a heated argument with him that "If I were your wife, I would put poison in your coffee," he replied, "And if I were your husband I would drink it" (Consuelo Vanderbilt Balsan, *Glitter and Gold,* 1952).

St. Augustine's Law to End All Laws

Necessity knows no law.

The thought seems to be proverbial. Prior to St. Augustine (354-430), it was expressed by Publilius Syrus (ca. 85-43 B.C.), one of whose maxims was "Necessity knows no law but to prevail." Later on – much later on, as it happens – Oliver Cromwell said in a 1654 speech to Parliament: "Necessity hath no law. Feigned necessities, imaginary necessities . . . are the greatest cozenage [i.e. frauds, deceptions] that men can put upon the Providence of God, and make pretenses to break known rules by."

See also **Maugham's Law, Prior's Precept,** and **Wycherley's Law.**

Austen's First Law

It is a truth universally acknowledged, that a single man in possession of a good fortune, must be in want of a wife.

Ms. Austen used this law as the first sentence of *Pride and Prejudice* (1813), and it is, in fact, the key to the novel, whose action revolves around Mrs. Bennet's quest to make good marriages for each of her five daughters. The novel's second sentence reinforces the opening one: "However little known the feelings or views of such a man may be on first entering a neighbourhood, this truth is so well fixed in the minds of the surrounding families that he is considered the rightful property of some one or other of their daughters." No doubt Mrs. Bennet would have agreed thoroughly with Ben Franklin's observation in a letter of June 25th, 1745, to a friend (identity not known) that "A single man . . . is an incomplete animal. He resembles the odd half of a pair of scissors." Completeness does not always guarantee satisfaction, however, as evidenced by **Gabor's Corollary**: "A man in love is incomplete until he is married. Then he is finished" (Zsa Zsa Gabor, *Newsweek*, March 28th, 1960).

Ms. Austen, by the way, was not yet twenty-one when she began writing this great novel in October of 1796. She finished it the following August. *Pride and Prejudice* was not published until 1813, however, due to what the *Encyclopaedia Britannica* (13th edition, 1926) gently terms "the blindness of publishers."

See also **Franklin's Laws**.

Austen's Second Law

If there is anything disagreeable going on, men are sure to get out of it.

This is from *Persuasion*, published in 1818, a year after Jane

Austen's death. An acute observer of provincial life, who recorded its texture in intricate detail, the author never married, managing somehow to get along without the dubious help of a man around her own house.

Men remained as recalcitrant as ever into the twentieth century, as noted by Jean Giradoux in *The Madwoman of Chaillot* (1945): "There is nothing so stubborn as a man when you want him to do something."

See also **Thatcher's Law.**

B

Bacon's Law

Money is like muck, not good except it be spread.

Francis Bacon (with all flags flying: Baron Verulam, Viscount St. Albans), evoked this law to explain why it was not good policy to allow "the Treasure and Moneyes" of a nation to be concentrated in a few hands. "For otherwise," he asserted, "a State may have a great Stock, and yet Starve. And Money is like Muck, not good except it be spread" ('Of Seditions and Troubles', *Essays*, 1625).

The baron was neither the first nor the last to articulate this principle. As far back as the sixth century B.C., Aesop noted in *The Miser and His Gold* that "Wealth unused might as well not exist," while, at the start of the twentieth century, Philander C. Johnson advised in *Senator Sorghum's Primer of Politics* (1906) that "A man fails to appreciate the value of money when he holds on to it so tight that he gets no benefit from it."

Bacon himself had considerable practical experience in statecraft, rising through a series of high positions to the Lord Chancellorship (1618-21). Certainly one of the wisest men in the kingdom (he also produced the aphorisms "Nature, to be commanded, must be obeyed" and "Knowledge is power"), he nevertheless lost power after admitting to having accepted bribes from participants in chancery suits. Thus freed, albeit unwillingly, from public responsibilities, he kept busy in private retirement, turning out philosophical, historical, and scientific works, including a third and enlarged edition of his *Essays*, which contains such other memorable statements as:

> *It is impossible to love and be wise* ('Of Love').

> *He that hath wife and children hath given hostages to fortune; for they are impediments to great enterprises, either of virtue or mischief* ('Of Marriage and Single Life').

> *Wives are young men's mistresses, companions for middle age, and old men's nurses* (Ibid).

> *In charity there is no excess* ('Of Goodness and Goodness of Nature').

> *The folly of one man is the fortune of another* ('Of Fortune').

> *He that will not apply new remedies must expect new evils; for time is the greatest innovator* ('Of Innovations').

> *If the hill will not come to Mahomet, Mahomet will come to the hill* ('Of Boldness').

> *Some books are to be tasted, others to be swallowed, and some few to be chewed and digested* ('Of Studies').

As for Bacon's money-muck law, it continues to crop up in various forms, not always with acknowledgment to Baron Verulam, Viscount St. Albans. Thus, the Texas wheeler-dealer, Clint Murchison, Jr., credited his father for the saying, "Money is like manure. If you spread it around, it does a lot of good. But if you pile it up in one place, it stinks like hell" (*Time*, June 16th, 1971). Another modern variant, "Money is like manure – it is meant to be spread around," appears in John Peers's *1,001 Logical Laws,* where it is called 'The Poverty Principle'.

See also **Aesop's Adages, Cavett's Law, Gresham's Law,** and **Senator Sorghum's Laws of Politics.**

Bailey's Rule

Threats without power are like powder without ball.

This principle was set forth by one of the first English lexicographers, Nathaniel Bailey, in his *Universal Etymological English Dictionary* (1721). Not much is known about Bailey except that he lived in Stepney, a London suburb, and was a schoolteacher and Seventh-Day Baptist. Bailey also deserves credit for being one of the few dictionary-makers prior to the 1960s who was brave enough to include 'fuck' (defined in Latin as *feminam subagitare*) and other common but 'impolite' terms.

Baker's Law of Inanimation

Inanimate objects are scientifically classified into three major categories – those that don't work, those that break down, and those that get lost.

In promulgating this law, Russell Baker pointed out in his column in the *New York Times* that the three kinds of inanimate objects have a common purpose to their existence: "The goal of all inanimate objects is to resist man and ultimately to defeat him" (June 18th, 1968). More than a century earlier, Ralph Waldo Emerson came close to stumbling upon this same insight in his essay on *Politics*, declaring that "Things have their laws as well as men; things refuse to be trifled with" (*Essays: Second Series*, 1844).

See also **Searle's Sage Sample.**

Baker's Laws of Progress

1. Progress is what people who are planning to do something really terrible almost always justify themselves on the grounds of.

2. Usually, terrible things that are done with the excuse

that progress requires them are not really progress at all, but just terrible things.

Russell Baker himself termed these 'Inside Facts About Progress' in *Poor Russell's Almanac* (1972) but they obviously have the force of law. His *Almanac* also includes other precepts of value as one travels down the highway of life. Among them:

Baker's Rules of the Road

1. The people who are always hankering for some golden yesteryear the loudest usually drive the newest cars.

2. There are no liberals behind steering wheels.

Baker's Secrets of Happiness

1. Happiness is when a wire has become disconnected under the dashboard and the motor is hissing and you go to a garage and the repairman says you have a "vacuum leak," and you ask how much it will cost to fix and he says "$1.75".

2. One snow in a winter is happiness. Two snows are too many. Three snows are a penance visited upon cities that are unjust. Wise is the man who goes to Yucatan after the first snow for he shall escape the ravages of dipsomania, self-pity and misanthropy, and his shoes shall not be ruined.

And for another view of how progress is made, see **Stalin's Law.**

Barnum's Law

There's a sucker born every minute.

The saying is irredeemably associated with the great nineteenth-century American showman Phineas Taylor Barnum despite efforts by Robert Pelton, curator of the

Barnum Museum in Bridgeport, Connecticut, to pin it on one of P.T.'s friends, a con man by the name of Joseph 'Paper Collar' Bessimer. Mr. Pelton may well be right, but Barnum gets popular credit for the remark because of his skill at roping in the credulous by the thousand. And he also knew how to get rid of them when he wanted to – as in his American Museum in New York City where he is said to have posted the sign 'This way to the egress', which led unlearned crowds along to the exit, thereby making room for new 'patrons'.

P. T. Barnum also has been credited with the observation that "You can fool most of the people most of the time," which is better known as **Lincoln's First Law**. All of which tends to give Barnum a blacker character than he deserves. The attractions that he staged were immensely popular and people didn't seem to mind if he occasionally put one over on them – 'humbugged' them, in the parlance of the time. Thus, the public forgave him after an autopsy indicated that Joice Heth, billed as George Washington's nurse, probably wasn't over 80 when she died in 1836, not 161 as claimed. (Barnum insisted that he himself had been taken in.) He also survived the admission that the famous Feejee Mermaid was a hoax, apparently manufactured by a Japanese fisherman who joined the top half of a monkey to the bottom half of a fish. On the other hand, Tom Thumb, Jenny Lind, and Jumbo were equally marvelous – and real.

Barnum, then, did not necessarily adhere to what commonly is regarded as the natural corollary to his law: "Never give a sucker an even break." (This has been embellished into "It's morally wrong to allow suckers to keep their money.") The corollary, dating from the 1920s, has been attributed to various authorities of that era, including Edward F. Albee, the circus-ticket seller who helped form the 400-theatre Keith-Albee vaudeville circuit; Wilson Mizner, celebrated wit of the 1920s; Mary Louise Cecilia 'Texas' Guinan, the entertainer and nightclub owner, who frequently welcomed patrons with "Hello Sucker"; and W. C. Fields, the nonpareil, who may have ad-libbed the quip in *Poppy*, a play by Dorothy Donnelly that was produced in 1923. Any one of them was perfectly capable of coming up with the line – or of stealing it and pretending to be the originator.

See also **Mizner's Law of Research**.

Bayly's Observation

Absence makes the heart grow fonder.

Thomas Haynes Bayly, early nineteenth-century English songwriter and playwright, may have cribbed this line in *Isle of Beauty* from the Roman poet Sextus Propertius, who put it this way in his second *Elegy: Semper in absentes felicior aestus amantes*. Some say neither Bayly nor Propertius got it right – that it is absinthe that makes the heart grow fonder or, a double pun attributed to Hugh Drummond: "Ladies and Gentlemen I give you a toast. It is 'Absinthe makes the tart grow fonder.'"

Bayly seems to have been essentially an optimist. In *Don Quixote*, Cervantes described "Absence [as] that common cure of love." For yet another pessimistic view of the effect of absence, see **Thomas's Law**, and for the all-too-common result of proximity, i.e. the absence of absence, see the third of **Aesop's Adages**.

Beaumarchais's Law

To make a living, craftiness is better than learnedness.

Pierre Augustin Caron de Beaumarchais included this insight in *The Marriage of Figaro*, which was a play before it became an opera. The crafty servant Figaro, hero of this comedy and

The Barber of Seville, had much in common with the author, whose accomplishments included distinguished service as a secret agent for the French and Spanish governments. (During the American Revolution, he ran a fleet of forty vessels to provide munitions to the rebel colonists.) *The Marriage of Figaro*, completed in 1778, was kept off the stage by Louis XVI until 1784. The king didn't approve of the author's radical sentiments, as exemplified by Figaro's monologue in act five: "What have you [the nobility] done to deserve such wealth? You took the trouble to be born and nothing else." The play was a huge success when finally produced, probably the greatest in the history of the French theatre. Even the nobility flocked to see it, despite its subtext, later characterised by Napoleon as the "revolution already in action."

Beaumont and Fletcher's Law

Beggars must be no choosers.

The line is from *The Scornful Lady* (ca. 1609), probably the first collaborative effort of Francis Beaumont and John Fletcher, but the thought is proverbial. John Heywood included "Beggars should be no choosers" in the first edition of his *Proverbs* (1546). Then there is the story about the English scholar Sir Maurice Bowra, who told a friend that he had finally decided to get married only to have the friend object to the woman in question, "But you can't marry anyone as plain as that." To which Sir Maurice replied, "My dear fellow, buggers can't be choosers" (from Francis King in Hugh Lloyd-Jones, *Maurice Bowra: a Celebration*, 1974).

The Beckner Effect

The common name in the bond market for the thunderous perturbations that frequently follow news flashes from Steve Beckner, in the Washington office of Market News Service.

As pointed out by Michael Lewis in the *New York Times Magazine* (October 1st, 1995), it doesn't matter to traders whether or not Beckner's news reports contain information that is intrinsically valuable: "All that matters is that a sufficient number of them [the traders] believe that others think they have value. They will then buy bonds because they think others will buy bonds." The ironic result is that the traders believe themselves to be at the mercy of an effect which they themselves have created.

Beer's Law

Absolutum obsoletum – if it works it's out of date. (Stafford Beer, *Brain of the Firm*, 1972).

See also **Herblock's Law**.

Beerbohm's First Law

Anything that is worth doing has been done frequently. Things hitherto undone should be given, I suspect, a wide berth.

Sir Max Beerbohm produced this general rule in an essay, 'From Bloomsbury to Bayswater', in *Mainly on the Air* (1946). A contemporary, Sir Arnold Bax, stumbled onto a variation of Beerbohm's Law, including two of the things to be avoided: "A sympathetic Scot summed it all up very neatly in the remark, 'You should make a point of trying every experience once, excepting incest and folk-dancing'"(*Farewell, My Youth*, 1943).

Beerbohm's Second Law

Mankind is divisible into two great classes: hosts and guests ('Hosts and Guests' in *And Even Now*, 1920).

See also **Archiolocus's Distinction**.

Behn's Law

Here today, gone tomorrow.

Novelist, dramatist, and spy (for King Charles II against the Dutch), Mrs. Aphra Behn was the first Englishwoman to support herself through literary endeavours – something that relatively few professional writers, regardless of sex, are able to do today. "Here today, gone tomorrow" probably is a proverbial expression, as old as the hills, so to speak, but the earliest known example of its use in writing comes from Mrs. Behn's play, *The Lucky Chance* (1686-87): "Faith, sir, we are here today, and gone tomorrow."

See also **Heraclitus's Law**.

Belli's Law

There is never a deed so foul that something couldn't be said for the guy; that's why there are lawyers. (Melvin Belli, *Los Angeles Times*, December 18th, 1981).

But see also **Dershowitz's Law**.

Bentham's Law

The greatest happiness of the greatest number is the foundation of morals and legislation.

The English philosopher and jurist Jeremy Bentham summed up his doctrine of utilitarianism in this manner. Others already had approached the idea in much the same terms, as Bentham himself realised. He noted in his *Commonplace Book*, published after his death in 1832 as part of his *Works*, that "Priestly was the first (unless it was Beccaria) who taught my lips to pronounce this sacred truth." Bentham may have been misremembering, however. Prior to Joseph Priestly and Cesare Beccaria-Bonesana, the same conclusion also had been reached by the Scottish philosopher Francis Hutcheson.

Moreover, Hutcheson expressed the thought in almost the same words as Bentham, declaring "That action is best which procures the greatest happiness for the greatest number" (*Enquiry Concerning Moral Good and Evil*, 1725). Bentham greatly developed the idea, however, devising an elaborate system of making moral decisions by calculating their consequences in terms of units of pleasure and pain. The system wasn't really workable, but Bentham's method of reasoning had profound social effects, especially on the law, where the utilitarian conclusion that punishment should be harsh enough to deter future crime, but no harsher, led to prison reform and other enlightened changes in the criminal code.

See also **Kant's Categorical Imperative**.

(Jeremy) Bernstein's First Law

All tests measure something.

Mr. Bernstein, a professor of physics at Stevens Institute of Technology in Hoboken, N.J., stumbled upon this "simple, almost self-evident principle" while contemplating the uses and abuses of IQ tests. To illustrate what he termed his 'First Law' (cleverly leaving himself room for promulgating another, should one come to mind) Mr. Bernstein reported in *Scientific American* that "I was once tested on my ability to crawl under a limbo stick after having drunk a jigger of Jamaican rum. I found that I could do it if the stick was set at my actual height." Applying this law to intelligence testing, he concluded that "IQ tests measure something. The problem is what to call it" (April 1995). Professor Bernstein's solution: the term 'IQ', or 'Intelligence Quota', with its unfortunate implication that a person with a small one is a moron, should be replaced by a new term, 'Quot', which would have no more stigma attached to it than comes from having a large or small telephone number.

(Theodore) Bernstein's First Law

A falling body always rolls to the most inaccessible spot.

As Theodore Bernstein, then assistant managing editor of the *New York Times*, explained in *The Careful Writer* (1965), this law applies generally to "such articles as cuff links, dimes, table-tennis balls, and caps of toothpaste tubes." In practical terms, what it means is that "if you drop a cuff link, it is useless to look at the open floor area near your feet. The only thing to do is to get down on all fours, preferably with a flashlight, and peer under the bed."

Rush's Corollary. When you drop change at a vending machine, the pennies will fall nearby while the other coins will roll out of sight (in Arthur Block, *The Complete Murphy's Law*, 1991).

Twain's Amendment. A coin, sleeve button, or a collar button dropped in a bedroom will hide itself and be hard to find. A handkerchief in a bed can't be found (Mark Twain, *Notebook*, Albert Bigelow Paine, ed., 1935).

Bernstein's First Law is the counterpart of **Sattler's Law** (theoretically, grapefruit juice could fly in any direction, but in practice it always hits you in the eye). It also has been recorded in more specific forms: see **Anthony's Law of the Workshop** and Murphy's First Law of Auto Repair in **Murphy's Law**.

(Theodore) Bernstein's Second Law

Bad words tend to drive out good ones, and when they do, the good ones never appreciate in value, sometimes maintain their value, but most often lose in value, whereas the bad words may remain bad or get better.

Theodore Bernstein modeled this law of language on **Gresham's Law of Coinage** ("bad money drives out good").

By 'bad word', Bernstein meant the secondary meanings of words that diverge from primary meanings but gradually come into use "because of ignorance, confusion, faddishness, or the importunities of slang" (*The Careful Writer*, 1965). As examples, he cited *awful* and *dreadful*, whose stark primary meanings lose force when the terms are used as commonplace expressions; *enormity*, whose genuine meaning tends to become lost when it is used in contexts where *enormousness* is meant; and *fruition*, a word that warrants preservation in the sense of "coming to fruit," but whose meaning is being blurred through use in place of *pleasure* or *gratification*. While fully recognising that words continually change in meaning to suit new needs as language evolves, Bernstein deplored "the displacement of good words by bad ones to no purpose, or to the detriment of good ones," and urged that the operation of his second law be resisted when it caused words to lose precision and vitality.

As often happens in the history of science, Bernstein's Second Law was independently discovered – or rediscovered, to be precise – by this author, who called it Gresham's Law of Language, in the first edition (1981) of *Rawson's Dictionary of Euphemisms & Other Doubletalk*. When words are drawn into service as euphemisms, according to this law (which might, upon reflection, well be called Rawson's Law), their underlying 'bad' or taboo meanings tend to drive competing 'good' meanings out of circulation. For example, *coition* and *intercourse* once were general terms for coming together (as in the coition, or conjunction, of planets) and communication (as between nations or inhabitants of different locales, especially with regard to commerce). The general terms have been so completely taken over by their specialised sexual meanings, however, that it is hardly possible to use the words nowadays in any other context. (One of the few exceptions is Intercourse, Pa., which actually was named with commercial trade in mind, not that other thing.) And going one step further, the tainting of 'good' words by their 'bad' meanings frequently results in the replacement of one euphemism by another. For example, *mad* has been euphemised successively as *crazy, insane, lunatic, mentally deranged,* and *mental;* countries that are poor and backward have metamorphosed from *underdeveloped* to *developing* to *lesser developed* nations; and children who do not keep up with their peers in school have been categorised variously as *dull, slow, retarded, exceptional* and *special.* This has been called (by some) Rawson's Law of Euphemistic Succession. See also **Gresham's Law.**

Berra's Law

The game isn't over until it's over.

Credit for this law generally is assigned to Hall-of-Fame baseball catcher, Lawrence Peter 'Yogi' Berra, on the basis of a remark he made in 1973 when the New York Mets, which he was then managing, were embroiled in a tight pennant race. Sometimes quoted in the form of "It ain't over until it's over," the saying is a condensation of the traditional wisdom that "The ball game isn't over until the last man is out."

Berra's Law has been cited so often in recent years that it has become practically a cliché. For example, Tammy Bakker, wife of Reverend Jim, the televangelist, claimed that "It's not over until it's over," as she pushed her way through a crowd of reporters following her husband's conviction on October 5th, 1989, for having sheared his flock too closely. (The jury found him guilty of twenty-four counts of fraud and conspiracy.) But Robert Maxwell, the late and unlamented publisher, betrayed some ignorance of contemporary American culture when he asserted during the course of his negotiations to purchase the *New York Daily News* in 1991 that "As Yogi Bear once said, a thing is not done until it is done."

Berra is one of those figures around whom sayings seem to collect. (He sometimes is credited with "The opera ain't over till the fat lady sings," but this line has been traced by Fred Shapiro, of Yale Law School, to a southern saying, "Church ain't out till the fat lady sings.") Some of Berra's bon mots may have been put into his mouth by sportswriters, but many have the genuine ring of a man who, as a player for the New York Yankees from 1946 to 1963, was influenced by the complex thought patterns of that team's manager; see **Stengel's Laws.** Herewith a selection from the wit and wisdom of the great Yogi:

It's like déjà vu all over again. (A suspicious quote, it not being like Mr. Berra to lapse into French.)

The future ain't what it used to be. (A kind of corollary to the above, this quote was cited in 1991 by General H. Norman Schwarzkopf in response to a question by an NBC News interviewer about his post-Persian Gulf war plans.)

The game is supposed to be fun. If you have a bad day, don't worry about it. You can't expect to get a hit every game. It gets late early out there. (On the difficulties of seeing a ball amid the shadows of left field in Yankee Stadium.)

Nobody goes there anymore; it's too crowded (sometimes rendered as "That place is so popular that nobody goes there anymore.") The 'Nobody goes' version is said by Yogi's wife and friends to be an actual remark. If so, it was an independent invention since, as pointed out by Ralph Keyes in *Nice Guys Finish Seventh*, the same line also appeared in a 1943 *New Yorker* short story by John McNulty.

Anybody who is popular is bound to be disliked.

When you arrive at a fork in the road, take it. (Or a variant, from Leon E. Panetta, then a member of the House of Representatives from California, "Like Yogi Berra said, when you reach the crossroads, take it" (*New York Times*, June 19th, 1990).

You can observe a lot by watching. (An actual remark, made during the press conference on October 24th, 1963, at which Mr. Berra was introduced as the new manager of the New York Yankees. It is in keeping with an explanation years earlier of how Bill Dickey taught him to be a catcher: "Bill is learnin' me his experiences.")

You've got to be very careful if you don't know where you are going, because you might not get there. (On the other hand, knowing where one is going is no guarantee of success, as Laurence Sterne noted in *A Sentimental Journey*, 1768: "I think there is a fatality in it – I seldom go to the place I set out for." And not knowing one's destination may even be an advantage; as Oliver Cromwell told the French ambassador in 1647: "A man never mounts so high as when he does not know where he is going.") See also Peter's Statement of Objectives in **The Peter Principle** and **Thoreau's Second Law.**

You can't win all the time. There are guys out there who are better than you. (But in Berra's case, not many, and he has ten World Series rings to prove it.)

See also **Chandler's Law.**

Bevan's Law

We know what happens to people who stay in the middle of the road. They get run over.

This pronouncement by Aneurin Bevan, leader of the radical wing of the British Labour Party and father of the National Health Service, was the quote of the week in the *Observer*

(December 9th, 1953). His dislike of middle-of-the-roaders was exceeded only by what he described in a 1948 speech as his "deep burning hatred for the Tory Party," whose members he regarded as "lower than vermin."

A partial exception to Bevan's Law was noted by Thomas C. Grey, author of *The Wallace Stevens Case: Law and the Practice of Poetry*, who told the *New York Times*: "Lawyers tend to be absolutists or disappointed absolutists, and Stevens represents something in between. He reminds us that there is more in the middle of the road than yellow lines and dead animals" (July 12th, 1991).

Bierce's Law

Calamities are of two kinds: misfortunes to ourselves and good fortune to others.

Ambrose Bierce mixed bits of wisdom such as this in with the cynical definitions that he composed for newspapers at intervals starting in 1881 and which were published in book form as *The Cynic's Word Book* (1906). This title was forced upon the author by the religious scruples of his employer at the time. In 1911, however, Bierce reissued the collection in expanded form under the title that he himself preferred and by which it is known today, *The Devil's Dictionary*.

Edmund Burke made the same point as the dyspeptic Mr. Bierce, albeit in reverse, when he announced that "I am convinced that we have a degree of delight, and that no small one, in the real misfortunes and pains of others" (*Philosophical Inquiry into the Origin of Our Ideas on the Sublime and Beautiful*, 1756).

See also **La Rochefoucauld's Rule** and **Vidal's Law**.

The Devil's Dictionary also included a number of what Bierce called "old saws fitted with new teeth," most of which have the force of law. Some examples:

A penny saved is a penny to squander.
A bad workman quarrels with the man who calls him that.
A bird in the hand is worth what it will bring.
Better late than before anybody has invited you.
Think twice before you speak to a friend in need.
Least said is soonest disavowed.
He laughs best who laughs least.
Where there's a will there's a won't.

Well known in his own day as a newspaper reporter, columnist, and literary arbiter (particularly for the young William Randolph Hearst's *San Francisco Examiner*), Bierce also wrote many short stories. The best ones derived from his own experiences in the Civil War in which he fought well, emerging as a brevet major and with a bullet that remained in his skull for the rest of his life. Always gloomy by nature and with a mordant wit (one of his stories begins, "Early one June morning in 1872 I murdered my father – an act which made a deep impression on me at the time"), Bierce became ever more bitter over the years as his marriage broke up and his sons died, one a suicide after a lover's quarrel and the other from pneumonia. Toward the end of 1913, he headed south to report on the Mexican revolution and was never heard from again. Occasional rumours of sightings of him surfaced in later years, but no one really knows when and where he died. *The Dictionary* constitutes his principal literary legacy.

For more Biercean wisdom, see **Descartes's Dictum** and **O'Malley's Observation**.

Billings's First Law

The wheel that squeaks the loudest is the one that gets the grease.

Josh Billings was the pen name of nineteenth-century American humorist Henry Wheeler Shaw, who specialised in humorous essays replete with such epigrams as this, from *The Kicker*.

Billings's Second Law

It is better to know nothing than to know what ain't so.

This is basically a proverb, as distilled by the Yankee humorist in his *Encyclopedia of Wit and Wisdom* (1874). Many other deep thinkers, including some with much more august reputations, have toyed with the same idea. Among them:

- **Thomas Jefferson.** Ignorance is preferable to error; and he is less remote from the truth who believes nothing, than he who believes what is wrong;

- **Friedrich Wilhelm Nietzsche.** Better know nothing than half-know many things;

- **John Maynard Keynes.** It is better to be approximately right than precisely wrong.

Still another variant, also attributed to Billings, was recorded by Albert Bigelow Paine in his 1912 biography of one of Billings's close friends, Mark Twain: "The difficulty is not that we know so much, but that we know so much that isn't so."

See also **Jefferson's Ukase.**

Billings's Third Law

As scarce as truth is, the supply has always been in excess of demand.

More wisdom from Henry Wheeler Shaw, a.k.a., Josh Billings; this is one of his *Affurisms*, included in *Josh Billings: His Sayings* (1865).

Blundell's Law

All books over five hundred pages that weren't written by Dickens or a dead Russian are better left on the shelf.

(William E. Blundell, *The Art and Craft of Feature Writing*, 1988).

Bogart's Rule

When a dog bites a man, that is not news, because it happens so often. But if a man bites a dog, that is news.

This working definition of news was attributed to John B. Bogart, city editor of the *New York Sun*, in Frank M. O'Brien's *The Story of the Sun* (1918). Bogart's boss, Charles A. Dana, also has been credited with it.

Bohr's Law

The crazier the theory, the more likely it is to be correct.

After Wolfgang Pauli expounded a radical theory of atomic particles at a conference in New York in 1958, Niels Bohr summarised the ensuing discussion, telling Pauli "We are all agreed that your theory is crazy. The question which divides us is whether it is crazy enough to have a chance of being correct. My own feeling is that it is not crazy enough." Freeman Dyson, who recalled this episode in *Scientific American* (September 1958), suggested that this rule applies to all 'crackpot' theories of elementary particles. "Most of the crackpot papers which are submitted to the *Physical Review* are rejected, not because it is impossible to understand them, but because it is possible," he continued. "Those which are impossible to understand are usually published. When the great innovation appears, it will almost certainly be in a muddled, incomplete and confusing form. To the discoverer himself it will be only half-understood; to everybody else it will be a mystery. For any speculation which does not at first glance look crazy, there is no hope."

Professor Dyson's comments apply to new ideas generally, not just theories about atomic particles. We have this on the authority of such eminent non-physicists as: Oliver Wendell Holmes, Sr., "There was never an idea stated that woke up men out of their stupid indifference but its originator was not spoken of as a crank" (*The Autocrat of the Breakfast Table*, 1858); Mark Twain, "The man with a new idea is a crank until it succeeds" ("Pudden'head Wilson's New Calendar," in *Following the Equator*, 1897), and George Bernard Shaw, "All great truths begin as blasphemies" (*Annajanska*, 1919).

See also **Butler's Observation**.

Boren's Guidelines for Bureaucrats

When in charge, ponder; when in trouble, delegate; when in doubt, mumble.

These rules for bureaucratic success have been adopted widely with minor changes in wording. For example, in delivering a eulogy at the funeral in 1991 of three-time New York City mayor Robert F. Wagner, one of his sons, Robert, Jr., said his father had jotted down some advice in the last weeks of his life, "probably not for the officials here but for his sons." The advice: "When in danger, ponder. When in trouble, delegate. And when in doubt, mumble." And Mayor Wagner, in fact, was noted for his cautious, methodical management style.

The rules were devised by James Boren, founder and president of NATAPROBU, the National Association of Professional Bureaucrats, and popularised through articles about him and his organisation in the *New York Times* (November 8th, 1970) and *Time* (November 23rd, 1970). Mr. Boren, an experienced governmental bureaucrat who had metamorphosed into an independent consultant, told *Time* that NATAPROBU had dedicated itself to "optimize the status quo by fostering adjustive adherence to procedural abstractions and rhetorical clearances." It also promoted "feasibility studies, reviews, surveys of plans, surveys of feasibility studies and surveys of reviews."

NATAPROBU was said to have three hundred members in 1970, but not much has been heard of it recently. It may have fallen prey to another of its objectives, which was to demonstrate "dynamic inactivism." Mr. Boren himself went on to greater things. In 1992 he ran for the presidency under the banner of the Apathy Party. Voter reaction was surprisingly apathetic, however, considering the likelihood that he could have delivered on his chief campaign promise, which was to supply the "bold, reckless, arrogant, ignorant leadership" that the public seemed to want.

Bouchier's Columbus Principle

Any new activity will cause more trouble than you can possibly imagine.

PBS correspondent David Bouchier enunciated this principle on Columbus Day 1996; hence its name. Mr. Bouchier was concerned especially with the ownership of cats, and his solution was simple: "Just don't start." The principle also applies to the sexual revolution, the technological revolution, world wars, and so on. Its validity has been demonstrated over and over again throughout history, from the most ancient times to the present – from Pandora of Greek myth, who out of curiosity opened her magical box (a jar, in some versions) and let loose a multitude of evils upon the world, to the probing intellects of today who have given us such wonders as junk food, junk bonds, and designer drugs. And, of course, there was the case of Christopher Columbus, who some think might better have stayed in bed.

Brandeis's Law

Crime is contagious. If the government becomes a lawbreaker, it breeds contempt for the law.

Supreme Court Justice Louis Brandeis made this observation in the course of a minority opinion in *Olmstead v. United States* (1928). In this case, the court decided 5-4 that wiretapping the telephones of a gang of bootleggers did not violate the Fourth Amendment's prohibition against unauthorised searches and seizures of evidence because government agents had placed the taps without actually trespassing upon the property of the defendants. Justice Brandeis took a broader view of the Fourth Amendment, arguing that it was intended to protect citizens from unjustifiable intrusions by the government by whatever means, including electronic or other measures not invented when the Bill of Rights was written.

Forty years later, in *Katz v. United States* (1967), the court came around to Brandeis's way of thinking, with Justice Potter Stewart holding for a 6-1 majority that physical intrusion is not the key factor in determining the legality of searches and seizure because "the Fourth Amendment protects people, not places."

Brecht's Law

Eats first, morals after.

Arguably the most basic law of all, this is a line from Berthold Brecht's *The Threepenny Opera* (1928). Another translation is "Grub first, then ethics." Brecht was a revolutionary Marxist, who left the comforts of Hollywood to return to his homeland in (East) Germany in 1948. It is hard to hold his politics against him, however, considering that he also managed in *The Threepenny Opera* to ask the question, some sixty years before the savings and loan scandals of the 1990s, "What is robbing a bank compared with founding a bank?"

See also **Sutton's Law**.

Bronfman's Law of Accumulation

To turn $100 into $110 is work. To turn $100 million into $110 million is inevitable.

From the wisdom of Edgar Bronfman, president of Seagram Company, Ltd., as distilled in *Newsweek* (December 2nd, 1985).

See also **Kahn and Egan's Law**.

Brooks's Law

If you've got it, flaunt it.

As the great Zero Mostel said, in full, in *The Producers* (1968), written and directed by Melvin Kaminsky (a.k.a. Mel Brooks), "That's it, baby, if you've got it, flaunt it."

This law has a natural corollary, as explained by Noel Perrin, Dartmouth professor and man-about-letters in a book review in the *New York Times*: "Most self-confident people are competitive, even aggressive. 'If you've got it, flaunt it' is their motto. 'If there's something you don't have, try to conceal it' is the corollary" (December 1st, 1991).

Mr. Brooks-Kaminsky also deserves to be remembered for the secrets of longevity, revealed in his album, *The 2,000-Year-Old Man:*

1. Don't run for a bus – there'll always be another.
2. Never, ever touch fried food.
3. Stay out of a Ferrari or any other small Italian car.
4. Eat fruit – a nectarine – even a rotten plum is good.

See also **Paige's Rules for Living**.

Browning's Observation

Less is more.

Though often associated with architect Mies van der Rohe, who popularised this as his motto while acting as director of the Bauhaus school (see also **Sullivan's Law**), the phrase actually was articulated first by Robert Browning in *Andrea* *del Sarto* (1855). The poem is cast in the form of a monologue by del Sarto to his wife Lucrezia. In the process, he reveals why his passion for his wife kept him from reaching the artistic heights of Michelangelo and Raphael, whose passion went into their paintings. Known to his contemporaries as 'The Faultless Painter,' he realises that his "forthright craftsman's hand" was too faultless:

> *Yet do much less, so much less, Someone says,*
> *(I know his name, no matter) so much less!*
> *Well, less is more, Lucrezia: I am judged.*

And he continues, in another famous phrase:

> *Ah, but a man's reach should exceed his grasp,*
> *Or what's a heaven for? all is silver-grey*
> *Placid and perfect with my art: the worse!*

Bucy's Law

Nothing is ever accomplished by a reasonable man.

Devised by Fred Bucy, executive vice president of Texas Instruments, the intent of this law was to describe the characteristic abrasiveness of managers in the business world, according to Thomas L. Martin Jr.'s *Malice in Blunderland* (1973). On close inspection, however, it looks much more like a justification for not worrying too much about other people's feelings no matter what one's field of endeavour. Non-businessmen of this sort whose names come quickly to mind include Columbus, Picasso, and General Douglas MacArthur.

Burke's Law

The only thing necessary for the triumph of evil is for good men to do nothing.

The only troubling thing about this ringing declaration is that it has never been found in the writings of Edmund Burke, eighteenth-century British statesman, political philosopher, and orator. Burke did express a similar thought, but much more floridly, declaring in a parliamentary speech that "When bad men combine, the good must associate; else they will fall one by one, an unpitied sacrifice in a contemptible struggle" (*Thoughts on the Cause of the Present Discontents*, April 23rd, 1770). Perhaps Burke's Law, as we now know it, is a popular paraphrase or distillation of the more formal statement. This is a rather long stretch, however. It seems at least as likely that Burke's Law is a spin-off of **Dante's Law** or an elaboration of **Goldsmith's Law**.

Burn's Law of Social Change

It usually takes about a century, or three generations, for a people, after a far-reaching social change, to get habits which are no longer really relevant out of their systems.

A. R. Burn went on to explain the operation of this law in *A Traveller's History of Greece* (1967) in this way: "The first generation of survivors are still brought up under the old order, and the second generation are people brought up by people who were brought up under the old order. This is one reason why a century, a period of about three generations, so often seems to have a distinctive character."

Slonimsky's Amendment. It takes approximately 20 years to make an artistic curiosity of a modernistic monstrosity and another 20 years to make it a masterpiece (Nicholas Slonimsky, *Lexicon of Musical Invective*, 1969).

See also **Laver's Law of Fashion.**

Burns's Law

The best-laid schemes o' mice an' men gang aft agley.

The line is from the next-to-last verse of 'To a Mouse'. The poem's subtitle, 'On Turning Her Up in Her Nest with the

Plough, November 1785', provides the context for the thought. Burns enlarged upon it in the manner:

> *But, Mousie, thou art no thy lane [not alone]*
> *In proving foresight may be vain:*
> *The best-laid schemes o' mice an' men,*
> > *Gang aft agley [awry]*
> *An' lea'e us nought but grief an' pain*
> > *For promis'd joy!*

Along with the mouse nest, then, it is clear that Burns also stumbled upon what is known today, rather less poetically, as the Doctrine of Unintended Consequences. See also **Murphy's Law** and **Spencer's Law**.

Burton's Rule

No rule is so general, which admits not some exception.

The Reverend Robert Burton's Rule, presented in *The Anatomy of Melancholy* (1621), has a fine ring to it but is logically inconsistent. As pointed out by Bill Boquist, of San Francisco, California, in a communication to *Harper's* (August, 1974):

> If for every rule there is an exception, then we have established that there is an exception for every rule. If we accept 'For every rule there is an exception' as a rule, then we must concede that there may not be an exception after all, since the rule states that there is always the possibility of an exception, and if we follow it to its logical end, we must agree that there can be no exception to the rule that for every rule there is an exception.

Burton's Rule is a variant of the proverbial wisdom (from the sixteenth century at least) that "The exception proves the rule", which also has led many people into deep waters logically. The most common mistake is that exceptions somehow validate rules. This is due to a misunderstanding: 'prove' here is being used in the sense of 'test' or 'make a trial of.' This was the dominant meaning of the word in the sixteenth and early seventeenth centuries, as in St. Paul's admonition – as it appears in the King James Bible of 1611 – "to prove all things." Thus, Reverend Burton to the contrary, the only thing an exception proves is that there is something wrong with the rule.

And this is how science progresses. When exceptions to theories are discovered, the theories – the rules – must either be refined to take the exceptions into account or discarded altogether. The scientific approach was stated succinctly by the French physiologist Claude Bernard: "Science admits no exceptions; otherwise there would be no determinism in science, or rather, there would be no science" (*Lessons from Experimental Pathology,* 1872). Sherlock Holmes had much the same idea in mind when he said, even more tersely, "An exception disproves the rule" (*The Sign of Four,* 1890).

See also **Macaulay's Maxim.**

(Nicholas Murray) Butler's Observation

An expert is one who knows more and more about less and less.

Nicholas Murray Butler is credited with making this observation during one of the many commencement addresses that he delivered as president of Columbia University, which he headed for forty-four years (1901-45).

Bohr's Amendment. An expert is a man who has made all the mistakes which can be made in a very narrow field (Niels Henrik David Bohr, as quoted by Edward Teller at the American embassy in London, November 10th, 1972).

Gropius's Rider. Specialists are people who always repeat the same mistakes (Walter Gropius, as quoted in *Contemporary Architects,* 1980).

Heisenberg's Optimistic Reflection. An expert is someone who knows some of the worst mistakes that can be made in his subject and how to avoid them (Werner Heisenberg, *Physics and Beyond,* 1969, A. J. Pomerans, tr., 1971).

Warren's Rule. To spot the expert, pick the one who predicts the job will take the longest and cost the most (in Arthur Bloch, *The Complete Murphy's Law,* 1991).

(Samuel) Butler's Law

Spare the rod and spoil the child.

This approach to child-rearing was by no means original to Samuel Butler, but his expression of it in *Hudibras* (1663) a mock-epic satirising the Puritans, appears to be the first statement of the law in what is considered to be its classic form. The complete couplet: "Love is a boy by poets stydled / Then spare the rod and spoil the child."

This is only one of many proverbial sayings in the poem, e.g. "make the fur fly," "made his mouth to water," "have a care o' the main chance," and "look before you ere you leap."

Buttered Toast, Law of

See **Payn's Law.**

Byron's Law

Truth is stranger than fiction.

This is the popular version of what George Noel Gordon, Lord Byron (1788-1824) actually wrote in *Don Juan* (Canto XIV, 1823):

'Tis strange – but true; for truth is always strange;
Stranger than fiction.

Byron probably latched onto a proverbial expression here. Almost a half century previously, Edmund Burke expressed the same thought in slightly different words: "When we speak of the commerce with our colonies, fiction lags after truth; invention is unfruitful, and imagination cold and barren" (*Second Speech on Conciliation with America*, March 22nd, 1775). Another traditional variant: "Truth is stranger than fiction, but not so popular." Then there is:

Mark Twain's Corollary. Truth is stranger than Fiction, but it is because Fiction is obliged to stick to possibilities; Truth isn't ('Pudd'nhead Wilson's New Calendar', in *Following the Equator*, 1897).

C

Caesar's Law

Caesar's wife must be above suspicion.

This law has been broadened considerably from its initial domestic application to become the standard by which the actions of government officials are judged, the theory being that those who partake of the public purse should avoid the appearance of impropriety (not to mention impropriety itself). Caesar did not actually articulate this law in the form in which it usually is cited today. What he really said when asked why he had divorced his wife Pompeia was, according to Plutarch, "I wished my wife to be not so much as suspected." And while regarded as a test of high morality today, Caesar's Law, as initially declared, has a strong odour of hypocrisy about it.

Caesar's comment was made while testifying at the trial in 62 B.C. of Publius Clodius for profaning a sacred rite, not Pompeia, though he may well have done both. At least, we have it on the authority of Plutarch that Clodius "was in love with Pompeia, and she had no aversion to him." All this became a matter of public record when it was discovered that the celebrants at an all-night fertility rite honouring *Bona Dea* (the Good Goddess), conducted by Pompeia and the Vestal Virgins in Caesar's own house (he was Chief Pontiff at the time), and from which men were strictly barred, had included Clodius – young, beardless, and licentious – dressed up as a girl. He had come to the house, hoping for what Plutarch terms an "interview" with Pompeia. While going through the house in search of her, he encountered Caesar's mother's maid, who asked him "to play with her, as the women did among themselves." Clodius declined but in so doing betrayed himself by the masculine sound of his voice.

Uproar! Clodius tried to hide but the women found him in a closet and kicked him out of the house. By the next day the story of what had happened was all over town. Caesar proceeded to part from his wife and Clodius was brought to trial for sacrilege. Allegations also were made of perjury, bribery, and the debauching of women – including his sisters. (They themselves were no angels. One of them, Clodia, became the 'Lesbia' who drove the poet Catallus to distraction. Another was nicknamed 'Quadrantia', because a lover had tricked her into surrendering herself for a purse of copper money instead of silver – the smallest copper coin being a quadrant.) But not to worry. Though Clodius had many enemies among the patricians, especially his aggrieved brothers-in-law, he was immensely popular with the masses and, hence, of political use to Caesar.

This, then, was the background to Caesar's testimony at the trial. Summoned as a witness against Clodius, Caesar said he had nothing to charge him with. Asked why, if that was so, he had divorced his wife, Caesar produced his famous reply. In the context, it amounted to an evasion and it helped get Clodius off the hook. Plutarch says most of the jurors gave "their opinions so written as to be illegible, that they might not be in danger from the people by condemning him, nor in disgrace with the nobility by acquitting him." Almost certainly they were bribed, and with Caesar's connivance. Thus exonerated, Clodius went on to become an important political ally of the man who was so concerned that his wife be above suspicion.

For more about Roman justice, see **Cicero's Laws for Historians.**

Caesar's Maxims

Julius Caesar was a profound student of human nature as well as a great general, and he was as good at marshaling words as men. (Plutarch tells us that he dictated while on horseback and often kept two or more secretaries busy simultaneously.) In addition to the law cited above, he made a number of other memorable observations in his own writings and as reported by others, including:

Men readily believe what they want to believe.

As a rule, men's minds are more deeply disturbed by what they do not see.

What we desire we readily believe, and what we ourselves think we expect others to think.

Chance, which means a great deal in all sorts of circumstances, but especially in war, can effect great changes with a very slight shift of the balance.

Avoid a strange and unfamiliar word as you would a dangerous reef.

If you must break the law, do it only to seize power: in all other cases observe it.

Cameron's Rule of Etiquette

You scratch my back, I'll scratch yours.

This rule is attributed to Simon Cameron, powerful Pennsylvanian politician, U.S. Senator, and first secretary of war in Abraham Lincoln's first administration. In practice, Secretary Cameron's mutual back-scratching bore a close resemblance to corruption, with an unseemly number of war contracts being awarded without competitive bidding to firms in his own state. He even scratched his own back, with much military traffic being routed over railroads in which he and the assistant secretary of war had direct financial interests. In all of this, Cameron was running true to form: Long before the war started, he was so widely believed to have cheated an Indian tribe on a supply contract that he was nicknamed 'the Winnebago Chief.'

Lincoln dealt with the Cameron scandal by asking for his resignation from the cabinet in January 1862. The House of Representatives launched an investigation that eventually resulted in a formal censure of the Secretary's conduct but Lincoln, an astute politician himself, spirited Cameron away in the meantime by naming him ambassador to Russia.

See also **Walpole's Law**.

Campbell's Law

It doesn't matter what you do, as long as you don't do it in public and frighten the horses.

This pronouncement traditionally is credited to Mrs. Patrick Campbell (1865-1940), though she lived well into the age of the automobile, which not only replaced the horse but completely changed courting customs. A celebrated actress (Shaw had her in mind when he wrote the role of Eliza Doolittle in *Pygmalion*), Mrs. Campbell also was famous for her wit. Another of her bon mots: "Marriage is a result of the longing for the deep, deep peace of the double bed after the hurley-burley of the chaise-longue." There speaks experience.

Camus's Regretful Conclusion

Alas, after a certain age, every man is responsible for his own face (Albert Camus, *The Fall*, 1956).

See also Orwell's Corollary to **De Maistre's Law**.

Cannon's Law

If you tell the boss you were late for work because you had a flat tyre, the next morning you will have a flat tyre (from the internet, January 8th, 1996).

A similar but more serious effect has been noticed by students, who explained away a day at the beach, or some similar absence, by telling the teacher that they had to attend the funeral of a greatly beloved aunt. This is almost guaranteed to bring on the aunt's death within the week.

Capone's Law

You can get a lot more done with a kind word and a gun than with a kind word alone.

This law was attributed to an outlaw – the gangster Al Capone – by economist Walter Heller. He was discussing the need for imposing wage and price controls to keep the inflation rate down instead of relying on presidential 'jawboning.' See also **Teddy Roosevelt's Law**.

Carlyle's First Law

The great law of culture is: Let each become all that he was created capable of being.

Thomas Carlyle, Scottish-born historian and philosopher, had an optimistic, rather romantic faith in the power of the individual. His bias was apparent from the beginning of his literary career, as evidenced by this law, taken from an 1827 essay in the *Edinburgh Review*.

Carlyle's Second Law

"Do the duty which lies nearest thee," which thou knowest to be a duty! The second duty will already have become clearer.

Thomas Carlyle also was known for his overbearing, brook-no-nonsense, apocalyptic style. The Second Law is from his philosophical satire, *Sartor Resartus* (Latin for 'The Tailor Re-tailored,' 1833-34).

Carlson's Corollary. Never go into a danger area unless it's your duty. Never hesitate if it is.

Lt. Col. Evans Fordyce Carlson, organiser of the Marine 2nd Raider 'Gung Ho' Battalion in World War II, wrote this in a letter to his former aide and close friend, 2nd Lt. Harry McCabe. According to Michael Blankfort's biography, *The Big Yankee: The Life of Carlson of the Raiders* (1947), McCabe continually consulted the letter as a guide to making decisions during the bloody battle of Iwo Jima in early 1945. Blankfort continues: "McCabe found it was his duty to go forward into a quarry, the center of a fierce fire-fight. He was wounded in his shoulder, refused evacuation; was wounded a few minutes later on the side of his head, refused evacuation again. The third bullet went through his head." Carlson's letter was found in his pocket.

Carothers's Insight

Something happens to a man when he puts on a necktie. It cuts off all the oxygen to his brain (A. J. Carothers, *The Secret of My Success*, 1987).

Carothers's Insight reinforces the validity of Henry David Thoreau's admonition: "Beware of all enterprises that require new clothes" (*Walden*, 1854).

Catt's Law

No written law has ever been more binding than unwritten custom supported by popular opinion.

Carrie Lane Chapman Catt, feminist, suffragette, and founder of the League of Women Voters, recognised the power of unwritten law with these words in a speech to the United States Senate on February 13th, 1900.

See also **Pindar's Law.**

Cavett's Law

As long as people will accept crap, it will be financially profitable to dispense it (Dick Cavett, *Playboy*, 1971).

See also **Bacon's Law.**

Cayo's Law

The only things that start on time are those that you're late for (wisdom from the internet, January 8th, 1996).

Cervantes's Law of Statistics

By a small sample we may judge of the whole piece.

Though remembered more as a writer than as a mathematician, it is clear from this line in *Don Quixote* (1605, 1615) that Miguel de Cervantes had a good grasp of statistical principles. Of course, the principles are subject to bending, as noted by Benjamin Disraeli: "There are three kinds of lies: lies, damned lies, and statistics" (as quoted by Mark Twain in his *Autobiography*, 1924).

Cervantes's knowledge of sampling techniques may have come from his regular employment as a purchasing agent for the Spanish navy – a job that paid so poorly that he was twice thrown into prison for debt.

Chandler's Law

You can't win them all.

Raymond Chandler, British-bred, American detective story writer, salted his hard-boiled prose with numerous insights into life generally. This universal law – the earliest occurrence of it in print according to *The Concise Oxford Dictionary of Proverbs* (1982) – appears in *The Long Goodbye* (1954). The line is delivered about half-way through the book by Roger Wade to Dr. Edward Loring: "Take it easy, Doc. You can't win them all." Neither Wade nor Loring are very nice men, but both are blessed with exceedingly attractive wives, as the detective hero, Philip Marlowe, has occasion to note in some detail.

See also **Berra's Law** for the great Yogi's explanation of why you can't win them all.

Chaucer's First Law

Time heals all wounds.

The basic thought, expressed by Chaucer in *Troilus and Criseyde* (ca. 1385), is proverbial. The Roman playwright Terence, writing in the second century B.C., brushed up against it in *The Self-Tormentor* ("Time removes distress"), while Sophocles, in the fifth century B.C., included it in *Oedipus Rex* ("Time eases all things"). Not all hands have agreed. According to a fragment from Demetrius, a philospher of the first century, A.D., "Time makes all things worse." But he was a member of the Cynic school of philosophy.

In our own time, the proverb was amended by Jane Sherwood Ace, who produced the elegant "Time wounds all heels." This version also crops up in *The Marx Brothers Go West* (1940), but Ms. Ace's husband Goodman gave her credit for orginating the spoonerism in *The Fine Art of Hypochondria; or, How Are You?* (1966). He might be suspected of bias in favour of his wife but for her renown as a specialist in malapropisms on 'The Easy Aces,' their long-running (1930-45) radio show. ("Congress is still in season" and "I'm really in a quarry" were other Jane Ace-isms.) For his part, Goodman Ace (1899-1982) deserves to be remembered for having discovered the secret formula for a care-free old age: ICRI = FI, which translates as "If You Can't Recall It, Forget It."

Chaucer's Second Law

Love is blind.

This basic law, as expressed here by Geoffrey Chaucer in *The Merchant's Tale* (ca. 1387-1400), is essentially proverbial. Back in the fourth century B.C., the Athenian playwright Menander put it this way: "Love blinds all men alike, both the reasonable and the foolish" *(Andria)*. And a couple of hundred years after Chaucer, Shakespeare added: "But love is blind, and lovers cannot see the pretty follies that they themselves commit" *(The Merchant of Venice)*. It was Chaucer, however, who also noted in *The Romance of the Rose* that love is especially blind at some times of the year: "Hard is the heart that loveth not in May."

Chaucer's Third Law

Murder will out.

In full, and in the original, from *The Prioress's Tale*: "Mordre wol out, certein, it wol not faille" (ca. 1387-1400). Like Chaucer's other laws, "Murder will out" probably is a proverbial expression. He himself reused it, twice within the space of six lines, in *The Nun's Priest's Tale*. Many other writers have expressed much the same thought, including Shakespeare ("Murder, though it hath no tongue, will speak," *Hamlet*, 1601), John Webster ("Murder shrieks out," *The Duchess of Malfi*, ca. 1613), William Congreve ("Love and murder will out," *The Double Dealer*, 1693), and Ralph Waldo Emerson ("murder will speak out of stone walls," (Harvard Divinity School commencement address, 1838).

Cheops's Law

No project was ever completed on time and within budget (internet, January 8th, 1996).

The great pyramid of Giza, erected in the early twenty-sixth century B.C. by the second pharaoh of the Fourth Dynasty, Khufu, known to Herodotus and hence, to most of us, as Cheops, is 756 feet square and originally rose to about 480 feet. It consists of well over two million blocks of stone, weighing an average of about two and one half tons apiece. (Some are as much as fifty tons.) All were wrestled into position by sheer muscle-power, with the aid of ramps, ropes, levers, and sleds. The original budget and construction schedule are not known, but considering the scale of the project, it would not be surprising if there were cost and time overruns. Rudyard Kipling, for one, seems to have suspected this, noting in *Departmental Ditties* (1912):

> *Who shall doubt the secret hid*
> *Under Cheops' pyramid*
> *Was that the contractor did*
> *Cheops out of several millions?*

See also the second of **Murphy's Laws**.

Cheshire's Law of the Social Jungle

Everything that goes up must come down.

As *Washington Post* society columnist Maxine Cheshire told *Life* magazine (February 28th, 1969): "I am going to write a Maxine Cheshire guide to social climbing and have it sold with the souvenir items. My law is 'Everything that goes up must come down.'" The basic thought is of considerable antiquity, of course, though the pre-Socratic Greek philosopher Heraclitus was not thinking of social climbing when he asserted in *On the Universe* that "The way up is the way down." Also pre-dating Ms. Cheshire, but by a rather lesser degree, was Wilson Mizner (1876-1933), who produced:

Mizner's Companion to Cheshire's Law. Be nice to people on your way up because you'll need them on your way down (as quoted in Alva Johnston's *The Incredible Mizners*).

See also **Heraclitus's Law** and **Mizner's Law of Research.**

Chisholm's Laws of Human Interaction

1. If anything can go wrong, it will.
2. When things are going well, something will go wrong.
3. Purposes, as understood by the purposer, will be judged otherwise by others.

Chisholm's First Law is the same as Murphy's Law but was discovered independently by Francis P. Chisholm, a professor of English at Wisconsin State College in River Falls, who described it in a paper, 'The Chisholm Effect,' originally published in *Motive* and introduced to a larger audience through inclusion in *A Stress Analysis of A Strapless Evening Gown And Other Essays For A Scientific Age* (Robert A. Baker, ed., 1963).

Professor Chisholm was inspired to develop his three laws by reports in early 1958 in *Astounding Science Fiction* of the frequent appearance in scientific labs and engineering contexts of the Finagle Factor and Diddle Constant. "No matter how carefully an experiment was set up, something *always* went wrong, usually in precisely the operation which *could not* go wrong. The difference between expected and achieved results could, in fact, be expressed in an exact relation, called the *Snafu equation*, involving the Finagle constants," said Chisholm. Generalising from these mostly pseudonymous reports, Chisholm produced his three laws, complete with corollaries. Thus, we have the set of laws, in full panoply, as revealed to the world by their discoverer:

Chisholm's First Law of Human Interaction. If anything can go wrong, it will.

> *Corollary:* If anything just can't go wrong, it will anyway.

Chisholm's Second Law of Human Interaction. When things are going well, something will go wrong.

> *First Corollary:* When things just can't get any worse, they will.

> *Second Corollary:* Anytime things appear to be going better, you have overlooked something.

Chisholm's Third Law of Human Interaction. Purposes, as understood by the purposer, will be misunderstood by others.

> *First Corollary:* If you explain so clearly that nobody can misunderstand, somebody will.

> *Second Corollary:* If you do something which you are sure will meet everybody's approval, somebody won't like it.

> *Third Corollary:* Procedures devised to implement the purpose won't quite work.

The Third Corollary to the Third Law closes the circle, as Professor Chisholm noted, by referring back to the First Law.

See also **Finagle's Law** and **Murphy's Law**.

Cicero's Laws for Historians

The first law is that the historian shall never dare to set down what is false; the second, that he shall never dare to conceal the truth; the third, that there shall be no suspicion in his work of either favouritism or prejudice.

These high standards for historians were set forth by Marcus Tullius Cicero, orator, lawyer, statesman, philosopher, and man of letters in *De Oratore* (55 B.C.), a treatise on the art of public speaking. Cicero virtually created Latin prose, transforming a tight, terse, utilitarian language, fit for merchants, lawyers, and soldiers, into a strong but supple one, capable of conveying subtle feelings and shades of meaning. His influence extends not only to later Latin writers but to writers in other languages influenced by Latin. Many of his thoughts are of continuing relevance. For instance:

The nobler a man is, the harder for him to suspect baseness in others *(Ad Quintum fratrem, I)*.

Nothing quite new is perfect *(Brutus)*.

There is nothing so ridiculous but some philosopher has said it *(De Divinatione)*.

The people's good is the highest law *(De Legibus)*.

Let the punishment match the offence *(De Legibus)*.

Nothing stands out so conspicuously, or remains so firmly fixed in the memory, as something in which you have blundered *(De Oratore)*.

The greatest pleasures are only narrowly separated from disgust *(De Oratore)*.

No one has the right to be sorry for himself for a misfortune that strikes everyone *(Epistulae ad Familiares, VI)*.

No thinker has ever . . . said that a change of mind was inconsistency *(Epistulae at Atticum, XVI)*.

Any man is liable to err, only a fool persists in error *(Philippics, XII)*.

We forget our pleasures, we remember our sufferings *(Pro Murena)*.

In time of war the laws are silent *(Pro Milone)*.

One should eat to live, not live to eat *(Rhetoricorum)*.

In the end, it was Cicero's words, as contained in the famous *Philippics*, that led to his death. The *Philippics* were a series of fourteen speeches in which Cicero, leading the group of senators who hoped to restore the Republic following the assassination of Julius Caesar in 44 B.C., bitterly attacked Marc Antony, who threatened to succeed Caesar as dictator. To fend off Marc Antony, Cicero supported Caesar's heir, the nineteen-year-old Octavian, hoping that veteran legionaries would remain loyal to him until new units could be raised and led by republican commanders. ("An excellent youth, who must be praised, used, and pushed aside," Cicero is supposed to have said of Octavian.) But young Octavian played a deeper game, one that eventually culminated with his metamorphosis into the Emperor Augustus. He aligned himself with Antony and Lepidus, who had led Caesar's cavalry, to form a new triumvirate that quickly gained control of Rome. Once in power, their first act was to condemn numerous opponents, including, at Antony's determined insistence, Cicero. Antony then dispatched a party of soldiers to find and kill him. This mission accomplished, Antony had Cicero's head and hands (because they had written the *Philippics*) displayed in the Forum on the very rostrum where he had gained his reputation as Rome's greatest orator. Antony's wife Fulvia stuck a hairpin through the tongue.

For more about the splendours of Roman civilisation, see **Caesar's Law**.

Clarke's Laws

1. When a distinguished but elderly scientist states that something is possible, he is almost certainly right. When he states that something is impossible, he is very probably wrong.

2. The only way of discovering the limits of the possible is to venture a little way past them into the impossible.

3. Any sufficiently advanced technology is indistinguishable from magic.

Arthur C. Clarke set forth these laws in *Profiles of the Future* (1962, rev. ed. 1972). A prolific author of science fiction, Mr. Clarke – trained in physics and mathematics – also was first to suggest, back in 1945, that a satellite in a synchronous orbit, where it stays above the same point on the earth's surface, would make an ideal vehicle for relaying radio, television, and telephone signals over the horizon.

The history of science is littered with examples of Clarke's First Law. For example, John Trowbridge, head of the physics department at Harvard University, said in 1880 – just a year after Einstein was born – that every important discovery in physics had already been made. Then there was Lord Rutherford, who led the way in discovering the structure of the atom but pooh-poohed the possibility of obtaining energy from this source, saying in 1933 that "Anyone who expects a source of power from the transformation of these atoms is talking moonshine."

In explaining his law, Clarke pointed out that "elderly" in science is not so elderly by other standards. In physics and mathematics, for example, anyone over thirty is "elderly." In other scientific fields, "senile decay" may be postponed into the forties. After the age of fifty, scientists "are good for nothing but board meetings and should at all costs be kept out of the laboratory."

Clarke said he had "modestly decided to stop" with three laws "as three laws were good enough for Newton," but that has not kept others from building upon his work. Thus, his third law has been extended in what is known as **Jones's Law** (though who Jones is, or was, is not known): "Anyone who make a significant contribution to any field of endeavor, and stays in that field long enough, becomes an obstruction to its progress – in direct proportion to the importance of the original contribution" (in Arthur Block, *The Complete Murphy's Law*, 1991).

And Isaac Asimov, reflecting upon his own valiant efforts to puncture popular beliefs in astrology, flying saucers, Velikovskianism, and so on, and while also admitting that he was "a little over thirty and have been a little over thirty for a long time," amended Clarke with:

Asimov's Corollary to Clarke's First Law. When, however, the lay public rallies around an idea that is denounced by distinguished but elderly scientists and supports that idea with great fervour and emotion – the distinguished but elderly scientists are then, after all, probably right (*The Skeptical Inquirer*, Spring, 1979).

The significance of age thirty also has been noted in non-scientific contexts; see **Weinberg's Laws.**

Clausewitz's Law

War is nothing more than the continuation of politics by other means.

Except for professional soldiers and other dyed-in-the-wool students of military affairs, the Prussian general, Karl von Clausewitz, is remembered today only for this single line from his principal work on military strategy, *On War* (1833). It took a twentieth-century Chinese statesman to complete the thought:

Zhou's Amendment to Clausewitz's Law. All diplomacy is a continuation of war by other means. (Zhou Enlai, as quoted by quoted by Edgar Snow, *Saturday Evening Post*, March 27th, 1954).

Prime Minister Zhou was following Chairman Mao's line,

of course. As far back as 1938, the chairman had declared in a lecture that "Politics is war without bloodshed while war is politics with bloodshed." This was the same year that Mao explained the source of political power at a meeting of the Chinese Communist Party's Central Committee: "Political power grows out of the barrel of a gun." (This is a deeply un-American principle, of course. When the U.S. uses military power to achieve political ends, strategicians speak instead in terms of "coercive dioplomacy.")

Cleaver's Law

You're either part of the solution or you're part of the problem.

The law is associated with Eldridge Cleaver, who, as a leader of the Black Panther party, was much in the news when he enunciated it in a speech in San Francisco in 1968. The thought, however, was in the air. Thus, Buell Gallagher, president of City College of New York – and not the type of person who would be likely to join Mr. Cleaver in mounting the barricades – told the graduating class of 1964, "Be part of the answer, not part of the problem, as the American revolution proceeds." See also **Peers's Law** and **Spencer's Law**.

(Bill) Clinton's Laws of Politics

From a late-night interview with B. Drummond Ayres, Jr., of the *New York Times* (September 17th, 1992), aboard Bill Clinton's airplane during the 1992 election:

1. Always be introduced by someone you've appointed to high office.

2. When you're starting to have a good time, you're supposed to be someplace else.

3. There is no such thing as enough money.

4. If someone tells you it's not a money problem, it's someone else's problem.

5. When someone tells you it's not personal, they're fixing to stick it to you.

6. Nearly everyone will lie to you given the right circumstance.

See also **O'Neill's Rule** and **Senator Sorghum's Laws of Politics**.

Cohen's Rules of Book Publishing

1. There is only one thing worse than losing an auction for a book – and that is winning it.

2. It is nearly always more profitable to leave your money in the bank than to venture into trade book publishing [i.e. fiction and non-fiction for general readers as opposed to textbooks, reference books, and so on], where a profit margin of even 5 percent is elusive.

3. No two people will agree on anything, even where to have lunch.

Roger Cohen, who discovered these rules while covering the book publishing beat for the *New York Times*, pointed out that the third rule is the most important one because it underscores a central fact about the business: "Nothing in publishing is demonstrably true. Optimism and pessimism, fact and rumor, statistics and guesswork mingle so completely that objective certitude and this industry bear as much relation to each other as Argentine steak and a vegetarian dinner" (September 2nd, 1991).

For more about publishing lunches, see **Creasey's Law**.

Coleridge's Law of Moral Polarity

When the maximum of one tendency has been attained, there is no gradual decrease, but a direct transition to its minimum, till the opposite tendency has attained its maximum.

Samuel Taylor Coleridge dispensed this scrap ("ort" for crossword puzzlers) of wisdom in *Table Talk* (April 25th, 1832). At the time, one suspects, he was sitting opposite a pendulum clock. Laudanum might also have helped.

Colson's Law

If you've got them by the balls, their hearts and minds will follow.

This law frequently is attributed to Charles T. Colson, special counsel to President Richard M. Nixon, somewhat unfairly because he did not originate this method of winning hearts and minds. The law actually arose as an ironic catchphrase during the war in Vietnam, where 'hearts and minds' was a slogan of the pacification program. But there is some rough justice here, too, since Colson kept a poster with this motto on the wall of his White House office, and he was well known for his take-no-prisoners approach to politics. For example, it was Colson who scared the pants off John Dean in 1971 by suggesting that the Brookings Institution in Washington, D.C., be firebombed so that one of Dean's men could slip into the building with firefighters and break into its vault amid the confusion. (Dean managed to get the plot nixed.)

The importance of winning hearts and minds has been understood for many years. As John Adams explained in a letter to Hezekiah Niles: "The Revolution was effected before the war commenced. The Revolution was in the hearts and minds of the people . . . The radical change in the principles, opinions, sentiments, and affections of the people was the real American Revolution" (February 2nd, 1818).

Comins's Law

People will accept your idea much more readily if you tell them Benjamin Franklin said it first.

David H. Comins, of Manchester, Connecticut, produced this law in a letter to *Harper's* in August, 1974. It is one of a number of laws submitted by readers to the magazine's 'Wraparound' section at the invitation of the editors. Of this group of laws, the best known is **Ettore's Law of Lines**.

Confucius's Law

Behave to everyone as if you were receiving a great guest; . . [do not] do to others what you would not wish done to yourself.

This declaration by Kung Fu Zi (Master Kung), or Confucius, in the more familiar, Latinised form of his name, is from the *Analects*, a collection of sayings and incidents from the life of the philosopher (551-479 B.C.). The *Analects* make up one of the 'The Four Books' attributed to Confucius and his disciples. Gathered together and published in 1190, they became the primary textbooks in Chinese education, serving as the basis for civil service examinations for some six hundred years, from about 1300 to 1905.

Confucius's Law is essentially the same as the Golden Rule, subsequently expressed by other thinkers in other ways. For example, Aristotle contended (about one hundred and fifty years after Confucius) that "We should behave to our friends as we would wish our friends to behave to us" (Diogenes Laertius, *Lives of Eminent Philosophers*), while Jesus Christ said in the Sermon on the Mount, "Therefore all things whatsoever ye would that men should do to you, do ye even so unto them: for this is the law and the prophets" (Matthew 7:12). And Philip Dormer Stanhope, fourth Earl of Chesterfield, who typically coated good advice with an unctuous, self-serving veneer, told his son, "Do as you would be done by, is the surest method of pleasing" (letter, October 9th, 1747). Then there is:

Henry Kissinger's Amendment (as reported in a biography of the former Secretary of State): "In a conversation with Golda Meir, Nixon once twisted the golden rule into a power game, telling her, 'My rule in international affairs is, "Do unto others as they would do unto you."' At which Kissinger interjected, 'Plus 10 percent'" (Walter Isaacson, *Kissinger*, 1992).

Confucius, Aristotle, Christ, Chesterfield, and apparently Nixon and Kissinger, too, share the underlying assumption that people agree generally on how they want to be treated – which is not always the case. For example, Henry David Thoreau was very suspicious of people who tried to do good to other people. From his retreat at Walden Pond, he asserted that "If I knew for a certainty that a man was coming to my house with the conscious design of doing me good, I should run for my life" ('Economy', *Walden*, 1854).

Other notable dissenters include George Bernard Shaw, who turned the Golden Rule upside down, asserting in *Man and Superman* (1903): "Do not do unto others as you would they should do unto you. Their tastes may not be the same." And Bishop Mandell Creighton, taking much the same tack as Thoreau, warned that "No people do so much harm as those who go about doing good" (in Louise Creighton, *Life*, 1904).

Then there is the modern, anonymous, and profoundly cynical version of the Golden Rule: "The guy with the gold gets to make the rules." This last one demonstrates, in case anyone has any doubts, that we no longer live in a Golden Age but one of Brass.

See also the first of **Shaw's Maxims** and **Kant's Categorical Imperative**.

Congreve's Conclusion

Hell hath no fury like a woman scorned.

This is the popular condensation of a couplet in the *The Mourning Bride* (1697) by William Congreve:

> *Heaven has no rage like love to hatred turned,*
> *Nor hell a fury like a woman scorned.*

Congreve apparently lifted the thought from *Love's Last Shift*, a play by Colley Cibber, that was produced a year earlier. In Cibber's version: "We shall find no fiend in hell can match the fury of a disappointed woman." The idea has since been further refined with the appearance of:

Connolly's Corollary. There's no fury like an ex-wife searching for a new lover (Cyril Connolly, *The Unquiet Grave*, 1945).

Friedman's Corollary. Hell hath no fury like a bureaucrat scorned (Milton Friedman, *Newsweek*, December 29th, 1975).

Gregory's Corollary. Hell hath no fury like a liberal scorned (Dick Gregory, quoted in Jonathon Green, *The Cynic's Lexicon*, 1984).

Connolly's Observation

Whom the gods wish to destroy they first call promising (Cyril Connolly, *Enemies of Promise*, 1938).

See also **Wilde's First Law**.

Conran's Law of Cooking

Life is too short to stuff a mushroom.

Shirley Conran used this personal motto as the epigraph to *Superwoman* (1975). It is unlikely that Ralph Waldo Emerson ever stuffed a mushroom, but he expressed much the same opinion as Ms. Conran, albeit in more detail in 'To J.W.' in his collected *Poems* (1847):

> *Life is too short to waste*
> *In critic peep or cynic bark,*
> *Quarrel or reprimand:*
> *'Twill soon be dark;*
> *Up! mind thine own aim, and*
> *God speed the mark!*

Conran's Law of Housework

It [housework] *expands to fill the time available plus half an hour: so obviously it is never finished.*

Elucidating this law in *Superwoman 2* (1977), Ms. Conran pointed out that "You cannot have everything and certainly cannot dust everything." Her solution: "Keep housework in its place, which you will remember, is underfoot."

See also **Parkinson's Law**.

The Cop's Law

It's better to be tried by twelve men than to be carried by six.

This is not so much a rule-of-thumb as a rule-of-forefinger, devised by police officers to justify the use of pistols in case of doubt (personal communication, Natalie Chapman, February 20th, 1990).

The Copernican Principle

Earth and earthlings are not at the centre of the universe.

Nicholas Copernicus (1473-1543) waited until he was on his deathbed (and no longer had any fear of ecclesiastical retribution) to publish his revolutionary *De Revolutionibus Orbium Coelestium*, in which he proposed the then mind-boggling theory that Earth was not at the centre of Everything. "Finally we shall place the Sun himself at the centre of the Universe," he wrote. "All this is suggested by the systematic procession of events and the harmony of the whole Universe, if only we face the facts, as they say, 'with both eyes open.'"

Subsequently, with the aid of telescopes (astronomers began squinting with one eye, not two, but saw further), it became clear that the 'Sun himself' is but one of billions of stars, situated along the outer edge of but one of billions of galaxies. From this, most cosmologists suppose that

1. some other stars must have planets;

2. some of these planets must have conditions suitable for supporting life;

3. life must have arisen on some of them, and

4. that some of these life forms must be (have been? will be?) intelligent in the sense that earthlings recognise intelligence.

No matter how great the odds against life arising on any particular planet of any particular star, our sun seems so typical of an immense number of stars that the final conclusion is hard to escape.

The implications of the Copernican Principle have been appreciated by acute observers for quite some time. For example, realising the the sun was just another star, Christiaan Huygens (1629-95), the exceedingly versatile Dutch astronomer, mathematician, and physicist (he built the finest telescopes of his time, determined the nature of Saturn's rings, made the first suggestion that light travels as a wave, and invented the pendulum clock, among other achievements), asked in his posthumously published *Cosmothereos*: "Why may not every one of these stars or suns have as great a retinue as our sun, of planets, with their moons to wait upon them?" Continuing this train of thought, he argued that the qualities of the planets in our solar system must be similar "to all those planets that surround that prodigious number of suns. They must have their plants and animals, nay and their rational creatures too, and those as great admirers, and as diligent observers of the heavens as ourselves."

The first planet circling a sun similar to ours, 51 Pegasus, was discovered in 1995.

Cornuel's Observation

No man is a hero to his valet.

Credit for this famous insight sometimes is given to Madame de Sévigné, but the observation actually was made first in this form by her contemporary, Madame Anne Bigot du Cornuel (1605-95), according to a letter of August 13th, 1728, of Madamoiselle Aissé. (*Aissé*, by the way, is a corruption of *Haidée*. The daughter of a Circassian chief, she was captured by the Turks, sold as a slave at about the age of four in 1698 to the French ambassador at Constantinople, and raised in France. She was famed for her beauty during her lifetime and for her letters afterward. She died in 1733. The first edition of her letters was edited in 1787 by Voltaire.) As for Madame du Cornuel: It seems probable that she made her remark about heros and their valets soon after reading Montaigne's *Essays*, in which he notes that "Many a man has been a wonder to the world, whose wife and valet have seen nothing in him that was even remarkable. Few men have been admired by their servants" (third edition, 1595).

The essential idea is much older, of course. Aesop, back in the sixth century B.C., knew full well what familiarity breeds; see the third of **Aesop's Adages**. Then there was Antigonus Gonatas (ca. 312-239 B.C.), the Macedonian king who refuted a flatterer's suggestion that he might be divine, saying

"The man who carries my chamberpot knows better." This, too, is a timeless thought. Thus, David Owen, author of *The Walls Around Us: The Thinking Person's Guide to How a House Works*, told the *New York Times* (September 26th, 1991): "No man is a hero in the eyes of his septic-tank pumper." Obviously, there is nothing new under the outhouse.

Costello's Conclusion

There are more horses' asses in this world than there are horses.

This bit of folk wisdom was conveyed to the author in a letter in 1983 from David F. Costello, author of *The Prairie World* and other books, and a keen-eyed observer of man as well as nature. A watered-down version of this observation is included in Paul Dickson's *The Official Rules* (1978) as Tishbein's Law: "There are more horses' backsides in the military service of the United States than there are horses." It is not known who Tishbein is or was, but the law was credited to him in this form at West Point, which suggests that it dates to the cavalry era.

Creasey's Law

Never buy an editor or publisher a lunch or a drink until he has bought an article, story or book from you. This rule is absolute and may be broken only at your peril.

British detective story writer John Creasey (1908-73), as quoted here by Bill Cole in the *New York Times* (September 3rd, 1989), had some inkling of what he was talking about, having suffered innumerable rejections before the first of his novels, *Seven Times Seven*, was published in 1932. Once having broken through, there was no holding him, and he went on to publish another five hundred or so detective stories, using numerous pseudonyms, the best known of which was J. J. Marric. Mr. Cole's round-up of comments about book publishing also included a reflection by Calvin Trillin:

Trillin's Corollary to Creasey's Law. The advance [against author's royalties] for a book should be at least as much as the cost of the lunch at which it was discussed.

See also **Cohen's Rules of Book Publishing.**

Crosby's Law of Advertising

The first law in advertising is to avoid the concrete promise – and cultivate the delightfully vague.

John Crosby, columnist, author, and most literate critic of an illiterate medium (television), made this observation in the *New York Herald Tribune* (August 18th, 1947).

Crystal's Law of Executive Pay

The smaller the company, the less a chief executive's compensation is related to the company's performance or size.

Graef S. Crystal, adjunct professor of business at the University of California in Berkeley, discovered this law after analysing the pay of chief executives of 1,936 quoted companies for 1994. At the 484 smallest companies in this group he found no link at all between the chief executive's compensation and corporate performance and only a tenuous relation between compensation and corporate size. "It's a table of random numbers, like throwing darts against a wall," Mr. Crystal told the *New York Times* (February 22nd, 1996).

Thus, Raymond L. Killian, head of Investment Technology Group, a New York company, was rewarded with $15.5 million dollars in salary and other benefits in 1994, while his company, with just 125 employees and revenues of $7.9 million, reported a $7.9 million loss for the year. Of course, many companies manage to pay their chief executives even while losing money on their operations. More startling, in a way, were the twelve companies in Mr. Crystal's sample that had after-tax profits – but did not make as much money as their chief executives.

The discrepancies between compensation (defined as cash salary plus stock options and other benefits), corporate performance (as measured by the gain in stock price and the value of reinvested dividends), and size (according to number of employees, invested capital, and revenues) appeared to be largely the result of the cosy informality of small companies. The chief executives of small companies may also be large shareholders in them, their compensation is determined almost totally by boards of directors rather than by formula or by achieving specific goals, and financial analysts and the media do not pay much attention to smaller firms. As Mr. Crystal told the *Times*: "Nobody's watching, nobody's looking under the rocks."

D

Dante's Law

The hottest places in hell are reserved for those who in a period of moral crisis maintain their neutrality.

President John F. Kennedy attributed this law to Dante in a talk that he gave in Bonn on June 24th, 1963. The occasion was the signing of a charter establishing the German Peace Corps. JFK had been struck by the quote some years before. In *A Thousand Days*, Arthur M. Schlesinger reported finding this line, along with others from Burke, Churchill, Jefferson, and so on, in a loose-leaf notebook that Kennedy kept in 1945-46. This particular line does not appear in Dante's works, however, and the young Kennedy's citations sometimes left something to be desired. (For example, he attributed **Hiram Johnson's Law** to Aeschylus.) Perhaps JFK telescoped the somewhat similar thought that does appear in Canto III of *The Inferno*, when Virgil tells Dante, just after the two pass through the gates of Hell (in John Ciardi's translation):

> *They [the nearly soulless] are mixed here with*
> *that despicable corps*
> *of angels who were neither for God nor Satan,*
> *but only for themselves. The High Creator*
> *scourged them from Heaven for its perfect beauty,*
> *and Hell will not receive them since the wicked*
> *might feel some glory over them.*

While those who profess neutrality may be barred from

hell, the road there is broad and remarkably easy to follow. As C.S. Lewis noted in *The Screwtape Letters* (1941): "The safest road to Hell is the gradual one – the gentle slope, soft underfoot, without sudden turnings, without milestones, without signposts." This was Mr. Lewis's update, in effect, of the Bible: "Wide is the gate, and broad is the way, that leadeth to destruction" (Matthew: 7:13).

See also **Burke's Law** and **Marx's Third Law**.

Dante's Observation

He listens well who takes notes.

The line (*Bene ascolta chi la nota*) is from Canto XV of *The Inferno* (pre-1321) by Dante Alighieri. The expression is proverbial in Italian.

(Charles) Darwin's Law

This preservation of favourable individual differences and variations, and the destruction of those that are injurious, I have called Natural Selection, or the Survival of the Fittest (The Origin of the Species, 1859).

Charles Darwin used the term 'natural selection' in contradistinction to the power of selection exercised by humans when breeding plants and animals. He took the phrase 'Survival of the Fittest' from Herbert Spencer, acknowledging in *The Origin of the Species* that it "is more accurate than Natural Selection" and "is sometimes equally convenient." See also **Spencer's Law**.

In Darwin's theory of evolution, natural selection is the mechanism that produces varieties of species (or "incipient species," as Darwin called them), new species, and new groups of species, or genera. He argued that these results stemmed from what he termed "the struggle for life":

Owing to this struggle, variations, however slight and from whatever cause proceeding, if they be in any degree profitable to the individuals of a species, in their infinitely complex relations to other organic beings and to their physical conditions of life, will tend to the preservation of such individuals, and will generally be inherited by their offspring. The offspring, also, will have a better chance of surviving, for, of the many individuals of any species which are periodically born, but a small number can survive.

The struggle for life, in turn, was, as implied here, a consequence of the astonishingly high rates at which plants and animals tend to reproduce.

See also **Malthus's Law** and **Wells's Second Law**.

(Sir Francis) Darwin's Law

In science, the credit goes to the man who convinces the world, not to the man to whom the idea occurs (Eugenics Review, *April 1914*).

Sir Francis (1848-1925) was the second son of Charles Darwin and a distinguished botanist in his own right. See also **The Matthew Effect**.

Data's Law

All things which can occur, do occur (Lieutenant Commander Data, in *Star Trek, The Next Generation*, repeat, many times, from 1987).

Data's Law refers to the weird world of quantum mechanics, as noted by Lawrence Krauss, author of *The Physics of Star Trek* (1995) in *Natural History* (June, 1996). *The Next Generation*'s android crew member was inspired to enunciate this law when a character named Worf began jumping wildly from one 'quantum reality' to another. Data's Law is another formulation of **Gell-Mann's Dictum**.

David's Qwerty Factor

The product that sets a de facto standard will dominate the marketplace whether or not it is the best one technologically.

The Qwerty Factor was the brainchild of Paul A. David, who unveiled it in 'Clio and the Economics of Qwerty,' a 1985 article in *American Economics Review*. Professor David, who doubles as a faculty member at Stanford University and a senior research fellow at All Souls College at Oxford University, demonstrated his idea with an analysis of the history of the typewriter. On the very first model, made in 1867 by Christopher Latham Sholes, the keyboard was arranged in alphabetic order. The keys kept jamming against each other, however, so Sholes tried other arrangements. First he put the most frequently used letters in the middle of the keyboard, the way a hand-typsetter's case was organised. When this set-up proved less than satisfactory, he went in the opposite direction, rearranging the keyboard so that the letters that occur together most often in writing were furthest apart. This resulted in 1872 in the familiar layout for which The Qwerty Factor is named, with the keys for the letters Q-W-E-R-T-Y being the first six in the top row of letters of typewriters and, nowadays, computer keyboards in the English-speaking world.

But is QWERTY the best system? Not everyone agrees. Other arrangements have been tried, such as DHIATENSOR, whose ten letters are said to spell 70 percent of the words in the English language, and the Dvorak Simplified Keyboard, whose proponents have established many records for speed typing. QWERTY rules, however, because touch-typing schools adopted it in the 1880s and it became the de facto standard. Once this happened, people and businesses found it too inconvenient to change to another system, even a possibly more efficient one.

And is all this just of academic interest? You can begin by asking Microsoft's Bill Gates, whose Windows operating system dominates the market even though most computer aficionados agree that Apple's system remains easier to use, despite the upgrades in Windows over the years. Windows became standard because Microsoft did a better job of marketing its system, especially to companies, and the advantage became self-reinforcing as more programs were written for it.

The Qwerty Factor also helps explain such other technological outcomes as the use of alternating current rather than direct current for transmitting power (Edison preferred the latter); the triumph of VHS over Beta videocassette tape, though most people who tried both thought that Beta was technically superior; and the adoption in the U.S. of light-water nuclear reactors although they are less efficient than gas-cooled reactors.

Poor Ralph Waldo Emerson probably is spinning in his grave; see **Emerson's Second Law**.

Davis's Commandment

The first and great commandment is, Don't let them scare you.

The commandment is from *But We Were Born Free* (1954), an attack on Senator Joseph McCarthy and other political witch-hunters, by Elmer Davis, writer, radio broadcaster, and head of the Office of War Information during World War II.

DeCaprio's Law

Everything takes more time and money (Annie DeCaprio, Highbridge, N.J., in *Harper's*, August 1974). See also the second of **Murphy's Laws**.

Decatur's Law

My country, right or wrong.

This is the popular, patriotic, telegraphed version of the toast that Commodore Stephen Decatur gave at a dinner in his honour in April, 1816, in Norfolk, Virginia. The ringing declaration is qualified somewhat in the fuller version, as reported in *Niles' Weekly Register* on April 20: "Our country! In her intercourse with foreign nations, may she always be in the right; but our country, right or wrong." Cooler heads have backed off even further. Thus, we have:

John Quincy Adams's Amendment. My toast would be, may our country always be successful, but whether successful or otherwise, always right (letter, August 1st, 1816).

Carl Schurz's Amendment. Our country, right or wrong. When right, to be kept right. When wrong, to be put right (speech, October 17th, 1899).

G.K. Chesterton's Disclaimer. "My country, right or wrong" is a thing no patriot would think of saying except in a desperate case. It is like saying, "My mother, drunk or sober" ('Defense of Patriotism' in *The Defendant*, 1901).

Deighton's Law

You can't make women happy. That's a kind of fundamental law of the universe. You try and make them happy and they'll never forgive you for revealing to them that they can't be (Len Deighton, *Spy Story*, 1985).

With all due respect to Mr. Deighton, the laws governing the male-female relationship are substantially more complicated, as shown by the following set of rules that was photocopied and circulated widely by students at The Taft School, in Watertown, Conn., and presumably elsewhere, in 1990:

The Rules

1. The Female always makes the rules.

2. The Rules are subject to change at any time without prior notification.

3. No male can possibly know all the Rules. (*Pace*, Mr. Deighton.)

4. If the Female suspects the Male knows all of the Rules, she must immediately change some or all of the rules.

5. The Female is *NEVER* wrong.

6. If the Female is wrong, it is because of a flagrant misunderstanding which was the result of something the Male did or said wrong.

7. If Rule 6 applies, the Male must apologise immediately for causing the misunderstanding.

8. The Female can change her mind at any given point in time.

9. The Male must never change his mind without written consent from the Female.

10. The Female has every right to be angry or upset at any time.

11. The Male must remain calm at all time, unless the Female wants him to be angry or upset.

12. The Female must under *NO CIRCUMSTANCES* let the Male know whether or not she wants him to be angry or upset.

13. Any attempt to document these Rules could result in bodily harm.

14. If the Female has PMS, all Rules are null and void.

Delmas's Unwritten Law

The right of any red-blooded male to kill anyone who fools around with his wife, daughter, mistress, or other female near and dear, and then to escape punishment by pleading temporary insanity – a right rarely extended to women in analogous circumstances. Obsolete?

The unwritten law has been invoked many times but most famously in American legal history in 1907 by Delphin Delmas, a California lawyer ("the little Napoleon of the West Coast bar"), who was hired by Harry K. Thaw's mother to defend her playboy son for having murdered the nation's leading architect, Stanford White. The woman in this instance was Evelyn Nesbit, Thaw's wife and previously White's mistress. (La Nesbit generally is remembered as 'The Girl in the Red Velvet Swing' – the swing being a prominent and apparently well-used appurtenance of White's penthouse apartment in New York's original Madison Square Garden, a building that he had designed.) Madly jealous of her previous lover, Thaw walked over to the architect's table at the Garden's rooftop dining theater on the night of June 25th, 1906, and shot him to death.

Almost everyone who knew Thaw or was connected with the case, including the district attorney who prosecuted him, thought he was profoundly crazy and should be consigned to a mental institution. When brought to trial the following year, however, Delmas tried to save Thaw from both asylum and prison by arguing that his client had been in the grip of a temporary insanity, which he termed "*dementia Americana, the unwritten law.*" The little Napoleon pulled out all stops:

> If Thaw is insane, it is with a species of insanity that is known from the Canadian border to the Gulf. If you expert gentlemen ask me to give it a name, I

suggest that you label it *dementia Americana*. It is that species of insanity that inspires every American to believe that his home is sacred. It is that species of insanity that persuades an American that whoever violates the sanctuary of his home or the purity of his wife or daughter has forfeited the protection of the laws of this state or any other state.

The jury deadlocked after forty-seven hours, seven members concluding that Thaw was sane enough to be convicted for murder while five voted for acquittal. At a second trial, however, enough evidence of Thaw's irrationality, dating to boyhood, was presented to persuade that jury to acquit him on grounds of insanity. Thaw spent most of the next fifteen years (with time out for one escape and one brief release) in the Mattewan State Asylum for the Criminally Insane (now known more blandly as the Correction Center for Medical Services). He died in 1947.

See also **McNaughton's Rule**.

Dershowitz's Rules

I have three rules. I never believe what the prosecutor or police say. I never believe what the media say, and I never believe what my client says (Alan M. Dershowitz, Harvard Law professor and advocate-at-large, *New York Times*, October, 28th, 1994).

But see also **Belli's Law**.

Descartes's Dictum

I think, therefore I am (Cogito, ergo sum).

This statement by René Descartes in the *Discourse on Method* (1637) is the single most famous line in the history of philosophy, but it was topped by a newspaperman, Ambrose

Bierce, who suggested in *The Devil's Dictionary* (1911) that the dictum might be improved to *Cogito cogito ergo cogito sum.* I think that I think, therefore I think that I am. This, said Mr. Bierce, would constitute "as close an approach to certainty as any philosopher has yet made."

See also **Bierce's Law.**

Dewdney's Law of Zero Return

Return on investment equals loss due to inflation plus taxes . . . which equals zero.

A. K. Dewdney proposed this law in *Scientific American* (November, 1990) with, he said, tongue firmly in cheek. Still, it highlights factors – inflation and taxes – not appreciated by many people when making financial decisions. Dewdney illustrated his law with the following example: Suppose that you have $10,000 to invest, that the interest rate is 9 percent, that the inflation rate is 5.5 percent, and that you are in the 35 percent tax bracket. The $10,000 would grow to $10,900 in a year, but taxes would cut the $900 in earnings to $585, while inflation would reduce the purchasing power of $10,585 to $10,002.83 – not quite a zero rate of return, but close enough to give any investor the shivers.

The Diddle Constant

See **Chisholm's Laws of Human Interaction.**

Dirksen's Three Laws of Politics

1. Get elected.
2. Get re-elected.
3. Don't get mad, get even.

Senator Everett McKinley Dirksen, Republican from Illinois, served in the United States Senate for thirteen years (1957-

69), ten of them as minority leader. The last of Senator Dirksen's rules often is attributed to Joseph Patrick Kennedy, father of John F.

See also (**John F.**) **Kennedy's Law**.

Disraeli's First Law

Never complain and never explain.

A stoic rule, attributed to Benjamin Disraeli, popular novelist, twice prime minister of Great Britain, and 1st Earl of Beaconsfield, by John Morley in his *Life of William Ewart Gladstone* (1903). In our own time, the *New York Times* credited Henry Ford II in its 1987 obituary of him with having said "Never complain, never explain" after being arrested for drunk driving. Victor Lasky picked up the phrase and helped popularise it by using it as the title of his 1981 biography of the younger Ford.

Disraeli's rule has been amended in various ways. Thus, Elbert Hubbard declared in his *Note Book* (1927): "Never Explain – your Friends do not need it and your Enemies will not believe you anyway." And Barber Conable, Republican congressman from upstate New York and later head of the World Bank, popularised the corollary: "Whenever you have to start explaining – you're in trouble."

Disraeli's Second Law

What we anticipate seldom occurs; what we least expected generally happens.

This line from the future prime minister's *Henrietta Temple* (1837) clearly anticipates Murphy's Law by well over a hundred years.

See also **Gumperson's Law**. Disraeli produced many other excellent epigrams. Among them:

Time is the great physician *(Henrietta Temple)*.

Justice is truth in action (speech, February 11th, 1851).

Finality is not the language of politics (speech, February 28th, 1859).

Never take anything for granted (speech, October 5th, 1864).

Change is inevitable. In a progressive country, change is constant (speech, October 29th, 1867).

There can be no economy where there is no efficiency (speech, October 3rd, 1868).

Every woman should marry – and no man (*Lothair*, 1870).

The secret of success is constancy of purpose (speech, June 24th, 1872).

The Dixon Effect

If you make enough predictions, a few are bound to be correct. The hits are likely to be remembered, the misses forgotten, and you will win fame and possibly fortune as a forecaster of the future.

The effect was named by John Allen Paulos for Jeanne Pinckert Dixon (1918-1997), whose predictions were purveyed to the masses mainly in supermarket tabloids where they were taken for gospel by the credulous. Professor Paulos contended in *Beyond Innumeracy* (1991) that the phenomenon whereby a few correct predictions are widely heralded and many false ones conveniently ignored "is quite widespread and contributes to the tendency we all have to read more significance into coincidences than is usually justified. We forget all the premonitions of disaster we've had that didn't predict the future and remember vividly those couple that seemed to do so. Instances of seemingly telepathic thought are reported to everyone we know; the incomparably vaster number of times this doesn't occur is too banal to mention."

Mrs. Dixon was most famous for the claim that she predicted the assassination of President John F. Kennedy some seven years before the event. In fact, as pointed out by Milbourne Christopher in *ESP, Seers & Psychics* (1970), the so-called prophecy was much less precise. The actual prediction, originally publicised in the May 13th, 1956, issue of *Parade*, a nationally circulated magazine supplement to Sunday newspapers, was that "As to the 1960 election, Mrs. Dixon thinks it will be dominated by labor and won by a Democrat. But he will be assassinated or die in office, though not necessarily in his first term." Thus, the prediction was right about the winner's party, wrong about the election being dominated by labor, did not mention Kennedy by name, and fudged on the manner and time of death. Also conveniently forgotten by Mrs. Dixon's fans is that closer to the election, in January 1960, she predicted in a nationally syndicated column by Ruth Montgomery that Kennedy would not gain the presidency. And that in June, Mrs. Dixon declared that "the symbol of the presidency is directly over the head of Vice-President Nixon" but "unless the Republican party really gets out and puts forth every effort it will topple." In Christopher's words: "Fire enough shots, riflemen agree, and eventually you'll hit the bull's-eye."

Among the other predictions for which Jeane Dixon is not remembered because they were not fulfilled:

- President Eisenhower soon will "appoint five-star General Douglas MacArthur to an exceedingly important post, probably an ambassadorship" (Montgomery column of January 1st, 1953).

- "In 1963, CIO President Walter Reuther will make known to his Union followers that he intends to run for President of the United States the following year" (Montgomery column, October 23rd, 1954).

- "Russia will be the first nation to put a man on the moon, probably in three years time" (in Montgomery's bestselling biography of Mrs. Dixon, *A Gift of Prophecy*, 1965).

- The war in Vietnam "will be over in ninety days" (a prediction that elicited cheers when shared with students in the University of Southern California's Hancock Auditorium on May 7th, 1966, just about seven years before the United States troops pulled out of that country).

And so it goes. Thomas E. Dewey never got the "powerful new post at Ike's side" that Jeane Dixon saw for him. The 1980s came and went without the Earth being struck by a monster comet or the United States electing a woman president. The Roman Catholic Church somehow managed to survive her prediction that it would dissolve prior to 1990.

In *Beyond Innumeracy*, Professor Paulos also shows how a wily prognosticator can create a reputation for infallibility, at least over a short run. Pretend you are the publisher of a stockmarket newsletter and you send out 64,000 letters, half predicting that the Dow Jones index will rise the next week and half that it will fall. The next week you send out 32,000 letters, but only to the people who had received the correct 'prediction' the previous week. Again, half the letters predict a rise and half a decline. Continue the process, mailing 16,000 letters in the third week, but only to those who received correct 'predictions' in week two. After six weeks, you'll have winnowed your universe down to 1,000 people who have received six correct 'predictions' in a row – and they should be ready to eat out of your hand. Tell them they must pay $1,000 to continue receiving your marvelous tipsheet. The next time you go to the post office, take a wheelbarrow. Your mailbox may be stuffed with $1,000,000.

See also **Firestone's Law of Forecasting.**

Drazen's Law of Restitution

The time it takes to rectify a situation is inversely proportional to the time it took to do the damage (in *A Writer's Companion*, Louis D. Rubin, Jr., ed., 1995).

See also **Fyfe's Laws of Revision**.

Duggan's Law of Scholarly Research

The most valuable quotation will be the one for which you cannot determine the source.

Michael A. Duggan (legally Kirk-Duggan since 1983), emeritus professor of business law and computer science of the University of Texas at Austin, propounded this law and its corollary in response to a request for submissions of new laws by Arthur Block in the first edition (1977) of his *Murphy's Law and Other Reason Why Things Go Wrong*. Professor Kirk-Duggan is the author of *Law & the Computer* and other works.

Corollary to Duggan's Law. The source for an unattributed quotation will appear in the most hostile review of your work.

See also **Faber's Second Law**.

Dumas's Law

Nothing succeeds like success (Alexandre Dumas, père, *Ange Pitou,* 1854). The expression is proverbial.

Wilde's Amendment. Nothing succeeds like excess (Oscar Wilde, *A Woman of No Importance*, 1893).

Hollywood's Iron Law. Nothing succeeds like failure (Sidney Zion, *New York*, January 24th, 1977). Zion introduced this law in an effort to explain why a Hollywood genius, after losing millions of dollars on a picture, is not canned along with the film, but given a fancier office, a better title, and more money to spend. In accordance with the law, "Only after nine straight flops was he eligible to become head of a studio."

See also **The Peter Principle**.

Durocher's Law

Nice guys finish last.

This is the popular, highly distilled version of what Brooklyn Dodger baseball manager Leo 'the Lip' Durocher said on July 5th, 1946, about the New York Giants. Explaining to a group of sportswriters why one had to be tough to be a winner, like his own first-place Dodgers, Durocher directed the attention of the scribes to the enemy dugout across the diamond. "Look over there," he said. "Do you know a nicer guy than [Giants' manager Mel] Ott? Or any of the other Giants? Why they are the nicest guys in the world! And where are they? In seventh place." The "seventh place" quickly was converted in the popular mind to "last place," the Giants finishing eighth that year. Durocher protested initially when the "last place" version of the quote was attributed to him, according to Ralph Keyes's *Nice Guys Finish Last*, but eventually grew tired of making denials. He entitled his 1975 autobiography *Nice Guys Finish Last*, and changed the wording of the quote in the book to conform more closely to what most people thought though he had said: "I called off his players' names as they came marching up the steps behind him. 'Walker, Cooper, Mize, Marshall, Kerr, Gordon, Thomson. Take a look at them. All nice guys. They'll finish last. Nice guys. Finish last.'"

The 'nice guys' had a measure of revenge, however. Although finishing in the cellar – the sub-basement, really, thirty-six games out of first – they managed to beat the league-leading Dodgers on the last day of the season, forcing them into a play-off with the St. Louis Cardinals, which the Cards won 2-0.

Permutations of Durocher's Law:

The First Rule of Public Speaking. Nice guys finish fast (*Reader's Digest*, June, 1976).

Kelley's Law. Last guys don't finish nice (Princeton professor Stanford Kelley, referring to the bitterness of political campaigns, as quoted by Alan L. Otten in the *Wall Street Journal*, February 26th, 1976).

See also **Lombardi's Law, Rice's Rule** and **Sutton's Law.**

E

Eban's Law

History teaches us that men and nations behave wisely once they have exhausted all other alternatives (Abba Eban, Israeli diplomat and politician, speech London, December 16th, 1970).

See also **Santayana's Law**.

Eddington's Theory

The number of different hypotheses erected to explain a given biological phenomenon is inversely proportional to available knowledge (in Arthur Block, *The Complete Murphy's Law*, 1991).

Eliot's Observation

Immature poets imitate, mature poets steal (T. S. Eliot, 'Philip Massinger', 1920).

Thus, George Gordon, Lord Byron demonstrated his maturity when he wrote in *Don Juan* (1819-24):

> *In her first passion woman loves her lover,*
> *In all others, all she loves is love.*

Or perhaps he would say, as modern moviemakers do when lifting scenes from their predecessors, that he was merely 'paying homage' to Françoise, Duc de la Rochefoucauld, whose *Maxims* (1665) included:

> *In their first passion, women love their lovers;*
> *in all the others, they love love.*

Another mature poet was John Donne (1572-1631), whose poem 'The Baite' begins:

> *Come live with me, and be my love,*
> *And we will some pleasures prove*
> *Of golden sands, and crystal brooks,*
> *With silken lines, and silver hooks.*

From this it appears that Donne's bedside reading almost certainly included a manuscript copy of Philip Marlowe's 'The Passionate Shepherd to His Love.' Composed in about 1589 though not formally published until 1600, 'The Passionate Shepherd' contains the verse:

> *Come live with me and be my love;*
> *And we will all the pleasures prove*
> *That valleys, groves, hills, and fields*
> *Woods or steepy mountain yields.*

Nobody has described the phenomenon more wittily than Jonathan Swift, who happily did so in rhyme in *On Poetry* (1733):

> *So, naturalists observe a flea*
> *Hath smaller fleas that on him pray;*
> *And these have smaller fleas to bite 'em,*
> *And so proceed* ad infinitum.
> *Thus every poet, in his kind,*
> *Is bit by him that comes behind.*

See also **Mizner's Law of Research.**

Emerson's First Law

A foolish consistency is the hobgoblin of little minds, adored by little statesmen and philosophers and divines. With consistency a great soul has simply nothing to do (Ralph Waldo Emerson, 'Self-Reliance' in *Essays: First Series*, 1841).

James's Emendation. The art of being wise is the art of knowing what to overlook (William James, *The Principles of Psychology*, 1890).

Fitzgerald's Corollary. The test of a first-rate intelligence is the ability to hold two opposed ideas in the mind at the same time, and still retain the ability to function (F. Scott Fitzgerald, *The Crack-Up*, 1936).

Berenson's Amendment. Consistency requires you to be as ignorant today as you were a year ago (Bernard Berenson, *Notebook*, 1892).

Whitman's Reconciliation of Emerson's Inconsistency. From Walt Whitman's 'Song of Myself' in *Leaves of Grass* (1855):

Do I contradict myself?
Very well then I contradict myself,
(I am large, I contain multitudes.)

Various large-minded people also have considered the question of little minds – and reached slightly different opinions. Thus, Benjamin Disraeli declared in *Sybil* (1845) that "Little things affect little minds," while Doris Lessing opined in 'A Woman on the Roof' in *A Man and Two Women* (1963) that "Small things amuse small minds."

Emerson's Second Law

If a man write a better book, preach a better sermon, or make a better mousetrap than his neighbor, tho' he build his house in the woods, the world will make a beaten path to his door.

The law does not appear in this form in any of Emerson's voluminous writings. The closest approach to it comes in a journal entry for February, 1855, in which the Sage of Concord observed that "I trust a good deal to common fame, as we all must. If a man has good corn, or wood, or boards, or pigs, to sell, or can make better chairs or knives, crucibles or church organs, than anybody else, you will find a broad-beaten road to his home." The more felicitous mousetrap version was preserved by Sarah S. B. Yule, who made a note of it when she attended a lecture by Emerson in 1871 in Oakland, California, and then included it in a book of sayings, with the sickly sweet title *Borrowings: A Collection of Helpful and Beautiful Thoughts*, which she and Mary S. Keene published in 1889. Emerson's mousetrap law was not extended for another century:

Shalett's Amendment to Emerson's Second Law. Build a better mousetrap and all of a sudden the mouse starts finding ways to get around your trap (Michael Shalett, *New York Times*, January 25th, 1996).

The 'better mousetrap' in this instance was a system pioneered by Mr. Shalett's company, Soundscan, for compiling *Billboard* magazine's charts of hit songs by tracking actual sales as recorded by barcodes at cash registers in thousands of music stores. Soundscan's method is far more reliable than the old, pre-1991 system of compiling the charts from oral reports of store managers. Not only were the managers' reports intrinsically inaccurate for being impressionistic, but the impressions frequently were influenced by free albums, concert tickets, vacations, and so on, from record companies that wished to push their products into the top slots.

Within several years, however, the mice had begun to learn ways of circumventing Mr. Shalett's mousetrap. For example, companies can boost sales by sending stores free copies of important new releases, or selling them four singles for the price of one, thus allowing them to discount list prices substantially. Some retailers also have been said to scan the same album more than once and to replace barcodes on older albums with those of new ones whose sales they want to inflate. The saving grace, one anonymous record company executive told the *Times*, is that Soundscan has proven that such tricks will only get a song so far. "You can fake it some of the way up the chart but you can't fake it all the way," he said. "What these things can only do is help expose a record. From that point on, it's up to the public to decide."

For other, profound exceptions to Emerson's Second Law, see **David's Qwerty Factor**.

Emerson's Third Law

The efforts which we make to escape our destiny only serve to lead us into it ('Fate' in *The Conduct of Life*, 1860).

'Destiny' is not a particularly popular explanation of events in our present scientific age. Today, when things go wrong, people are more likely to talk in terms of the Law of Unintended Consequences.

See **Sophocles' First Law** and **Spencer's Law**.

Erasmus's Law

The grass is always greener on the other side of the fence.

The Dutch scholar and theologian Desiderius Erasmus is unlikely to have been the first to make this observation but his expression of it in *Adages* (1545) is the earliest recorded version in *A Dictionary of American Proverbs* (Wolfgang Meider et. al, eds., 1992). Folk wisdom has produced many variations, among them "Grass always seems greener in foreign fields," "Grass is always greener in somebody else's back yard," and "The grass may be greener across the street, but watch out for the barbed wire."

The effect of distance upon our perceptions is not limited to the greenness of grass. For example, Arthur Bloch included the following two rules in *The Complete Murphy's Law* (1991):

Fuller's Law of Journalism. The farther away the disaster or accident occurs, the greater the number of dead and injured required for it to become a story.

Loftus's Theory on Personnel Recruitment. Faraway talent always seems better than home-grown talent.

See also **Alinsky's Law, Finnegan's Law,** and **Riley's Law.**

Ettore's Law of Lines

The other line moves faster.

Barbara Ettore, a resident of New York City, who appears to have learned about lines (queues) the hard way, explained the implications of her law in a communication to *Harper's* (August 1974): "This applies to all lines – bank, supermarket, toll booth, customs, and so on. And don't try to change lines. The Other Line – the one you were in originally – will then move faster." Ettore's Law seems to have attained the widest circulation of a group of laws that appeared in this issue of *Harper's*. For other examples, see **Comin's Law, Lowery's Law** and **Robinson's Law.**

Other deep thinkers with time on their hands have proposed similar laws, including:

Vaughan's Version of the Law of Lines. At bank, post office or supermarket, there is one universal law which you ignore at your own peril: the shortest line moves the slowest" (Bill Vaughan, *Reader's Digest*, July 1977).

Sheinwold's Law of Lanes. When traffic halts on a four-lane highway, it's a law of nature that the other lanes move while your lane stays glued to the road (Alfred Sheinwold, *New York Post,* March 8th, 1972).

See also **Gumperson's Law, Keppner's Law,** and **Steinbeck's Law of Traveling.**

Euripides' First Law

There is no wind that always blows a storm.

Appearing in *Alcestis* (438 B.C.), the earliest play by Euripides that has been preserved, this is the classical statement of the proverbial "It is an ill wind that blows no good." Or – as musicians have said of the oboe – "It is an ill wind that nobody blows good."

Euripides' Second Law

In this world second thoughts, it seems, are best (Hippolytus, 428 B.C.).

Euripides' Third Law

The lucky person passes for a genius (Herakleidae, ca. 428 B.C.).

But it may not be wise to point this out to the 'genius.' As E. B. White pointed out nearly twenty-four hundred years later: "Luck is not something you can mention in the presence of self-made men" ('Control', in *One Man's Meat*, 1944).

But see also **Pasteur's Observation** and **Rickey's Law.**

F

Faber's First Law

If there isn't a law, there will be (headline for an article by Timesman Harold Faber, the *New York Times Magazine*, March 17th, 1968, and in his *The Book of Laws*, 1979).

Faber's Second Law

The number of errors in any piece of writing is directly proportional to the amount of reliance on secondary sources (Harold Faber, *The Book of Laws*, 1979).

See also **Duggan's Law of Scholarly Research.**

Falk's Distinction

Some people in the world are important. All the rest wish they were.

Mr. Richard R. Falk, a practitioner of the fine art of public relations – a press agent or flack, in other words – proudly told the *New York Times* (November 6th, 1971) that he was the model for the loathsome P.R. man in the 1957 film *Sweet Smell of Success* (script by Clifford Odets and Ernest Lehman). Mr. Falk's accomplishments included carrying a cross up Broadway, dressing up a model in a bikini of frankfurters, and getting March 21st to be declared Fragrance Day. Other tidbits of his wisdom: "Newspaper editors have got to fill the white space between the ads"; "You make it a little fantastic or humorous, bring in enough pseudo-facts, and the papers will buy it," and "I know what editors want." His standard guarantee, he said, was that everything he wrote was 50 percent true. In keeping with this, he said that his autobiography would be entitled *Liar for Hire*.

Fetridge's Law

Important things that are supposed to happen do not happen, especially when people are looking, or, conversely, things that are supposed to not happen do happen, especially when people are looking.

This law was named for Claude Fetridge, a radio engineer for NBC, according to H. Allen Smith's *A Short History of Fingers* (1963). The occasion was Mr. Fetridge's attempt in 1936 to broadcast the departure of the famous swallows of the mission of San Juan Capistrano on their annual migration, which occurs like clockwork every October 23rd. The NBC crew traveled at some expense to the mission in Southern California, arriving in plenty of time to set up their sound equipment for the marvelous event, and a nationwide audience waited to hear the whirring sound of millions of wings. But nothing happened. The swallows, it turned out, had left a day ahead of time, perhaps because this was a leap year. Whatever, the expected event did not happen, and Mr. Fetridge earned a measure of immortality.

Fetridge's Law has universal application. For example, as noted by Mr. Smith, the dog that will jump over a stick a thousand times a day for its owner in private will balk when a neighbour is invited to watch. The baby that says "Dada" in front of its proud parents will either screech or go totally silent when friends are summoned to witness the performance. The car that develops deathly rattles on the road will only hum smoothly when brought to the garage so the mechanic can diagnose the problem. And so on. Mr. Smith even managed to turn the law to his advantage. Recognising its reliability, he reported that "whenever I get a rattle in my car I simply drive rapidly to the garage, turn in, back around, pause briefly so the car can sense the presence of a skilled mechanic, and then drive home – my difficulty is cleared up without my ever speaking to the garage people."

Frank's Corollary to Fetridge's Law. One's ability to perform a given task competently decreases in proportion to the number of people watching (Mark R. Frank, *Omni*, May 1979).

Hartley's Corollary to Fetridge's Law. The probability of someone watching you is proportional to the stupidity of your action (internet collection of laws, January 8th, 1996).

See also **Gumperson's Law, Rawson's Third Law** and **Sattler's Law.**

Feuerbach's Law of Consumption

Man is what he eats (Ludwig Feuerbach, *Blätter für Literarische Unterhaltung*, November 12th, 1850).

Walter de la Mare propounded the feminine corollary to Feuerbach's Law in 'Miss T' in *Peacock Pie* (1913):

> *It's a very odd thing –*
> *As odd as can be –*
> *That whatever Miss T eats*
> *Turns into Miss T.*

See also **Woollcott's Law.**

Finagle's Law

If anything can go wrong with an experiment, it will.

First Corollary. If an experiment works, something has gone wrong.

Second Corollary (a.k.a. Fett's Law of the Lab). Never attempt to replicate a successful experiment.

Finagle's law is just a special case of Murphy's Law, which, as it happens, sometimes is credited to Finagle. Thus, the English archaeologist Geoffrey Bibby described a complication in a dig on the island of Bahrain in the Arabian Gulf in these terms: "And then – by what I believe is known as Finagle's Law, which says that what can go wrong will go wrong – an Islamic well had been driven down precisely on the line which we had chosen for our main section" *(Looking for Dilmun,* 1969). Mr. Bibby also noted another common archaeological example of this law at work: "The disposal of earth dug up in the course of an excavation is always a headache, for unless it is dumped a very expensive distance from the diggings it always proves to have been piled precisely where you want to dig the following year."

Mr. Finagle has been credited with many other laws. He appears to be a fictitious character, however. The name itself is a word of American origin, traced so far only to 1926; it may be related to the English dialectical *fainaigue,* to fiddle, to cheat, to renege (as at cards). Among Finagle's other laws:

No matter what the result of an experiment, there will always be someone (1) eager to misinterpret it, (2) fake it, (3) believe it proves his or her own pet theory.

Experiments should be reproducible – that is, all should fail in the same way.

In any collection of data, the obviously correct figure, which doesn't need to be checked, is a mistake.

First Corollary. No one whom you ask for help will see the error.

Second Corollary. Everyone who stops by with unsought advice will spot the mistake immediately.

Once a job has been fouled up, any attempt to improve it will just make it worse, sometimes much worse.

See also **Chisholm's Laws of Human Interaction**.

Finnegan's Law

The further away the future is, the better it looks (in *Organic Gardening*, June 1978).

This is the temporal counterpart to the spatial truism about the grass always being greener on the other side of the fence; see **Erasmus's Law**.

Rawson's Corollary to Finnegan's Law. The more distant the past, the better it looks. This is why older people, looking back to their youth, tend to think that bygone times were better times – and, a corollary to the corollary, that the younger generation is going to the dogs. It also helps explain the common myth that the earliest years of humanity were a Golden Age, a time of innocence, when spring reigned perpetually, people neither argued nor fought, and the rivers flowed with milk and honey.

Firestone's Law of Forecasting

Chicken Little only has to be right once (item from the internet, January 8th, 1996).

See also **The Dixon Effect**.

Fitzsimmons's Law

The bigger they come, the harder they fall.

The law often is attributed to Robert ('Ruby Bob') Fitzsimmons, heavyweight boxing champion in 1897-99, who supposedly made this boast prior to meeting the much larger James J. Jeffries in 1899. But Fitzsimmons might also have picked the saying up from one of his predecessors as champion, John L. Sullivan (1882-92) or James J. ('Gentleman Jim') Corbett (1892-97). Whatever, the phrase was used so often that it had become a cliché in both the United States and Great Britain by the time of World War I. Variations include "The taller they are, the further they fall" and "The harder you fall, the higher you bounce."

p.s. Fitzsimmons lost.

Flintstone's Teachings

Fred Flintstone has unwittingly inculcated timeless rules in the minds of millions of young viewers of the animated TV series about him and his Stone Age family. As distilled by Thomas Fields-Meyer and Richard L. Meyer in an OpEd-page piece in the *New York Times* (March 23rd, 1993), they are:

1.   Never underestimate the strength of a child.
2.   Never bet more than you have.
3.   Wealthy oil men drive big cars.
4.   Pets make excellent companions.
5.   Never put Superglue in a bowling ball.
6.   It's possible to have pollution-free cars.
7.   Never leave a child unattended.
8.   Household appliances have minds of their own.
9.   Never put too many items on a drive-in tray.
10. Car-pooling can work.
11. It's a good idea to remember your anniversary.
12. The little guy can beat the system.
13. Good stone walls make good neighbours.
14. Expectant fathers do crazy things.
15. Friendship is important.

Forbes's Law

Money isn't everything as long as you have enough (Malcolm S. Forbes, publisher, balloonist, bon vivant, and father of Steve 'flat tax' Forbes, in Jon Winokur, *Friendly Advice*, 1991).

Ford's Commandment

Use it or lose it.

The commandment by auto-maker Henry Ford has the ring of a proverb but is not listed in the *Dictionary of American Proverbs* (which does include such near-relatives as "Use what you would not lose" and "Use it but don't abuse it"). In full, what Ford said was "Money is like an arm or leg: use it or lose it" *(New York Times*, November 8th, 1931). Or as the legal maxim has it, "Rights are lost by disuse." Of course, any self-respecting lawyer is able to argue both sides of the same question, which has led to the formulation of an opposing maxim: "A right sometimes sleeps but it never dies."

Forrester's Laws

1. In complicated situations, efforts to improve things often tend to make them worse, sometimes much worse, on occasions calamitous.

2. In a complex social system, the obvious commonsense solution to a problem will turn out to be wrong most of the time (Jay W. Forrester, quoted in the *New York Times*, June 4th, 1971, and October 10th, 1971, respectively).

For examples of why things go wrong, see **Spencer's Law**.

Franklin's Laws

Benjamin Franklin produced some original laws in his *Poor Richard's Almanack*, published annually for the years from 1733 to 1758, and a bestseller in its time (some ten thousand copies a year), but he also drew heavily on earlier authors and collections of proverbs, sometimes improving old sayings in the process. Herewith a sampling of his wisdom from the almanacs, with a few other tidbits thrown in:

After three days men grow weary of a wench, a guest, and weather rainy (Almanack, 1733) **Corollary**. Fish and visitors smell in three days (*Almanack*, 1736).

Where there's marriage without love, there will be love without marriage (Almanack, 1734).

And for more about Franklin's thoughts on marriage, see **Austen's First Law**.

Necessity never made a good bargain (Almanack, 1735).

Early to bed, early to rise, makes a man healthy, wealthy, and wise (Almanack, 1735). **Corollary**. He that riseth late, must trot all day, and shall scarce overtake his business at night (*Almanack*, 1742). **Thurber's Amendment to Franklin's Corollary.** Early to rise and early to bed makes a male healthy and wealthy and dead (James Thurber, 'The Shrike and the Chipmunk', in *Fables for Our Time*, 1940).

He that lives upon hope, dies farting (Almanack, 1736). Franklin cleaned this up for the last edition of his *Almanack*, amending the law to "He that lives upon hope will die fasting."

Experience keeps a dear school, but fools will learn in no other (Almanack, 1743).

There are no gains without pains (Almanack, 1745). Adlai Stevenson reused this when accepting the Democratic Party's presidential nomination in 1952. See also **Friedman's Law**.

Time is money (Advice to a Young Tradesman, 1748). **Corollary**. Lost time is never found again (*Almanack*, 1748).

Little strokes fell great oaks (Almanack, 1750).

A little neglect may breed great mischief – for want of a nail the shoe was lost; for want of a shoe the horse was lost; and for want of a horse the rider was lost (Almanack, 1758). This progression sometimes is continued: "and for want of a rider the battle was lost."

Half a truth is often a great lie (Almanack, 1758).

In this world nothing is certain but death and taxes (letter to Jean-Baptiste Le Roy, November 13th, 1789).

See also **Gumperson's Law.**

Friedman's Law

There's no such thing as a free lunch.

This is one of the most basic of all laws, the economist's equivalent of such physical principles as the laws of conservation of energy and matter, of the equivalence of action and reaction (for every force there is an equal and opposite force), and of the famous second law of thermodynamics, which requires, among other things, that the growth of order in any closed system be paid for by increasing disorder, or entropy, within a wider environment. (In the end, some billions of years from now, the free lunch will be over, according to this law, when the disordering tendency has permeated completely the widest possible environment. At this point, everything will be very chilly. Physicists refer to this as "the heat death of the universe."

See also the *Almanack* entry for 1745 in **Franklin's Laws, Murphy's Fifth Law,** and Mrs. Parkinson's contribution to **Parkinson's Law.**

The free lunch law generally is associated with economist Milton Friedman, who popularised it in his *Newsweek* columns and then used it as the title of a book in 1975. Professor Friedman did not originate the law, however. It appears in many earlier works. Barry Commoner employed it in a discussion of ecology in the *New Yorker* in 1971. Science fiction writer Robert Heinlein used it in the form of an acronym, TANSTAAFL ("There ain't no such thing as a free lunch") in *The Moon Is a Harsh Mistress* in 1968. Financial writer Burton Crane employed the "ain't" form in *The Sophisticated Investor* in 1959. Incoming New York City mayor Fiorello La Guardia proclaimed the end of the free meal i.e. graft, at city hall in 1934 with the words, *"E finita la cuccagna!"* The trail is indistinct, but the phrase most likely dates to the nineteenth century, when bars commonly offered 'free' sandwiches to attract customers at noontime. Anyone who walked into a bar and started eating a sandwich without buying a drink, however, quickly found out that the lunch was not really free – probably by being tossed out on his ear.

Fuller's Observation

It is always darkest just before the day dawneth (Thomas Fuller, *Pisgah Sight*, 1650).

Reverend Fuller, a popular preacher as well as a writer, was appointed chaplain to Charles II after the merry monarch's restoration to the throne in 1660. The next year, Reverend Fuller died. Mount Pisgah is the eminence that Moses climbed in order to view the promised land, which God had forbidden him to enter. Shortly thereafter, Moses died.

Henry Wadsworth Longfellow cribbed from Fuller in *The Baron of St. Castine:* "The nearer the dawn, the darker the night" *(Tales of Wayside Inn,* 1863-74).

A modern amendment of Fuller's Observation is "It's always darkest just before it's totally black," attributed by Senator John McCain (R., Ariz.) to Chairman Mao Zedong *(New York Times,* December 22nd, 1989). The Senator may have had tongue in cheek, but the sentiment reflects the tenor of our times as accurately as Fuller reflected his.

Fyfe's Laws of Revision

1. Information necessitating a change of design will be conveyed to the designer after and only after the design is complete. *Corollary.* In simple cases, presenting one obvious right way versus one obvious wrong way, it is often wiser to choose the wrong way so as to expedite subsequent revision.

2. The more innocuous the modification appears to be, the further its influence will extend and the more necessary the design will have to be redrawn.

3. If, when completion of a design is imminent, field dimensions are finally supplied as they actually are instead of as they were meant to be, it is always simpler to start over again from scratch. *Corollary.* It is usually impractical to worry beforehand about interferences – if you have none, someone will make one for you.

Fyfe's Laws were included in a collection of laws that was snatched out of the electronic ether, i.e. the internet, January 8th, 1996.

See also **Drazen's Law of Restitution**.

G

Galbraith's First Law

The greater the wealth, the thicker will be the dirt.

This indubitably describes a tendency of our time. John Kenneth Galbraith enunciated this law in *The Affluent Society* (1958) when explaining the difficulties of obtaining a "social balance" between private consumption and public services. "The more goods people procure, the more packages they discard and the more trash that must be carried away," he explained. "If appropriate sanitation services are not provided, the counterpart of increasing opulence will be deepening filth. The greater the wealth, the thicker will be the dirt."

Los Angeles provided Mr. Galbraith's "near-classic" example of the problem of the social balance: "Magnificently efficient factories and oil refineries, a lavish supply of automobiles, a vast consumption of handsomely packaged products, coupled for many years with the absence of a municipal trash collection service which forced the use of home incinerators, made the air nearly unbreathable for an appreciable part of each year."

See also **Toffler's Law** and **Veblen's Law**. An eminent economist (in more ways than one, being well over six and one-half feet tall), Mr. Galbraith also made keen observations in other fields; see below.

Galbraith's Second Law

The more underdeveloped the country, the more overdeveloped the women.

Mr. Galbraith's mind was not occupied entirely by humdrum affairs of state when he served as ambassador to India, judging from this observation in a letter of April 27th, 1961, to President John F. Kennedy. "Being Ambassador to India is the nearest thing yet devised to a male chastity belt. But one can still gaze wistfully," he added.

Gelb's Observation

Operations tend to set a lot of policies in concrete (Leslie Gelb, *New York Times Magazine,* January 18th, 1981).

Mr. Gelb wrote with unusual authority on the subject of policies and operations, having interrupted his journalistic career at the *New York Times* in the 1960s to serve as head of the Defense Department's Office of Policy Planning, in which capacity he directed the task force that prepared the *History of U.S. Decision-Making Process on Vietnam Policy,* a.k.a. *The Pentagon Papers.*

Gell-Mann's Dictum

Whatever isn't forbidden is required.

Corollary. If there's no reason why something shouldn't exist, then it must exist (Murray Gell-Mann, in Paul Dickson, *The Official Rules,* 1978).

The Dictum (a strengthening of Schiller's "Whatever is not forbidden is permitted," in *Wallenstein's Camp,* 1789) fits with the system devised in early 1961 by Professor Gell-Mann, of the California Institute of Technology (and independently by Yuval Ne'eman, an Israeli Army engineer-turned-physicist), to make sense out of the confusingly large number of elementary particles discovered during the preceding decade. By analysing symmetries and patterns of violations of symmetries, the new system explained why particles were exactly what they were and predicted the existence of as yet undiscovered ones. It was called 'the eightfold way' because it involved the operation of eight quantum numbers and because of a remark attributed to Buddha: "Now this, O monks, is noble truth that leads to cessation of pain: this is the noble Eightfold Way: namely, right views, right intention, right speech, right action, right living, right effort, right mindedness, right concentration."

Although devised for the quirky world of subatomic quarks, Gell-Mann's Dictum, which predicts that if there is no rule against something happening, then it must inevitably happen – is paralleled exactly in the everyday macroscopic world by **Murphy's Law**.

Gerrold's Law

A little ignorance can go a long way (from the internet, January 8th, 1996).

This is probably the same Gerrold who is responsible for the **Laws of Infernal Dynamics**; see below.

Gerrold's Laws of Infernal Dynamics

1. An object in motion will always be heading in the wrong direction.

2. An object at rest will always be in the wrong place.

3. The energy required to change either one of these states will always be more than you wish to expend, but never so much as to make the task totally impossible.

Attributed to David Gerrold, columnist and writer for *Starlog* magazine in Paul Dickson's *The Official Rules*, 1978, these laws have endured. With some changes in wording, they were included in a collection of laws that was plucked from the internet on January 8th, 1996.

See also **Gerrold's Law**.

Gibbon's Law

All that is human must retrograde if it does not advance.

Edward Gibbon reached this conclusion while researching the thirteen-hundred-year period covered in *The History of the Decline and Fall of the Roman Empire*. His six-volume history took him more than a dozen years to write, and his thoughts upon completing it also are worth recording for they epitomise those of many writers upon finishing admittedly less monumental works. It was nearing midnight on June 27th, 1787, when he wrote the last lines of the last page. Putting down his pen, he walked out into his moonlit garden. "I will not dissemble the first emotions of joy on the recovery of my freedom, and, perhaps, the establishment of my fame," he reflected. "But my pride was soon humbled, and a sober melancholy was spread over my mind by the idea that I had taken everlasting leave of an old and agreeable companion, and that whatsoever might be the future date of my *History*, the life of the historian must be short and precarious."

This was about as emotional as Gibbon ever got. His history already had been much praised, the first volume especially, but he survived with equanimity one of the harder literary knocks on record. In the words of William Henry, Duke of Gloucester, upon being presented by the author with volume two of his *History* in 1781: "Another damned, thick, square book! Always scribble, scribble, scribble! Eh! Mr. Gibbon?"

See also **Eleanour Roosevelt's Second Law**.

Gilbert's Law of Appearances

Things are seldom what they seem, / Skim milk masquerades as cream (W. S. Gilbert, *H.M.S. Pinafore*, 1878).

Gilbert's Law expresses the same thought as Shakespeare's "all that glisters is not gold" *(The Merchant of Venice*, 1596-97), which, in turn, is a proverb whose roots have been traced back to classical times. Bartlett's *Familiar Quotations* cites a Latin translation of Aristotle's *Elenchi* as the ultimate source: "Yellow-coloured objects appear to be gold."

Machiavelli's Corollary. The great majority of mankind are satisfied with appearances, as though they were realities and are often more influenced by the things that seem than by those that are (Niccolò Machiavelli, *Discourses on the First Ten Books of Titus Livius*, 1513-17).

See also **Agnes Allen's Law, Kelly's Law, Lasch's Law, Shannon's Law of Administration,** and the last of **Wilde's Other Laws.**

Goldsmith's Law

Silence gives consent.

Oliver Goldsmith included this law in his comedy *The Good-Natur'd Man*, produced in 1768. In our own time, the Reverend Martin Luther King, Jr., put a greater onus on those who remain silent with the more explicit corollary: "He who accepts evil without protesting against it is really cooperating with it" *(Stride Toward Freedom)*. Of course, this has much in common with Christ's uncompromising injunction: "He who is not with me is against me" (Matthew 12:30).

See also **Burke's Law.**

Gomez's Law

If you don't throw it, they can't hit it.

Yankee pitcher Vernon 'Lefty' Gomez may not have put it in exactly these words, but this apparently is what he thought when facing Jimmie Foxx one day in 1937. The count was two and two, so the story goes. Yankee catcher Bill Dickey gave Gomez a sign, but the pitcher shook him off. Dickey gave him the sign for another pitch, and again Gomez declined to throw. Dickey continued, running through his full repertoire, and Gomez continued to shake his head. Finally, the catcher ran out to the mound. "What do you want to throw," he asked. "Hell," said Gomez, "I don't want to throw this guy anything." Eventually, of course, Gomez did make another pitch – and it wound up in the stands in left field.

Gomez was a good pitcher, with a lifetime record of 189 victories against 102 defeats, but Foxx was a better batter, with 534 home runs in his career (currently fourteenth on the all-time list) and 1,921 runs batted in (seventh on the all-time list).

Gordon's Rule of Evolving Bryographic Systems

While bryographic plants are typically encountered in substrata of earthy or mineral matter in concreted state, discrete substrata elements occasionally display a roughly spherical configuration which, in the presence of suitable gravitational and other effects, lends itself to combine translatory and rotational motion. One notices in such cases an absence of the otherwise typical accretion of bryophyta. We therefore conclude that a rolling stone gathers no moss.

Gordon apparently is a fictitious character. Reprints of this rule from the 1970s, describe him as 'Professor Gordon,' but do not include his full name and academic affiliation. Gordon's conclusion is of considerable antiquity, of course. See **Publilius's Maxims (no. 524).**

Gresham's Law

Bad money drives out good – meaning that debased or underweight coins will drive good money out of circulation, as people squirrel away the more valuable coins in mattresses and other hiding places.

The law was named in 1857 by H. D. Macleod, a Scottish economist, who thought that Sir Thomas Gresham, sixteenth-century London merchant, founder of the Royal Exchange, and financial adviser to the Crown, had been the first to state the principle. But Macleod was wrong. The law had been understood and explained by earlier monetary theorists, including Nicolaus Koppernick, who doubled as an astronomer and who is better known as Copernicus. Even the ancient Greeks were familiar with the principle. Thus, Aristophanes noted how brass coins replaced gold in *The Frogs,* a play that was first produced in 405 B.C. only a couple of centuries after the invention of coinage in Lydia (ca. 630 B.C.). From the translation by Dudley Fitts:

> *Yet there are sensible men and good in Athene's city,*
> *True as ancient coin, gold against modern brass.*

The principle embodied in Gresham's Law has widespread applications. Thus, Terry Teachout proposed a variant, which he called **Grisham's Law** (after bestselling novelist John): "In popular culture, trash gets trashier over time" *(New York Times Book Review,* August 27th, 1995). Other authorities have reached similar conclusions. Speaking of the communications business, Lee Loevinger, a onetime FCC commissioner, said "Bad news drives good news out of the media" (in Paul Dickson, *The Official Rules,* 1978), while Marvin Kitman, glomming onto a truth, as humorists are wont to do, pointed out that "Pure drivel tends to drive ordinary drivel off the TV screen" (Arthur Bloch, *The Complete Murphy's Law,* 1991). See also **(Theodore) Bernstein's Second Law.**

Gummidge's Law

The amount of expertise varies in inverse proportion to the number of statements understood by the general public.

Dr. Gummidge, a professor of sociology at Instant College, propounded this law during a conversation with a student that was recorded in a 'Time Essay' *(Time,* December 30th, 1966). The exchange went like this:

Gummidge: Remember Gummidge's Law and you will never be Found Out: The amount of expertise varies in inverse proportion to the number of statements understood by the General Public.

Student: In other words?

Gummidge: In other words, never say "In other words." That will force you to clarify your statements. Keep all pronuncianmentos orotund and hazy. Suppose your mother comes to school and asks how you are doing. Do I reply: "He is at the bottom of his class – lazy and good-for-nothing"?

Student: Why not? Everybody else does.

Gummidge: I am not everyone else. I reply: "The student in question is performing minimally for his peer group and is an emerging underachiever."

Gumperson's Law

The contradictory of a welcome probability will assert itself whenever such an eventuality is likely to be most frustrating or, in other words, the outcome of a given desired probability will be inverse to the degree of desirability.

Sometimes called The Law of Perverse Opposites, Gumperson's Law dictates that there are always plenty of parking spaces on the other side of the street, that the person who buys the most raffle tickets has the least chance of winning, that the woman at the race track who bets according to the colours of jockeys' shirts will do better than the man who has spent hundreds of hours poring over past-performance charts, and that the same person who needs two boxes of matches to start a fire in a fireplace will cause a forest fire by tossing a cigarette stub out of a car window.

The law was attributed to R. F. Gumperson, when introduced to the world in the November 1957 issue of *Changing Times,* but the real author, according to Paul Dickson's *The Official Rules,* was John H. Hazard, subsequently the magazine's executive editor. Mr. Dickson also relayed Gumperson's Proof: "The most undesirable things are the most certain (e.g. death and taxes)." This last, a play on one of **Franklin's Law,** was attributed to a Martin S. Kottmeyer, of Carlyle, Ill.

An especially horrible example of Gumperson's Law in operation is embodied in:

The Law of Inverse Proportion of Social Intercourse. The possibility of a young man meeting a desirable and receptive young female increases by pyramidal progression when he is already in the company of (1) a date, (2) his wife, (3) a better-looking and richer male friend (Ronald Beifield, quoted by Alan L. Otten, the *Wall Street Journal,* February 2nd, 1975).

Or, as former Green Bay Packer football star and man-about-town Paul Hornung is said to have said: "Never get married in the morning, 'cause you may never know who you'll meet that night" (in William Safire and Leonard Safir, *Good Advice,* 1982).

See also **Disraeli's Second Law, Ettore's Law of Lines** and **Fetridge's Law.**

Gunter's Laws of Air Travel

1. When you are served a meal aboard an aircraft, the aircraft will encounter turbulence.

2. The strength of the turbulence is directly proportional to the temperature of your coffee (internet collection of laws, January 8th, 1996).

The Gunter here most likely derives from Edmund Gunter (1581-1626), an English mathematician, whose name has been perpetuated through association with several practical inventions. (Ironically, his contributions to mathematics – he introduced the words *cosine* and *cotangent* – have been pretty much forgotten.) The inventions included Gunter's Chain, a 100-link chain used by surveyors, and Gunter's Scale, a slide-rule used in solving problems in navigation, trigonometry, and so on. Meanwhile, a gunter is a sail that operates somewhat like a slide-rule, being attached to a spar that slides up and down a short mast.

See also **Hoyle's Rule**.

H

Haight's Brokerage Law

When the market is stable, it is a good time to buy, but when it is going up, buy quickly to catch the rising tide. When the market is going down, however, it is a good time to buy as it will soon turn up. When it has been going down for some time ("crash" is a nasty word, not to be used), it must be at the bottom and can only go up, so BUY, BUY, BUY. Bye-bye! (from the wisdom of Keith Haight, ex-broker, May 1991).

Greenberg's Corollary. Don't ask the barber if you need a haircut (Daniel Greenberg, the *Wall Street Journal*, September 18th, 1977).

Haldane's Observation

The universe is not only queerer than we suppose, but queerer than we can *suppose.*

The British geneticist J. B. S. Haldane, best known for his part in developing the mathematical foundation for the theory of natural selection, qualified this observation as a 'suspicion' in the title essay of *Possible Worlds and Other Essays* (1927). In full, he wrote:

> Now, my own suspicion is that the universe is not only queerer than we suppose, but queerer than we *can* suppose. I have read and heard many attempts at a systematic account of it, from materialism and

theosophy to the Christian system or that of Kant, and I have always felt that they were much too simple. I suspect that there are more things in heaven and earth than are dreamed of, or can be dreamed of, in any philosophy. That is the reason why I have no philosophy myself, and must be my excuse for dreaming.

Haldane was selling himself short; he was not actually so lacking in the philosophical department. A lifelong Marxist, he believed that any form of government – indeed, authority of any kind – was intrinsically bad. He broke with the Communist Party in 1950 on account of Stalin's support of T. D. Lysenko, whose genetic theories, emphasising the role of environment over heredity, became party dogma in the USSR, and he protested British policies in Egypt by leaving his post as professor at London University in 1957 and moving permanently to India. (One of the unexpected pleasures of his emigration was that it allowed him to dispense with shoes and socks in favour of sandals: "Sixty years in socks is enough.") He also chaired the government committee that produced what is known as the Haldane Principle – a method of organisation that is not employed as widely as it might be – i.e. that government research and development efforts should be carried out by independent agencies rather than by the departments that will benefit from their results.

The philosophical antithesis of Haldane's Observation is Einstein's belief that the principles of the universe are knowable, as expressed in a letter to Max Born, that "*He* [God] does not play dice" (December 4th, 1926). This was in keeping with his 1921 remark that "God is subtle but he is not malicious" (later carved above the fireplace of the Common Room in Fine Hall at Princeton University). Commenting on Einstein's comment, however, the cosmologist Stephen Hawking came down on Haldane's side, contending in a 1975 *Nature* article that "God not only plays dice, He sometimes throws the dice where they cannot be seen."

See also **Bohr's Law, Heisenberg's Uncertainty Principle**, and the Corollary to the Rider to the Second Amendment of **Murphy's Law.**

Haldeman's Law

Once the toothpaste is out of the tube, it's going to be very tough to get it back in.

White House chief-of-staff H. R. 'Bob' Haldeman imparted this bit of wisdom to presidential counsel John W. Dean III in a telephone call on April 8th, 1973, just before Dean was to meet with federal prosecutors to discuss his role in the great Watergate cover-up (Dean, *Blind Ambition,* 1976).

The container metaphor for limiting the scandal was common within the sacred precincts of the White House. For example, referring to the various, nefarious operations that E. Howard Hunt and the plumbers had pulled off in addition to the Watergate break-in, President Nixon opined, "Oh well, this is a can of worms, as you know; a lot of this stuff went on" (White House tape, September 15th, 1972). Later, discussing Mr. Hunt's threat to go public about all the "seamy things" he had done for the White House unless he received $122,000, Mr. Nixon said that "It seems to me that we have to keep the cap on the bottle that much or we don't have any options" (White House tape, March 21st, 1973). Similar laws include:

The Law of Canned Worms. Once you open a can of worms, the only way to get them back in is to obtain a larger can.

The Digger's Dilemma. More dirt comes out of a hole than you can get back into it.

The First Law of Holes (especially relevant for people in politics). If you are in one, stop digging.

See also **Horace's Law.**

The Hart Rule

Anything any politician did with a woman other than his wife prior to May 5, 1987, ought to be allowed to go unrevealed.

The Hart here is Gary, former Democratic senator from Colorado, whose denial on May 5th, 1987, that he had ever spent "an evening, a night" with a woman other than Mrs. Hart, was contradicted by enough evidence to force him to abandon his campaign for his party's 1988 presidential nomination. (Reporters had staked out his Washington town house the previous weekend, spotting the departure of a Ms. Donna Earle Rice, who, it turned out, also had accompanied Mr. Hart on a cruise to the Bahamas aboard the good ship *Monkey Business* – and there were pictures of the fun couple to prove it.) All this was fresh in the memory of a Virginia Republican, John Buckley, who propounded the Hart Rule three years later when Democratic senator Charles S. Robb was fending off allegations that he had had an affair with a former representative of the state in the Miss US Pagent. (Mr. Robb admitted only to indiscreet "socializing.") Mr. Buckley's point was that "Intense scrutiny of candidates' lives is an unpleasant fact of life in politics today . . . After Gary Hart's exposure, politicians were on notice that their behavior had to change" *(Roanoke Times & World,* April 28th, 1991, in Anne H. Soukhanov, *Word Watch,* 1995).

The Hawthorne Law

The simple act of studying the performance of workers or students will cause their productivity or test scores to improve.

The law derives from studies conducted by a research team from the Harvard Business School at Western Electric Company's Hawthorne Works near Chicago between 1924 and 1932. The researchers wanted to determine the relationship between the work environment and productivity. They did such things as increase light levels. Better lighting led – not too surprisingly – to better productivity. But then they lowered light levels – and surprise! – productivity increased again. Eventually, the researchers groped their way to the answer. A factory is a social situation; workers are human beings. The assembly-line workers – the study group consisted of five young women – interpreted any change as evidence of management's interest and goodwill, and they responded accordingly. The increase in productivity or performance that results from the law is known as the Hawthorne Effect, as in "In the Oak School experiment the fact that university researchers . . . were interested in the school may have led to a general improvement of morale and effort on the part of the teachers. In any case, the possibility of a Hawthorne Effect cannot be ruled out either in this experiment or in other studies of education practices" (*Scientific American*, April, 1968).

See also **Heisenberg's Uncertainty Principle**.

Heisenberg's Uncertainty Principle

The act of measurement affects whatever is being measured so that reality can never be known precisely.

Werner Heisenberg was wrestling with the problem of pinpointing the positions of subatomic particles when he discovered this principle in 1927. Suppose one wants to know the exact position of an electron. Hypothetically, this could be done by illuminating the electron with light or another form of radiation. To determine the electron's position with precision, the wave length of the light would have to be shorter than the dimensions of the particle itself. The electron is so small, however, that even this minute amount of light would cause it to change its position. Continuing this line of reasoning, Heisenberg found that it is impossible to specify position and velocity simultaneously. In fact, there is an inverse relationship. The more accurately position is measured, the less accurately velocity can be defined. And vice versa: The more accurately velocity is measured, the more uncertainty there is about position.

All this may seem terribly abstruse, but it is not. The Uncertainty Principle calls into question the traditional notion of cause and effect. This has troubled many philosophers and physicists, Einstein among them (see **Haldane's Observation**). The saving grace is that cause-and-effect determinations can be made statistically: While it is impossible to say what any one particle will do, the aggregate behaviour of a large body of particles can be predicted because on average each follows certain laws.

The Uncertainty Principle applies to many measurements in ordinary life, too. Tiny uncertainties, which loom large in the small-scale microscopic world, generally are masked in the large-scale macroscopic one, but they exist nevertheless. For example, people assume that thermometer readings are accurate, forgetting that the instrument absorbs some heat from the tub of warm water, human body, etc., whose heat is being measured; thus the very act of measurement causes a change in the original temperature of the water, etc. Similarly, some air is let out of a tyre when an air-pressure gauge is attached to it and an electric current is diminished slightly by the movement of the needle on the gauge that is used to read it. In social situations, too, the simple presence of an observer – an anthropologist at a tribal ceremony, a news reporter at a schoolboard meeting, or a TV camera in a courtroom – generally influences the course of events to some uncertain degree as they are recorded. The distortion that results from measurement or observation is called the Heisenberg Effect, as in "No one does or can do the same thing on stage that he does unobserved. It's the popularised Heisenberg effect. The act of observing inevitably changes the process under observation" (*New York Times Magazine*, May 15th, 1977).

Fortunately, the statistical approach also helps make sense of the macroscopic world. As Sherlock Holmes observed to Dr. Watson: "You can, for example, never foretell what any one man will do, but you can say with precision what an average number will be up to (*The Sign of Four*, 1890). Fans of the great Sherlock will be pleased to note that he had this insight nearly forty years before Heisenberg had his.

See also **Butler's Observation, The Hawthorne Law, Heraclitus's Law, Pascal's Law,** and **Spencer's Law.**

Heller's Catch-22

See **Morton's Fork.**

Hendrickson's Law

If you have enough meetings over a long enough period of time, the meetings become more important than the problem the meetings were intended to solve (E. R. Henrickson, president of Environmental Engineering, Inc., Gainsville, Florida, in Thomas L. Martin, Jr., *Malice in Blunderland,* 1973). For more about meetings, see **Kirkland's Law.**

Hensley's Law

The less teeth the women have, the better the bar.

The tavern in this case was the venerable Schooner Wharf Bar on Key West Bight, a remnant of the original seaport in rapidly developing Key West, Florida. When Clyde Hensley, co-owner with his wife Brigit of the local Travelers Palm inn, introduced Charles Kuralt to the Schooner Wharf Bar, the regulars in the thatched roof establishment were "drinking their Mother's Milks fast and looking over their shoulders for the bulldozers" (*Charles Kuralt's America,* 1995). And the women weren't wearing their dentures.

Heraclitus's Law

You can't step twice into the same river, for other waters are ever flowing on to you.

Heraclitus of Ephesus (ca. 540-ca. 480 B.C.) apparently wrote only one book, *On the Universe,* and it has been lost except insofar as other ancient authors quoted from it. The idea of continual change was central to his philosophy. Diogenes Laertius quoted him in *Lives of Eminent Philosophers* as maintaining that "Nothing endures but change." Plato, in his dialogue, Cratylus, attributed to Heraclitus the statement that "Everything flows, nothing stays still."

Just what Heraclitus meant by all this is a subject of debate. Was he referring to continuous, measured change over time? This is the kind of change to which Marcus Aurelius referred in the second century A.D. in his *Meditations*: "Time is a sort of river of passing events, and strong is its current; no sooner is a thing brought to sight than it is swept by and another takes its place, and this too will be swept away." Or as William James, who coined the phrase "stream of consciousness," put it: "Let anyone try, I will not say to arrest, but to notice or attend to, the present moment of time. One of the most baffling experiences occurs. Where is it, this present? It has melted in our grasp, fled ere we could touch it, gone in the instant of becoming" (*The Principles of Psychology,* 1890).

On the other hand, Heraclitus could also have been advancing a more radical idea, comparing all natural objects to a river, in which case the apparent stability of the world around us is nothing but a phantasm and we would be precluded from apprehending reality. Since he does not question the evidence of the senses in the other snippets of his works that have been preserved, he probably meant the former, a more comforting thought. Plato's *Cratylus* continued the second line of inquiry, however, reaching the unsettling conclusion that you cannot even step into the same river once. In this connection, see also **Heisenberg's Uncertainty Principle**.

Swift's Corollary. There is nothing in this world constant, but inconstancy (Jonathan Swift, *A Critical Essay upon the Faculties of the Mind*, 1707).

Karr's Amendment. The more things change, the more they remain the same (*Plus ça change, plus c'est le même chose*). The journalist and author Alphonse Karr was referring to revolutions specifically in this famous statement from the January, 1849, issue of his satircal monthly, *Les Guêpes*.

Carr's Corollary to Karr's Amendment. Change is certain. Progress is not (E. H. Carr, *From Napoleon to Stalin and Other Essays*, 1980).

See also **Behn's Law, Cheshire's Law of the Social Jungle, Swift's First Law, Santayana's Law,** and **Wolfe's Law.**

Herblock's Law

If it's good, they'll stop making it.

Though generally attributed to political cartoonist Herblock (short for Herbert Lawrence Block), the law may not have originated with him. According to a syndicated column by Sydney J. Harris on December 28th, 1977, Herblock came up with the law when production of his favourite carbon drawing stick was discontinued. Nearly two years earlier, however, Alan L. Otten quoted Jane Otten and Russell Baker as having observed independently that "If it works well, they'll stop making it." Mr. Otten termed this 'The Perversity of Objects Precept' (*Wall Street Journal*, February 26th,

1976). And in the preceding decade, a very similar thought, "If it's good and I want it, they don't make it anymore," was expressed by Elizabeth C. Finegan to Harold Faber in a letter of March 17th, 1968 (Faber, *The Book of Laws*, 1979). Thus, Herblock's Law looks very much like a modern proverb about the orneriness of modern life. It even has a companion, which is not as well known, but should be:

Gerhardt's Law. If you find something you like, buy a lifetime supply – they're going to stop making it (in John Peers, *1,001 Logical Laws . . .* , 1979).

See also **Arnold's Laws of Documentation** and **Beer's Law.**

Herodotus's Law

Circumstances rule men; men do not rule circumstances.

Herodotus put these words into the mouth of Artabanus, uncle of Xerxes, in his history of the Greco-Persian wars of 500-479 B.C. Artabanus had misgivings about the Persian king's plan to invade Greece. The comment that Herodotus attributed to him came as part of a warning to Xerxes that he was taking a great risk simply because of the size of his navy. He had so many ships that it would not be possible to find safe harbours for all of them if a storm arose along the way. In that circumstance, he faced disaster. Artabanus recommended proceeding in accordance with what modern strategicians call 'a worst-case scenario.' In his words: "Methinks it is best for men, when they take counsel, to be timorous, and imagine all possible calamities." Xerxes thanked Artabanus for his advice but did not take it, replying "Fear not all things alike, nor count up every risk. For if in each matter that comes before us thou wilt look to all possible chances, never wilt thou achieve anything." In the end, of course, Xerxes returned home in defeat, having sacrificed many lives and lost much treasure, all to no avail.

The fatalism of Herodotus's Law was echoed in similar words by Abraham Lincoln when explaining how changing circumstances had led him to shift from a policy of not interfering with slavery to one of emancipation: "I claim not to have controlled events, but confess plainly that events have controlled me" (letter, April 4th, 1864, in David Herbert Donald, *Lincoln*, 1995).

Herodotus's Law was updated in a more cynical manner, appropriate to the present age, by writer-director-actor John Huston in *Chinatown* (1978):

Huston's Corollary. Given the right circumstances, people will do anything.

See also **Lincoln's First Law.**

Hippocrates' First Law

For extreme illnesses extreme treatments are most fitting.

This aphorism may or may not represent the actual words of the so-called Father of Medicine (ca. 460-380 B.C.). It is part of The Hippocratic Collection, a potpourri of anonymous essays and fragments thereof, which may have come from the library at his medical school on the island of Cos. Whether or not Hippocrates actually proposed this rule, it almost certainly reflected his thinking and, hence, shaped that of later generations. Thus, in *Hamlet* (1600-01), Claudius, King of Denmark, contemplates the removal of his dangerous step-son in these terms:

> *Diseases desperate grown*
> *By desperate appliance are removed*
> *Or not all.*

Guy Fawkes, who sought to blow up King James I and the rest of the government on the opening day of Parliament in 1605 by placing barrels of gunpowder beneath the House of

Lords, must have been a theatre-goer. At any rate, he used the same justification in almost the same words after he was arrested and brought to the king's bedchamber for questioning. Expressing no regrets except for the failure of the scheme, Fawkes declared that "Desperate diseases require desperate remedies." After suitable tortures, he revealed the names of other members of the plot and was executed on January 31st, 1606. King James, no doubt, would have subscribed to the maxim of Publilius Syrus: "There are some remedies worse than the disease."

See also **Publilius's Maxims**.

Hippocrates' Second Law

Life is short, the art long, opportunity fleeting, experience treacherous, judgment difficult.

This observation by Hippocrates is perhaps more widely known in its Latin condensation by Seneca, *Vita brevis est, ars longa*. This last has led to risqué puns, such as the epitaph on the headstone of one Willie Longbottom who died aged 6: 'Ars Longa, Vita brevis.'

Hobson's Choice

No real choice – that is, Hobson's choice or none.

The rule is credited to Thomas Hobson (1544-1631), keeper of an inn and stable in Cambridge. He became famous, if not notorious, among university students for his practice of not allowing them to select which of his horses they wanted to rent. Realising that if given a free choice, the scholars would invariably pick the best mounts, then ride them hard, Hobson rotated the horses in his stable, and permitted each customer to take only the best rested animal. Sir Richard Steele described Hobson's system in the *Spectator* (October 14th, 1712) this way: "When a man came for a horse, he was led to into the stable, where there was a great choice, but he obliged him to take the horse which stood next to the stable door; so that every customer alike was well served according to his chance, and every horse ridden with the same justice. From whence it became a proverb, when ought to be your election was forced upon you, to say 'Hobson's choice.'"

In this ointment, there is but one small fly. In October, 1617, fourteen years before Mr. Hobson's death, Richard Cocks, a merchant then residing in Japan, reported in a letter back home that "We are then put to a Hodgson's choise to take such previleges as they will give us, or else goe without." So, perhaps, *Hobson's choice* should be *Hodgson's choice*. On the other hand, Mr. Hobson already had been in business for many years in 1617 (he was 86 when he died of the plague) and spelling was not standardised in the early seventeenth century. Between *Hobson* and *Hodgson*, the reader may take his or her *choise*.

See also **Shakespeare's First Law.**

Hoffer's Observation

When people are free to do as they please, they usually imitate each other. Originality is deliberate and forced, and partakes of the nature of protest (Eric Hoffer, *The Passionate State of Mind*, 1955).

Hofstadter's Law

It always takes longer than you expect, even when you take into account Hofstadter's law.

Douglas R. Hofstadter introduced this law in connection with a discussion of chess-playing computers in *Gödel, Escher, Bach: An Eternal Golden Braid*. People are not nearly as good as computers at recursive analysis – the figuring out for every piece on the board of long chains of possible moves, the best replies to them, the best counter-moves, and so on. Yet top-level players were beating machines consistently. Much of the art seemed to be in the ability of humans to focus on particular positions instead of following every possible line of play to its conclusion.

> In the early days of computer chess, people used to estimate that it would be ten years until a computer (or program) was world champion. But after ten years had passed, it seemed that the day a computer would become world champion was still more than ten years away," wrote Mr. Hofstadter, suggesting that this itself was "just one more piece of evidence for the rather recursive *Hofstadter's Law.*

Gödel, Escher, Bach was published in 1979. In 1996, IBM's Deep Blue opened a six-game match with world champion Gary Kasparov by defeating him. It did this by leading the champion into a complex position in which it benefited from its superior powers of recursive analysis. Mr. Kasparov learned his lesson quickly, simplifying positions in subsequent games and winning the series. But Deep Blue also improved its game. In a rematch in May of 1997, the machine finally defeated the world champion.

See also the second of **Murphy's Laws.**

Holmes's First Law

Eliminate all other factors, and the one which remains will be the truth.

Sherlock Holmes enunciated this law in *The Sign of Four* (1890), as recounted by his friend and roommate, John H. Watson, M.D., with the assistance of Sir Arthur Conan Doyle. Holmes, last reported to be living in well-deserved retirement on the southern slopes of the Sussex Downs, where he busies himself keeping bees, restated this law in slightly different form in 'The Adventure of the Beryl Coronet': "It is an old maxim of mine that when you have excluded the impossible, whatever remains, however improbable, must be the truth."

Wilde's Amendment. Truth is rarely pure and never simple (*The Importance of Being Earnest*, 1895).

See also **Papagiannis's Law.**

Holmes's Second Law

It is a capital mistake to theorise before one has data.

Sherlock Holmes set forth this law while investigating 'A Scandal in Bohemia' (1891) – an especially memorable case because during it he met his only love, Irene Adler, henceforth referred to by him as "the woman." Holmes provided an explanation along with his law, saying: "It is a capital mistake to theorise before one has data. Insensibly one begins to twist facts to suit theories, instead of theories to suit facts." Later, in *The Valley of Fear*, the great detective (or "unofficial consulting detective," as he styled himself) reformulated the law in a conversation with a police inspector, declaring that "The temptation to form premature theories upon insufficient data is the bane of our profession."

It follows from all this that obtaining data is of primary importance. As Holmes himself exclaimed: "Data! Data! Data! I can't make bricks without clay" ('The Adventure of the Copper Beeches'). The raw data must be examined carefully, however, for as Holmes pointed out in 'The Boscombe Valley Mystery', "There is nothing more deceptive than an obvious fact." It also is necessary to pay attention to the tiniest details. Thus, Holmes noted in 'A Case of Identity': "It has long been an axiom of mine that little things are infinitely the most important."

See also **Meyer's Law.**

Hopper's Law

If you do something once, people will call it an accident. If you do it twice, they call it a coincidence. But do it a third time and you've just proven a natural law (quoted in Ethlie A. Vare and Greg Ptacek, *Mothers of Invention*, 1989).

Grace Murray Hopper, a mathematician with a Ph.D. from Yale, was one of the first computer programmers. She entered the field in 1943 as a naval lieutenant assigned to the Bureau of Ordnance Computation Project at Harvard University. Lt. Hopper worked initially on the Mark I, an electromechanical ancestor of the modern computer. Over the years, both as a civilian and after her recall into the Navy in 1966 (she retired as rear admiral), she made many contributions to computing technology, particularly in the development and standardisation of programming languages.

Curiously, Admiral Hopper's most long-lasting contribution may have been the one to which she gave the least amount of thought: popularising the use of 'bug' to refer to a defect in a program or a computer. The first computer 'bug' was a real one, a moth, that had got into the Mark I on an August night in 1945. Her account of the episode was included in the *New York Times* obituary of her (January 3rd, 1992): "Things were going badly, there was something wrong in one of the circuits. Finally, someone located the trouble spot and, using ordinary tweezers, removed the problem, a two-inch moth. From then on, when anything went wrong with a computer, we said it had bugs in it." In the general sense of a defect or fault in a machine or plan, 'bug' pre-dates the computer age, however. The oldest example of the word's use in this way in the *Oxford English Dictionary* comes from an 1899 report in the *Pall Mall Gazette* of Thomas Alva Edison "discovering 'a bug' in his phonograph" – an expression, the report continued, "for solving a difficulty and implying that some imaginary insect has secreted itself inside and is causing all the trouble." Thus, Admiral Hopper's contribution looks like an independent re-invention inspired by the fortuitous intervention of an actual bug in the Mark I.

Horace's Law

Once a word has been allowed to escape, it cannot be recalled.

The first century B.C. poet Horace – Quintus Horatius Flaccus in full and in Latin – was a full-time writer (thanks to the patronage of Gaius Cilnius Maecenas, whose generosity toward young artists – Vergil was another of his beneficiaries – made *Maecenas* a byword for any patron, especially a supporter of the arts). Over a thirty-five-year period, Horace composed nearly 10,000 lines, all of his works apparently having survived. This law is contained in Book 18 of his *Epistles*.

Other writers before and after Horace have expressed the same thought. For example, a fragment from one of the plays of Menander, who lived in the fourth century B.C. but whose works were almost unknown until 1905 when parts of them were discovered on a papyrus in Egypt, includes the line, "It is as easy to recall a stone thrown violently from the hand as a word which has left your tongue." In the fourteenth century, Geoffrey Chaucer put it this way in 'The Maniciple's Tale': "Thing that is seyd, is seyd; and forth it gooth." And still later, in the seventeenth century, Thomas Fuller asserted that "Time and words can't be recalled" (*Gnomologia*).

Horace's Law was restated in less poetic but eminently practical terms in 1990 by Peter Commandy, conductor of a survival course for teachers in the New York City school system. Explaining why he counseled teachers not to interrupt or talk back even when being berated or insulted, he told John Kifner of the *New York Times*, "What I'm combatting is the most powerful weapon in the world. It's not an Uzi, not a cannon. It's the human tongue. It's the most negative force in the world. Once something has been said, you can't get it back" (June 2nd). Even the words "calm down" can escalate an argument, said Mr. Commandy, since they imply that what's upsetting the other person is not terribly important. Mr. Commandy's theory was that teachers should always listen, always give respect, and he offered a foolproof method for preventing oneself from interrupting another person: Put the tip of your tongue on the roof of your mouth, just behind your two front teeth. Try it. You won't be able to say a word.

See also **Haldeman's Law** and the last of **Publilius's Maxims**.

Hoyle's Rule

When in doubt, take the trick.

The Hoyle here is Edmond, long-lived (1672-1769) author of books on whist and other card games; this is rule twelve for whist in the first edition of *Hoyle's Games* (1746). His name was disseminated widely by plagiarists who used it to market their own rule books, whence the phrase "according to Hoyle." The phrase, curiously, has been dated only to the early twentieth century. Previously, Americans said "according to Gunter," referring to the English mathematician Edmund Gunter. The English, meanwhile, used "according to Cocker" in the same sense, Edward Cocker being the supposed author of *Arithmetick* (1678), a text that went through 112 editions. (More plagiarism: Another man, John Hawkins, apparently wrote Cocker's book, which was not published until three years after he died. Augustus de Morgan, who tracked down the forgery in the mid-nineteenth century, observed that "This same Edward Cocker must have had a great reputation, since a bad book under his name pushed out the good ones.")

Variations on Hoyle's Rule include:

Twain's Corollary. When in doubt tell the truth ('Pudd'nhead Wilson's New Calendar' in *Following the Equator*, 1897).

The Coward's Creed. When in doubt, don't. (Often suggested to people contemplating marriage).

See also **Gunter's Law of Air Travel**.

Hungerford's Law

Beauty is in the eye of the beholder.

The Irish writer Margaret Wolfe Hungerford churned out millions of words in more than thirty novels, but she is remembered mainly for this single line from *Molly Bawn* (1878).

(Aldous) Huxley's Law

Official dignity tends to increase in inverse ratio to the importance of the country in which the office is held.

Huxley produced this law in *Beyond the Mexique Bay*, published in 1934, two years after his best remembered book, *Brave New World*.

(Sir Julian) Huxley's Law

Sooner or later, false thinking brings wrong conduct.

Brother to Aldous, and another of many distinguished members of the Huxley family, Sir Julian was a scientist, science writer, humanist, and first director general of the United Nations Educational, Scientific, and Cultural Organization (UNESCO). This is from his *Essays of a Biologist* (1923).

I

Imhoff's Law

The organisation of any bureaucracy is very much like a septic tank. The really big chunks always rise to the top.

This law was attributed to Professor John Imhoff, head of the Department of Industrial Engineering at the University of Arkansas, Fayetteville, by Thomas L. Martin, in *Malice in Blunderland* (1973). The insight came naturally to Professor Imhoff – it was in his genes, so to speak – since, as Mr. Martin pointed out, "A distant cousin, Karl Imhoff, invented the Imhoff Septic Tank of international fame."

The natural complement to Imhoff's Law is:

Rusk's Law of Delegation. Where an exaggerated emphasis is placed upon delegation, responsibility, like sediment, sinks to the bottom (in Arthur Bloch, *The Complete Murphy's Law*, 1991).

Irving's Acute Observation

A sharp tongue is the only edge tool that grows keener with constant use.

This insight is from Washington Irving's *Rip Van Winkle* (1819), about a man who takes a nap and doesn't wake up for twenty years. Far and away the most popular story that Irving ever wrote, it is based on a folk tale. An ancestral version, about a sheepherder who takes a fifty-seven-year long nap, appears in the works of Diogenes Laertius, about whom nothing is known except that he was alive and writing in the third century.

Ito's Rules

Rule 1. Be cautious, careful and when in doubt, keep your mouth shut. Rule 2. When tempted to say something, take a deep breath and refer to Rule 1 (Judge Lance A. Ito, outlining the principles that he planned to apply in the forthcoming murder trial of O. J. Simpson, *New York Times,* July 23rd, 1994).

J

Jefferson's Ukase

Delay is preferable to error.

Thomas Jefferson made this observation in a letter to George Washington on May 16th, 1792. ('Delay' was not the only thing he preferred to error; see also **Billings's Second Law**.) The virtues of delay have been noted by many others, including the man who nearly beat Jefferson in the race for the presidency in 1800, getting as many votes as him in the electoral college, only to lose when the tie was broken by the House of Representatives: "Never do today what you can do as well tomorrow. Delay may give clearer light as to what is best to be done" (Aaron Burr, in James Parton, *The Life and Times of Aaron Burr*, 1857). See also **Senator Sorghum's Laws of Politics**.

History's quintessential delayer is Quintus Fabius Maximus, who bought time for Rome to build a new army during the second Punic War by avoiding battle with Hannibal. "By delaying he preserved the state," wrote Quintus Ennius in his *Annals*, a history of Rome. Fabian's strategy is memorialised with two words in the English language. The first is *cunctation*, which is not as bad as it sounds, denoting merely a delay (from *Cunctator*, the delayer, the nickname that the Romans gave to Fabian). The second is the adjective *Fabian* for characterising a cautious policy of favouring social change while avoiding direct confrontation with the state – especially as exemplified by the Fabian

Society, organised in 1884 to promote socialism in Great Britain.

p.s. Fabian's delaying tactics may have preserved the state in the long run, but the immediate pay-off was dismal. The new army that the Romans assembled while he was in the field soon suffered one of the great military defeats of all time. Taking the offensive under more aggressive commanders (the Romans changed generals every year), the new army attacked Hannibal's Carthaginians at Cannae in 216 B.C. The much smaller Carthaginian force gave way in the centre; then Hannibal managed to encircle the Romans, in effect, striking on both wings and in the rear (an 'envelopment' in technical, military terms). The historian Polybius reports that the Romans lost nearly 80,000 men, the Carthaginians just 5,700.

Jo Bob's Rule

The meanest and the biggest get to make all the rules.

This rule allowed Jo Bob Williams, an immense pro football lineman, to do anything he wanted at a wild postgame party in *North Dallas Forty*, the 1979 film made from Peter Gent's 1973 novel of the same title. Phil Elliott, an offensive end and the protagonist of the story, cited this rule as his reason for declining to interfere with Mr. Williams, then holding a fully-clad woman high in the air, preparatory to tossing her into a swimming pool. The flavour of the off-field lives of the players on this team is further conveyed by one of the reveries of Elliott: "From somewhere in the recesses of my ravaged brain I recalled an early doping maxim bequeathed to me by a friend now doing two to life in Huntsville for possession: no matter what happens, he said, always pass the joint first."

All this is entirely fictional, of course, though it is worth noting that before Mr. Gent took up book writing, he was an offensive end for the Dallas Cowboys.

(Byron) Johnson's Laws of Bureaucratic Success

1. Never do anything for the first time.

2. Make only big mistakes – they will pass unnoticed

> (Byron L. Johnson and Robert Ewegen,
> *B.S.: The Bureaucratic Syndrome*, 1982).

See also **Senator Sorghum's Laws of Politics**.

(Hiram) Johnson's Law

The first casualty when war comes is truth.

This law commonly is attributed to Senator Hiram W. Johnson, of California, who supposedly made the remark in the course of a Senate debate in 1918. Written evidence is lacking, but the thought is consistent with his views. A Progressive (Theodore Roosevelt's running mate in 1912) who turned into an isolationist Republican, Johnson opposed U.S. entry into World Wars I and II. Curiously, much the same idea also was expressed by another Johnson – Samuel, the so-called Great Cham of Literature – albeit in more circuitous fashion: "Among the calamities of war, may be justly numbered the diminution of the love of truth, by the falsehoods which interest dictates, and credulity encourages" (*The Idler*, November 11th, 1730).

Hiram Johnson, meanwhile, though tagged as 'Holy Hiram' by his political opponents, also should be remembered for possessing a remarkable talent for invective, one that outshines even the most vitriolic of modern politicians. Thus, when running for governor of California in 1910, he was goaded by the *Los Angeles Times* into counter-attacking its publisher in these terms: "In the city of San Francisco we have drunk to the very dregs of infamy; we have had vile officials; we have had rotten newspapers. But we have nothing so vile, nothing so low, nothing so debased, nothing so infamous in

San Francisco as Harrison Gray Otis. He sits there in senile dementia, with gangrened heart and rotting brain, grimacing at every reform, chattering impotently at all things that are decent; frothing, fuming, violently gibbering, going down to his grave in snarling infamy" (in Marshall Berges, *The Life and Times of Los Angeles*, 1984).

Jones's Law

Friends may come and go, but enemies accumulate. (Thomas Jones, quoted by Alan L. Otten, the *Wall Street Journal*, February 20th, 1975).

This law, which may or may not have been originated by Mr. Jones, has since become a popular saying in political circles. For example, Peggy Noonan, speechwriter for President George ("a kinder, gentler nation," "a thousand points of light") Bush, cited it in an interview on the Charlie Rose television show on January 6th, 1994.

See also **McLaughry's Law**.

K

Kahn's Law

If you can't explain what you're doing in simple English, you are probably doing something wrong (Alfred Kahn, *Time*, May 8th, 1978).

See also **McNaughton's Rule**.

Kahn and Egan's Law

The rich get rich and the poor get poorer.

The line is from *Ain't We Got Fun* by Gus Kahn and Raymond B. Egan. The verse in full goes: "There's nothing surer, / The rich get rich and the poor get poorer, / In the meantime, in between time / Ain't we got fun." This was written in 1921, with the 'meantime' lasting eight years – until the great crash of 1929.

The basic thought has been around for a while. John Ray included 'Money begets money' in his 1670 collection of *English Proverbs*.

See also **Bronfman's Law of Accumulation**.

Kant's Categorical Imperative

Act only on that maxim which you can at the same time wish that it should become a universal law.

Though expressed in convoluted terms, this principle from Immanuel Kant's *Foundations of the Metaphysics of Morals*

(1797) is essentially a generalised form of the Golden Rule. Kant's prose is famously dense, so much so that German students have been known to read him in English, finding his train of thought easier to comprehend in translation than in the original.

See also **Bentham's Law** and **Confucius's Law.**

Kautilya's Observation

The enemy of my enemy is my friend.

Often described as an Arab proverb, this insight actually comes from the *Arthasastra*, a pre-fourth century B.C. Sanskrit text on statecraft by Kautilya, a guru of an Indian king, Chandragupta Maurya. This law was much cited in the United States during the build-up to the Gulf war of 1991 as justification for seeking the cooperation of Syria in defeating Iraq. Both Kautilya's Observation and its corollary, "The friends of my friends are my friends," should be taken with a grain of salt. As playwright Garson Kanin told a meeting of the the the Authors League on February 22nd, 1989: "There's an old almanac saw that 'The friends of my friends are my friends.' Nothing could be less certain."

Billingsley's Amendment. The worst enemy you can have is one who was once your best friend (Sherman Billingsley, proprietor of New York City's famed Stork Club from 1929 to its closing in 1965, in notes for an autobiography that he never got around to finishing, *New York Times*, July 1st, 1996).

Kelly's Law

Nothing is ever as simple as it first seems (*Farmer's Almanac*, 1978; an observation by an otherwise unknown and unheralded Kelly).

See also **Gilbert's Law of Appearances.**

(John F.) Kennedy's Law

Life is unfair.

Questioned at a White House press conference on March 23rd, 1962, about the apparent unfairness of the first American advisers being killed in Vietnam while the rest of the nation was enjoying the benefits of peace and prosperity, President John F. Kennedy, drawing on his own experience in World War II, replied: "There is always inequity in life. Some men are killed in a war and some are wounded, and some men never leave the country . . . Life is unfair." This law was echoed on the *M.A.S.H.* television series: "There are certain rules about war, and rule number one is that young men die, and rule number two is that doctors can't change rule number one" (rerun, August 6th, 1991).

Another much-quoted Kennedy rule for living, "Don't get mad, get even," may actually have been coined by his father, Joseph Patrick, or by another member of the older generation. See **Dirksen's Three Laws of Politics**.

Sad to report, the provenance of the equally famous "Forgive but never forget," also is somewhat cloudy. The sentiment was attributed to JFK by his speechwriter and special counsel, Theodore C. Sorensen, in a 1968 television interview. The pragmatic Kennedy was perfectly capable of reaching this conclusion on his own, but it also seems possible that he half-remembered Aesop's tale, 'The Man and the Serpent', whose moral is that "Injuries may be forgiven but not forgotten." The psychiatrist Thomas Szass amplified this in *The Second Sin* (1973): "The stupid neither forgive nor forget; the naive forgive and forget; the wise forgive but do not forget."

Finally, wise souls with short memories may take consolation from the plight of the monarch in Lewis Carroll's *Through the Looking-Glass* (1872):

"The horror of that moment," the King went on, "I shall never, *never* forget."

"You will, though," the Queen said, "if you don't make a memorandum of it."

(John P.) Kennedy's Law

All is fair in love and war.

The statement sounds as though it should go back to Homer's time at least, but the earliest known specimen of it in writing, according to *A Dictionary of American Proverbs* (1992), comes from a novel that was published as recently as 1835: *Horse-Shoe Robinson*, by John Pendleton Kennedy, who wrote under the name of Mark Littleton. A Marylander, Pendleton had a distinguished public career, serving in Congress and as secretary of the navy (in which capacity he organised Perry's expedition to Japan), but literary affairs were what really interested him. He wrote political satires, novels about plantation life, and was an early supporter of Edgar A. Poe (as Poe styled himself). He based *Horse-Shoe Robinson* on the recollections of a Revolutionary War veteran, whom he had met on a visit to South Carolina.

(Robert F.) Kennedy's Law

About one-fifth of the people are against everything all the time (speech, University of Pennsylvania, May 6th, 1964).

See also **Woody Allen's Observation**.

Keppner's Law

You never find an article you have lost until you replace it (Otto Keppner, Wardsboro, Vt., communication to *Harper's*, August, 1974).

Kerr's Law

If you can keep your head when all about you are losing theirs, it's just possible that you haven't understood the situation.

Ms. Jean Kerr helped popularise this law in her bestselling *Please Don't Eat the Daisies* (1957). She cited it as something "someone pointed out recently." The saying sometimes is referred to as 'The Navy Law', apparently because it is posted in the wardrooms of some ships, but it has long since escaped its moorings, e.g. "As Ed Murrow once said about Vietnam, anyone who isn't confused doesn't really understand the situation" (Walter Bryan, *The Improbable Irish*, 1969). Other variations on the theme include:

Commoner's Law. When you fully understand the situation, it is worse than you think (Barry Commoner, *Life*, December, 1979).

Mondale's Law. If you are sure you understand everything that is going on, you are hopelessly confused (Walter Mondale, quoted by Ann Landers, syndicated column, March 26th, 1978).

Nelson's Law of Momentum. If you don't make big yardage on the first and second down, you're in trouble, and if you don't think so, you are really in trouble and you don't understand the situation (Dave Nelson, *New York Times*, October 5th, 1971).

Mrs. Peter's Law. Today, if you're not confused, you're just not thinking clearly (Irene Peter, in Laurence J. Peter, *Peter's Quotations*, 1977).

See also **The Peter Principle**.

What appears to be an early allusion to the law comes from Rudyard Kipling's 'If–', in *Rewards and Fairies* (1910): "If you can keep your head when all about you / Are losing theirs and blaming it on you." Which leads to a vitally important insight, named for a possibly mythical Mr. Jones, about whom nothing is known, not even his first name:

Jones's Law. The man who smiles when things go wrong has thought of someone he can blame it on.

Kipling's Law of Blackmail

If once you have paid him the Dane-geld / You never get rid of the Dane (Rudyard Kipling, 'Dane-geld', in *History of England*, 1911).

The Danegeld was a national tax, imposed on the English in order to get funds to give to the Danes in the northern part of the country in return for halting their raids to the south. The Danegeld was first levied in 991 by Ethelred II, better remembered as Ethelred the Unready. As Kipling noted, the Danes did not go away. Neither did the tax. Once Ethelred and his successors discovered this remarkable source of income, they collected it at intervals until 1163, long after the Danish threat had subsided. Among the kings who levied it were Canute, himself a Dane, and William the Conqueror, who had the Domesday Book compiled in order to facilitate gathering of the tax. The Danegeld, then, was the granddaddy of the modern income tax. See also **Schonberg's Law.**

Kipling's Laws of the Jungle

Now these are the Laws of the Jungle, and many and mighty are they; / But the head and the hoof of the Law and the haunch and the hump is – Obey!

This is the conclusion of Rudyard Kipling's 'The Law of the Jungle' in *The Second Jungle Book* (1895). The poem begins with the admonition:

> *Now this is the Law of the Jungle – as old and as true as the sky;*

And the Wolf that shall keep it may prosper, but the Wolf that shall break it must die.

Kirkland's Law

The usefulness of any meeting is inversely proportional to the size of the group (Lane Kirkland, in the *Wall Street Journal*, March 3rd, 1974).

Mr. Kirkland should know whereof he spoke, having sat through a great many meetings while president of the A.F.L.-C.I.O. He also deserves credit for "Everything outside the A.F.L.-C.I.O. is Hoboken," an exclusionary definition of general utility since it can be recast to put down almost anyone or anything. For example: Everything outside the National Association of Manufacturers is Hoboken. Everything outside the National Organization of Women is Hoboken. Everything outside East Hampton is Hoboken. But note that the principle of symmetry is not obeyed: Everything outside Hoboken is not East Hampton. On the contrary, as the world turns, it often seems that everything outside Hoboken is just another kind of Hoboken.

For more about meetings, see **Hendrickson's Law,** Parkinson's Law of Triviality in **Parkinson's Law,** and **Shanahan's Law.**

Kissinger's Law

The absence of alternatives clears the mind marvelously (Henry A. Kissinger, in Peter Potter, *All About Success*, 1988).

Kissinger's Law is similar to a more pointed remark by Samuel Johnson: "When a man knows he is to be hanged in a fortnight, it concentrates his mind wonderfully" (September 19th, 1777, in *Boswell's Life of Johnson*, 1791).

Just what led Kissinger to his insight is not known, but Johnson's remark was practically Nixonian in its disingenuity.

This was his answer when asked if had authored an unusually forceful sermon by a minister, Dr. William Dodd, who was scheduled to be hanged for forgery. In truth, Johnson had written the sermon as well as petitions in Dr. Dodds's name for clemency. He evaded the question, however, because he thought it would be wrong to take credit for words that he had allowed another man to pass off as his own – at least while the appeals might still do the man some good. Dr. Dodds went to the scaffold on June 27th and Johnson fessed up, giving Boswell his copies of all the original papers on September 15th.

Koppett's Law

Whatever creates the greatest inconvenience for the largest number of people must happen (Leonard Koppett, *New York Times*, October 19th, 1977).

Probably because Mr. Koppett was a member of the *New York Times* sports department, Harold Faber, another *Times* man, categorised this as one of the laws of sports in his *Book of Laws* (1977). With all due respect to Mr. Faber, however, the law has much broader implications as, for example, anyone who has ever depended on the New York City subways can tell you. It is, in fact a near relative of **Murphy's Law**.

Koppett's Observation

A simple story, however inaccurate or misleading, is preferred to a complicated explanation, however true (Leonard Koppett, *A Concise History of Baseball*, ms, 1996).

Mr. Koppett referred here specifically to the history of baseball. For example, for many years most baseball fans preferred to believe the simple myth that the rules for the national pastime sprang full-blown from the brow of Abner

Doubleday, a boy from rural Cooperstown, N.Y., who went on to become a Civil War general. In truth, however, the game evolved in New York City in the early 1840s from cricket, rounders, and what was variously known as town ball, Boston Ball, or the Massachusetts game.

Of course, the psychological tropism toward simple stories, or explanations, is not always misplaced; see **Ockham's Razor.**

Krauthammer's Tirana Index

The higher the vote any government wins in an election the more tyrannical it is.

The Index, named for the capital of Albania, was devised by columnist Charles Krauthammer following that country's 1982 election in which a slate backed by the local dictator Enver Hoxha eked out a victory of 1,627,959 to 1 (cited in *New Yorker*, June 21st, 1993).

Kristol's Law

Being frustrated is disagreeable, but the real disasters of life begin when you get what you want (Irving Kristol, quoted by George F. Will, in *Newsweek*, November 28th, 1977).

See also **Shaw's Quandary** and **Wilde's First Law.**

L

La Bruyère's Law

Men fall from great fortune because of the same shortcomings that led to their rise.

This line from Jean de La Bruyère's *Characters of Theophrastus* (1688) would have made a fine epitaph for Richard M. Nixon.

Laingren's Law

Human beings are like tea bags. You don't know your own strength until you get into hot water.

Bruce Laingren discovered this law – a process of self-discovery, really – while undergoing the rigours of 444 days as a hostage in Iran in 1979-81. He cited it in *Time* (August 26th, 1991) in connection with an article about the differences in the physical and emotional states of two other hostages who had just been released after five years of captivity in Lebanon.

Lance's Law

If it ain't broke, don't fix it.

A bit of folk wisdom popularised by Bert Lance, Director of the Office of Management and Budget, under President Jimmy Carter. The equivalent of the proverbial (since Chaucer's time, at least) "Leave well enough alone," this was

Mr. Lance's standard for determining which governmental departments should be reorganised. As elucidated in *Nation's Business*: "Bert Lance believes he can save Uncle Sam billions if he can get the government to adopt a single motto: 'If it ain't broke, don't fix it.' He explains: 'That's the trouble with government: Fixing things that aren't broken and not fixing things that are broken" (May 27th, 1977).

Lance's Law applies equally well to automobiles, television sets, faucets, and other appurtenances of civilisation. Nevertheless, misguided attempts have been made to improve upon it, e.g. the title of a 1991 book by Robert J. Kriegel and Louis Patler, *If It Ain't Broke . . . Break It!: And other Unconventional Wisdom for the Business World*. Then there was the capsule description of part two of a TV series *Thriving on Chaos*: "'If it ain't broke, fix it anyway.' Large corporations that have reorganized" (*New York Times*, January 18th, 1990).

Anticipating Lance's Law in different respects are:

Churchill's Law. Beware of needless innovations, especially when guided by logic (speech, December 17th, 1942).

Scott's Law. When a man has not a good reason for doing a thing, he has one good reason for letting it alone (Sir Walter Scott, quoted in Laurence J. Peter, *The Peter Prescription*, 1972).

And if you don't let it alone, it may break; see **Zahner's Law**.

Lansky's Insight

Some people never learn to be good. One quarter of us is good. Three quarters is bad. That's a tough fight, three against one.

This morsel of wisdom from gangster Meyer Lansky was preserved for posterity thanks to an FBI bug, according to

Robert Lacy's *Little Man: Meyer Lansky amd the Gangster Life* (1991). Mr. Lansky's associates were much impressed by his formidable intellect. "That Meyer!" one of them (Bugsy Siegel or Joe Adonis) is reported to have said, "Can you believe it? He's a member of the Book-of-the-Month Club!"

Lardner's Law

Two can live cheaper than one.

The observation has an ageless, proverbial ring, but the earliest example of it in the *Oxford Dictionary of American Proverbs* is relatively recent, coming from Ring Lardner's *Big Town* (1921). The folk, in their infinite wisdom, have embellished it in various ways, e.g. "Two can live as cheap as one if one's a horse and the other is a sparrow" and "Two can live as cheaply as one only if one doesn't eat."

La Rochefoucauld's Rule

In the misfortunes of our best friends, we find something that is not displeasing.

This is one of the *Maximes* (1665) of François, Duc de La Rouchefoucauld. Other reflections by him along this line include "We all have strength enough to endure the misfortunes of others" and "If we had no faults of our own, we would not take such pleasure in noticing those of others."

The seven hundred or so maxims of La Rochefoucauld, some as long as a half page but most only two or three lines in length, were recognised immediately as literary gems. It is hard to escape the conclusion, however, that their biting quality stems from the disappointments of a man who had been on the losing side in the Fronde revolt of 1648-52, then had to spend most of the remaining four decades of his life out of the political and social mainstream. See also **Bierce's Law** and **Vidal's Law**.

Lasch's Law

Nothing succeeds like the appearance of success (Christopher Lasch, *The Culture of Narcissism*, 1979).

See also **Gilbert's Law of Appearances**.

Lauder's Law

When a person with experience meets a person with money, the person with experience will get the money. And the person with the money will get some experience (Leonard Lauder, speech, February, 1985, discussing the early years of the Estée Lauder company).

Wilde's Addendum. Experience is the name everyone gives to their mistakes (Oscar Wilde, *Lady Windermere's Fan*, 1892).

Laver's Law of Fashion

The same costume will be:

Indecent	10 years before its time
Shameless	5 years before its time
Outré (daring)	1 year before its time
Smart	
Dowdy	1 year after its time
Hideous	10 years after its time
Ridiculous	20 years after its time
Amusing	30 years after its time
Quaint	50 years after its time
Charming	70 years after its time
Romantic	100 years after its time
Beautiful	150 years after its time

(from James Laver's *Taste and Fashion*, 1937)

See also **Burn's Law of Social Change**.

Leopold's First Law

A thing is right when it tends to preserve the integrity, stability, and beauty of the biotic community. It is wrong when it tends otherwise.

This statement from 'The Land Ethic', the concluding essay in *A Sand County Almanac* (1949), sums up Aldo Leopold's argument for for considering questions of land use in ethical and aesthetic as well as economic terms. "A system of conservation based solely on economic self-interest is hopelessly lopsided," he maintained. "It tends to ignore, and thus eventually to eliminate many elements in the land community that lack commercial value, but that are (as far as we know) essential to its healthy functioning. It assumes, falsely, I think, that the economic parts of the biotic clock will function without the uneconomic parts."

This was radical stuff in the 1940s and is still not widely accepted by many land owners and users – especially loggers, miners, ranchers, and property developers.

Leopold's Second Law

The first requisite of intelligent tinkering is to save all the pieces (Aldo Leopold, quoted in *Washingtonian*, September, 1978).

Liddell Hart's Maxims

Captain Sir Basil Henry Liddell Hart, one of the most influential military thinkers of the twentieth century, distilled the essence of strategy and tactics into eight maxims. His ideas apply not just to the battlefield, but to politics, business, and sex – to any problem or activity that involves a conflict of wills. As expressed in his classic work, *Strategy* (second edition, 1967), the eight maxims are:

1. Adjust your end to your means – in effect, don't bite off more than you can chew.

2. Keep your objective always in mind, adapting plans to circumstances, remembering that there are more ways than one of gaining an objective, and making sure that attainment of intermediate objectives is worthwhile. "To wander down a side-track is bad, but to reach a dead end is worse."

3. Choose the line (or course) of least expectation, i.e. put yourself in your opponent's shoes and take the line of action that he (or she) is least likely to foresee or forestall.

4. Exploit the line of least resistance – providing, of course, that it leads toward your ultimate objective.

5. Pursue a line of operation that offers alternate objectives. Your opponent will not be sure which objective to defend most strongly and you will have a better chance of gaining at least one of them – whichever he (or she) guards least – and perhaps of achieving one after the other.

6. Make sure that your plans and dispositions of forces are flexible. Any plan should provide for a next step, quickly carried out, in case of success or failure or – the more common outcome in war – partial success. (See also **Publilius's Maxims, no. 469.**)

7. Do not throw your weight into an offensive while your opponent is on guard. Unless the enemy is much inferior in strength, wait until his (or her) power of resistance or evasion is paralysed by disorganisation and demoralisation before making a real attack.

8. Do not renew an attack along the same line, or in the same manner, after it has once failed. Bringing up reinforcements is not enough since the enemy is likely to do the same and his (or her) success in repulsing you will have strengthened his (or her) morale.

"The essential truth underlying these maxims," wrote Liddell Hart, "is that, for success, two major problems must be solved – *dislocation and exploitation*. One precedes and the other follows the actual blow – which in comparison is a simple act. You cannot hit the enemy with effect unless you have first created the opportunity; you cannot make that effect decisive unless you exploit the second opportunity that comes before he can recover."

On a still more profound level, Liddell Hart was advocating "the strategy of the indirect approach." Explaining how this strategy applies to other aspects of life, Liddell Hart said:

> The direct assault of new ideas provokes a stubborn resistance, thus intensifying the difficulty of producing a change of outlook. Conversion is achieved more easily and rapidly by unsuspected infiltration of a different idea or by an argument that turns the flank of instinctive opposition . . . In commerce, the suggestion that there is a bargain to be secured is far more potent than any direct appeal to buy. And in any sphere it is proverbial that the surest way of gaining a superior's acceptance of a new idea is to persuade him that it is his idea! As in war, the aim is to weaken resistance before attempting to overcome it; and the effect is best attained by drawing the other party out of his defences.

In the military realm, Liddell Hart's theories about mechanised warfare, mobility, surprise attack, and air warfare, developed during the 1920s and 1930s, were put into practice in World War II, initially and with great effectiveness by the Germans with their blitzkrieg (i.e. lightning war) offensives. His enemies acknowledged their debt. General Heinz Guderian, who established the panzer units in the German army, said "I was one of Captain Liddell Hart's disciples in tank affairs." And Field Marshal Erwin Rommel opined that "The British would have been able to prevent the greatest part of their defeats if they had paid attention to the modern theories expounded by Liddell Hart before the war."

Liebling's Law

If you try hard enough, you can always manage to boot yourself in the posterior (A. J. Liebling, quoted in the *New York Post*, September 9th, 1968).

A variant, requiring even greater athletic ability, and also attributed to Mr. Liebling: "If you are smart enough you can kick yourself in the pants, grab yourself by the back of the collar, and throw yourself out on the sidewalk" (in Louis D. Rubin, Jr., ed., with Jerry Leath Mills, *A Writer's Companion*, 1995).

Lincoln's First Law

You can fool all of the people some of the time and some of the people all of the time, but you can't fool all of the people all of the time.

Advertising people and other cynics have expressed doubts about the validity of this rule, leading to the following amendments:

F.P.A.'s Amendment. The trouble with this country is that there are too many politicians who believe, with a conviction based on experience, that you can fool all of the people all of the time (Frankling Pierce Adams, *Nods and Becks*, 1944).

Thurber's Amendment. You can fool too many of the people too much of the time (James Thurber, 'The Owl Who Was God' in *Fables for Our Time*, 1940).

Levine's Amendment. You can fool all of the people if the advertising is right and the budget is big enough (movie mogul Joseph E. Levine, in Robert W. Kent, *Money Talks*, 1985).

Captain Penny's Amendment. You can fool all of the people some of the time, and some of the people all the time, but you can't fool Mom (internet collection of laws, January 8th, 1996).

Lincoln's observation first appeared in print in Alexander K. McClure's *'Abe' Lincoln's Yarns and Stories* (1904). The president is supposed to have made the statement to a caller at the White House. In full, the quote reads: "If you once forfeit the confidence of your fellow citizens, you can never regain their respect and esteem. It is true that you may fool all the people some of the time; you can even fool some of the people all the time, but you can't fool all of the people all of the time."

The Lindley Rule for Reporting

The reporter must take complete responsibility for whatever he or she writes, without giving any hint of the source of the information that has been provided on the basis of "not for attribution" or as "deep background."

This rule is named for journalist Ernest K. Lindley, who informed William Safire in 1968 that it "was laid down early in the Truman Administration to enable high-ranking officials to discuss important matters – especially those involving international and military affairs – without being quoted or referred to in any way. It was, and is, a rule of no attribution – thus differing from the usual 'background rule' pemitting attribution to 'official sources' or 'U.S. officials,' etc." (*Safire's Political Dictionary*, 2008).

Difficulties with the Lindley Rule that have brought it into some disfavour are:

1. It can lead to cosy collusion between the media and government officials.

2. It frees leakmeisters from taking responsibility for what they say.

3. It eases the burden on reporters to report exactly what is said.

4. It forces the public to accept as a matter of faith that the reporter hasn't just made up the story out of whole cloth.

The Lindley Rule probably should be repealed.

Locke's Law

One day you're a peacock, the next day you're a feather duster.

David H. Locke, Republican minority leader in the Massachusetts senate, did not take credit for originating this "expression in politics." The metaphor certainly has the hallmarks of age, but it is not listed in standard sources and so will be assigned here to him until other evidence comes to hand. The feather duster in this particular instance was state Governor Michael Dukakis, whose approval rating in a state poll had plunged to 41 percent just six months after he had run for president (*New York Times*, May 2nd, 1989).

Lombardi's Law

Winning isn't everything, it's the only thing.

This law always will be associated with American football coach Vincent Lombardi, who raised the lowly Green Bay Packers to glory, winning the first two Super Bowls in 1968 and 1969, but he did not originate it. The line appears in a 1953 movie, *Trouble Along the Way*, in which John Wayne plays a football coach at a small Roman Catholic School, and it was articulated before that in real life by Red Sanders, who coached football at UCLA at the time the movie was made.

Respectfully Quoted, published by the Library of Congress, reports that Sanders employed it as early as 1948 at Vanderbilt, where he coached before moving to UCLA. The exhortation could well be much older.

Coach Lombardi tried more than once to deny the quote, maintaining that what he really said was that winning isn't everything but that wanting – or making the effort – to win is. In the charged atmosphere of the locker room, the thought may well have been compressed. At least, it was the stronger, harsher form that Green Bay guard Jerry Kramer remembered in his best-selling *Instant Replay* (1968), which popularised the saying.

See also **Durocher's Law** and **Rice's Rule**.

Longworth's Law

You can't make a soufflé rise twice.

An acute analysis attributed to Alice Roosevelt Longworth, of Thomas E. Dewey's chances of winning the presidency on his second attempt (1948). Mrs. Longworth, daughter of President Teddy, widow of Speaker of the House Nicholas, and longtime grande dame of Washington society, was famed for her sharp tongue. She popularised the remarks that Dewey looked like "the little man on the wedding cake," and that President Coolidge looked as if he had been "weaned on a pickle." Of her own father, she is said to have said that he "always wanted to be the corpse at every funeral, the bride at every wedding and the baby at every christening." And she owned a sofa pillow with the embroidered maxim, "If you can't say something good about someone, sit right here by me" (*Time*, December 9th, 1966).

See also **Luce's Law** and **Stalin's Law**.

Loos's Law

Gentlemen prefer blondes. (Anita Loos, book title, 1925).

Less well remembered, perhaps justly so, is the 1928 sequel, *But Gentlemen Marry Brunettes.*

Lowell's Law

If we see light at the end of the tunnel, / It's the light of the oncoming train.

These lines from Robert Lowell's *Day by Day* (1977) sometimes appear in amended form as Rowe's Rule, by an otherwise unidentified Rowe: "The odds are 6 to 5 that the light at the end of the tunnel is a headlight of an oncoming express train" (in Paul Dickson, *The Official Rules*, 1978).

Both Lowell's Law and Rowe's Rule are spin-offs from the blindly optimistic phrase that was used so often during the Vietnam war, e.g. by President Lyndon Johnson in a speech on September 21st, 1966: "I believe there is a light at the end of what has been a long and lonely tunnel."

Rowe's 6-to-5 odds are in keeping with – and perhaps stem from – **Runyon's First Law**, which applies to life generally rather than train tunnels particularly.

Lowery's Law

Just when you get really good at something, you don't need it anymore (William P. Lowery, Sidney, Illinois, *Harper's*, August 1974).

Another law attributed to a Lowery, probably not William, which has appeared in different legal collections dating from the 1970s and which remains current (found in abbreviated form on the internet, January 8th, 1996), is: "If it jams, force it. If it breaks, it needed replacing anyway."

See also **Anthony's Law of Force.**

Luce's Law

No good deed ever goes unpunished.

Another woman (see **Longworth's Law** above) with an exceptionally sharp tongue, Clare Boothe Luce, editor, playwright, diplomat, and wife of Time, Inc., publisher Henry, might never have got off this zinger, though it is commonly attributed to her. Other candidates for the honour include publisher Walter Annenberg, the British playwright Joe Orton, Sir Noel Coward, and Oscar Wilde. The Reverend William Sloane Coffin used a variant in an October 1984 speech on behalf of a program for protecting refugees: "In my experience, good deeds usually do not go unpunished." The true, original author of the sentiment probably is the prolific Mr. Anonymous, who flourished shortly after Aesop concluded in 'The Lion and the Mouse' that "No act of kindness, no matter how small, is wasted."

The political counterpart of Luce's Law is D'Amato's Law. Thus, referring to New York senator Alphonse D'Amato's success in obtaining campaign funds, a fellow Republican, John Buckley, said that D'Amato has "raised to a high art the practice of insuring that no good deed goes uncollected" (*New York Times Magazine*, October 27th, 1991).

M

Macaulay's Maxim

Nothing is so useless as a general maxim (Thomas Babington, Lord Macaulay, 'Machiavelli', in the *Edinburgh Review*, March, 1827).

Samuel Taylor Coleridge may have been a reader of the *Review*. At any rate, he converted Macaulay's Maxim into a vivid image just three months later: "A man of maxims only is like a Cyclops with one eye, and that eye placed in the back of the head" (*Table-Talk*, June 24th, 1827).

See also **Burton's Rule** and **Montagu's Motto**.

Maddocks's Law of Literature

Novelists with the most damned consciences tend to write the most blessed prose.

Reviewing Thomas Keneally's *A Dutiful Daughter* in *Time* magazine, Melvin Maddocks introduced this law in this manner: "One of the soundest laws of modern literature goes like this: Novelists with the most damned consciences tend to write the most blessed prose. On the lengthy roster headed, of course, by Joyce, Thomas Kenneally supplies another case in point" (June 7th, 1971).

De Maistre's Law

Every nation has the government it deserves. (Joseph de Maistre, *Letter to X*, 1811).

De Maistre was thinking particularly of the unsettled state of affairs in Europe following the French revolution. The only government of which he really approved was that of the pope, whose powers he believed should be absolute, untempered by councils, nations, or, least of all, the judgments of individuals. The foundation of social order, he argued in a famous essay, was the executioner.

Orwell's Corollary. At 50, everyone has the face he deserves (George Orwell, notebook, April 17th, 1949, in *Collected Essays*, 1968). But Orwell never had the chance to check this one out in his own shaving mirror, being not yet 50 when he died in 1950. These words are the last ones in his notebook.

See also **Camus's Regretful Conclusion** and **Senator Sorghum's Laws of Politics**.

Malthus's Law

Population, when unchecked, increases in a geometrical ratio. Subsistence increases only in an arithmetical ratio.

Thomas Robert Malthus reasoned in *An Essay on the Principle of Population* (1798) that improvements in living standards among the poorest people were doomed to failure because of this law. While the means of subsistence might increase steadily, they would do so, he argued, only in an arithmetic ratio or series (such as 3, 6, or 12), and thus would be overwhelmed by increasing numbers of people, with population growing in a geometric progression (e.g. 3, 9, 27, 81). But for the effects of war, pestilence, famine, and – a possible palliative that he recommended in an 1803 revision, "moral restraint," meaning premarital chastity and postponement of marriage – population would always increase faster than food supplies.

Malthus's Law may not be exactly right. Two hundred years have gone by, and humanity has managed so far to escape the Malthusian bind, thanks to the opening of new areas to farming and improvements in agricultural techniques. Still, with the world population now doubling about every fifty years, it is hard to argue with the trend of his conclusions or, short of embracing war, pestilence, and famine, to visualise a solution to the population problem other than what some people call "immoral restraint," i.e. birth control.

Malthus's essay strongly influenced the thinking of both Charles Darwin and Alfred Wallace, who independently produced the theory of evolution. It was from Malthus that Darwin picked up the phrase 'the struggle for existence.' Discussing the fecundity of nature in *The Origin of the Species* (1859), Darwin wrote:

> As more individuals are produced than can possibly survive, there must in every case be a struggle for existence, either one individual with another of the same species, or with the individuals of distinct species, or with the physical conditions of life. It is the doctrine of Malthus applied with manifold force to the whole animal and vegetable kingdoms; for in this case there can be no artificial increase of food, and no prudential restraint from marriage. Although some species may be increasing, more or less rapidly, in numbers, all cannot do so, for the world would not hold them.

The realisation of the struggle for existence led Darwin and Wallace to ask – in Wallace's words now – "Why do some die and some live? And the answer was clearly, that on the whole the best fitted live" (*My Life*, 1905).

See also **Charles Darwin's Law.**

Manes's Law of Computer Enhancement

Rare is the "improvement" that will ever repay the time lost in performing it.

Computer columnist Stephen Manes stumbled onto this law while trying to give his machine a brain transplant that would double its thinking speed. He continued: "Installs 'in just minutes,' says the advertising. Right; in this case, 600 or so. In the attempt to save milliseconds, minutes and even hours have an uncanny way of disappearing forever" (*New York Times*, April 12th, 1994).

Marcy's Law

To the victor belong the spoils.

This rule was enunciated on January 25th, 1832, by William Learned Marcy of New York in a Senate speech defending President Andrew Jackson's appointment of Martin Van Buren as ambassador to Great Britain. Quoth the Senator:

> It may be, sir, that the politicians of the United States are not as fastidious as some gentlemen are, as to disclosing the principles on which they act. They boldly preach what they practice. When they are contending for victory, they avow their intention of enjoying the fruits of it. If they are defeated, they expect to retire from office. If they are successful, they claim as a matter of right, the advantages of success. They see nothing wrong in the rule, that to the victor belong the spoils of the enemy.

Marcy's Law was presaged in 1830 by Representative J. S. Johnson, who put it this way: "The country is treated as a conquered province, and the offices distributed among the victors as the spoils of war." And toward the end of the century, Richard Croker, the Tammany boss in New York City, explained: "Politics are impossible without spoils . . . You have to deal with men as they are . . . you must bribe the masses with spoils."

The corollary to Marcy's Law is contained in the political proverb, "Root, hog, or die" – or in full, as set forth in *Calumet and War Club* (1836): "Root, hog, or die – work for your office or leave it – support the party, right or wrong – are the terms of the agreement."

Marcy himself subsequently backed away from his law as succeeding administrations improved the spoils system to the point that incoming presidents began evicting officeholders even if they had been appointed by presidents of the same party. "They have it that I am the author of the office seeker's doctrine, that 'to the victor belong the spoils,'" said Marcy, "but I certainly should never recommend the policy of pillaging my own camp."

Marcy's Law has been largely nullified in recent decades by the Supreme Court of the United States, which has produced a series of decisions that protect government employees – and independent contractors, too, as of 1996 – from patronage dismissals and from being denied jobs or promotions on account of their political affiliation. But for these rulings, the incoming Clinton administration could have avoided a scandal simply by firing everyone in the White House travel office in 1993 instead of searching around, ineptly as it turned out, for legal reasons to dismiss them. Senator Marcy would have not understood what the brouhaha was all about.

Martial's Law

Conceal a flaw, and the world will imagine the worst (*Epigrams*, 1st century A.D.).

Martin's Law

You're not drunk if you can lay on the floor without holding on.

Dean Martin popularised this law in a drunk shtick that he performed with the two other members of the Rat Pack (Frank Sinatra and Sammy Davis, Jr.) but credited it to an older imbiber, Joe E. Lewis.

Marx's First Law

From each according to his abilities, to each according to his needs.

Karl Marx popularised the phrase but did not originate it. He acknowledged this himself, carefully enclosing the statement within quotation marks in his *Critique of the Gotha Program* (1875). Bartlett's *Familiar Quotations* notes that Marx probably was quoting (or thought he was quoting, his version actually amounting to a paraphrase) a passage from *Organisation du Travail* (1840), by Louis Blanc, or *Le Code de la Nature* (1755), by a Morelly, a political theorist who anticipated Rousseau to some extent and about whom nothing is known, not even his first name. Of course, the essential idea of Marx's First Law also appears in the Bible: "Neither was there any among them that lacked: for as many as were possessors of lands or houses sold them, and brought the prices of the things that were sold, And laid *them* down at the apostles' feet: and distribution was made unto every man according as he had need" (Acts, 4:34-35).

Marx's Second Law

Historical events occur twice – the first time as tragedy, the second as farce.

This observation by Karl Marx appears in his *The Eighteenth*

Brumaire of Louis Bonaparte (1852). It is his riff on Georg Wihelm Hegel's dictum that "People and governments have never learned anything from history" (*Philosophy of History*, 1832).

See also **Santayana's Law.**

Marx's Third Law

The road to Hell is paved with good intentions.

Karl Marx included this traffic warning in *Das Kapital* (1867-83). The thought was not original to him. "Hell is paved with good intentions" appears in John Ray's 1670 collection of *English Proverbs*. Another version, "Hell is full of good intentions or desires," is attributed to St. Bernard of Clairvaux, founder of the Cistercian order, who lived in the twelfth century.

Wilde's Corollary. It is always with the best intentions that the worst work is done (Oscar Wilde, *Intentions*, 1891).

Humphrey's Amendment. The Senate is a place filled with goodwill and good intentions, and if the road to hell is paved with them, then it's a pretty good detour" (Hubert H. Humphrey, quoted in *Newsweek*, January 23, 1978).

As for St. Bernard: He also has been credited with "Love me love my dog" (*Qui me amat, amat et canem meum*, Who loves me will love my dog also). This Bernard has nothing to do with the large dogs that bring little casks of brandy to snowbound travelers in the mountains. The dogs got their name from the St. Bernard passes over the Alps, and the passes, in turn, got their name from St. Bernard of Menthon, who established a hospice on the Great St. Bernard pass toward the end of the tenth century. And p.s. The dogs really did help rescue people.

See also **Dante's Law** and **Spencer's Law.**

The Matthew Effect

The tendency in the scientific community to give all credit for discoveries to the senior members of a team while giving short shrift to junior members for work that they have carried out and sometimes conceived.

A classic example of the Matthew Effect is the case of Jocelyn Bell, an English graduate student who in October 1967 noted 'a bit of scruff' in the tape output of a radio telescope and recognised it, although she was examining a hundred feet of tape daily, as the same bit of scruff she had noticed two months earlier. Further observations established that this scruff was actually a burst of pulses exactly one and one-third seconds apart. When Ms. Bell conveyed this information to her team leader, Anthony Hewish, he replied "Oh, that settles it. It must be man-made." Continuing observations, however, established that the object was too far away to be man-made. It turned out to be a pulsar, the first to be discovered. During the following December and January, Ms. Bell also discovered the second, third, and fourth pulsars. To find the last two, she had to run through about three miles of tape.

In 1974, a Nobel prize was awarded to astronomers for the first time. The prize was shared by Martin Ryle, director of the radio observatory at Cambridge University for his role in developing new kinds of radio telescopes, and by Anthony Hewish for his "decisive role in the discovery of pulsars." Ms. Bell's contribution went unnoticed.

The Matthew Effect is so-named from the Gospel according to Matthew, verse 13:12: "For unto every one that hath shall be given, and he shall have abundance: but from him that hath not shall be taken away even that which he hath."

To the German naturalist Friedrich Heinrich Alexander, Baron von Humboldt (he of the Pacific's Humboldt Current) is credited the corollary: "There are three stages in the popular attitude toward a great discovery; first, men doubt its existence, next they deny its importance, and finally they give the credit to someone else."

See also **Sir Francis Darwin's Law**.

Maugham's Law

You can't learn too soon that the most useful thing about a principle is that it can always be sacrificed to expediency (W. Somerset Maugham, *The Circle*, 1921).

See also **St. Augustine's Law to End All Laws**.

McGeary's Law

The more noise a man or a motor makes, the less power there is available (W. R. McGeary, in Peter Potter, *All About Success*, 1988).

McGovern's Law

The longer the title, the less important the job.

George McGovern discovered this law in 1960, when president-elect John F. Kennedy sought to persuade the South Dakota Democrat that the post of director of the Food for Peace Program was more important than that of secretary of agriculture (in Paul Dickson, *The Official Rules*, 1978). But McGovern, temporarily out of a job because he had given up his House seat in order to run for the Senate, then lost, accepted the directorship anyway.

A few exceptions exist to McGovern's Law. Thus, 'executive vice president' carries more weight than 'vice president', though neither are as important as the plain, unadorned 'president'. The law holds true in most bureaucracies, however, with 'secretaries' outranking 'assistant secretaries' and 'deputy assistant secretaries', while simple 'generals' order 'lieutenant generals' about and 'colonels' tell 'lieutenant colonels' what to do.

The longest title on record for the most menial position is the Personal Assistant to the Secretary (Special Activities), who worked for Joseph A. Califano, when he served as secretary of Health, Education and Welfare in the Carter administration. The Personal Assistant, etc.'s job description, as approved by Mr. Califano, began: "This position is to provide a confidential assistant to the Secretary to assist in providing a broad range of services for special activities." It continued for another 389 words, not one of which was 'cook', which is what the Personal Assistant, etc., was hired at $12,763 per annum to do. For his mastery of bureaucratese, Mr. Califano was selected by the National Council of Teachers of English as one of the winners of its 1977 Doublespeak Awards.

See also The Lateral Arabesque in **The Peter Principle**.

McGregor's Revised Maxim

The shortest distance between two points is under construction (internet collection of laws, January 8th, 1996).

McLaughry's Law

To make an enemy, do someone a favour (James McLaughry, quoted by Alan L. Otten, in the *Wall Street Journal*, February 20th, 1975). See also **Jones's Law**.

McNaughton's Rule

Any argument worth making within a bureaucracy must be capable of being expressed in a simple declarative sentence that is obviously true once stated (John McNaughton, quoted by Alan L. Otten, in the *Wall Street Journal*, March 3rd,

1974). See also **Kahn's Law, Orwell's Laws of Language,** and **Rosten's Other Laws (no. 3).**

McNaughton's Rule should not be confused with the McNaughten Rules, long the criteria for determining insanity in criminal cases. These rules stemmed from the answers by the fifteen judges in the House of Lords to a series of questions that were posed to them following the acquittal in 1843 on grounds of insanity of Daniel M'Naghten (a.k.a. McNaghten, McNaughten, Macnaughton, etc.) for murdering Edward Drummond, private secretary to the prime minister, Sir Robert Peel. In essence, the rules provided that a person was criminally responsible for a deed unless it could be shown that he was labouring under a delusion at the time of its commission that prevented him from understanding either the nature and quality of his act or that it was wrong. In practice, this standard leaves a lot to be desired – it does not take into account, for example, the person who acts under a compulsion though he may have some sense of right and wrong – and it has been tempered over time. For a classic American insanity defense, see **Delmas's Unwritten Law.**

Mencken's First Law

No man ever went broke underestimating the intelligence of the American public (H. L. Mencken, attributed).

Variants of this, also attributed to the Sage of Baltimore, include "No man ever went broke underestimating the taste of the American people" and "Never overestimate the intelligence of the voter." The basic law may well be a popular condensation of a wordier comment by Mencken: "No one in this world, so far as I know – and I have searched the records for years, and employed agents to help me – has ever lost money by underestimating the intelligence of the great masses of the plain people" (*Chicago Tribune*, September 19th, 1926).

Mezzrow's Amendment. The great American public likes nothing better than to be roped in, and the tighter you squeeze 'em the more you please 'em (Milton 'Mezz' Mezzrow and Bernard Wolfe, *Really the Blues*, 1946). Mr. Mezzrow said that he learned this lesson in 1925 while playing saxophone in a downtown Chicago club, where even the smallest party couldn't get in and get out without dropping at least two grand for the night. The name of the joint was the Deauville, "pronounced Doughville."

Mencken's Second Law

Nine times out of ten, in the arts as in life, there is actually no truth to be discovered; there is only error to be exposed (H. L. Mencken, *Prejudices, Third Series*, 1922).

The 90 percent benchmark also appears in other contexts. For example:

Roosevelt's Wise Distinction. Nine-tenths of wisdom is being wise in time (Theodore Roosevelt, speech, June 14th, 1917).

The 90-90 Rule of Project Schedules. The first 90 percent of the tasks takes 10 percent of the time and the other 10 percent takes the other 90 percent (in John Peers, *1001 Logical Laws*, 1979).

Carter's Legal Ruling. 90 percent of our lawyers serve 10 percent of our people. We are over-lawyered and under-represented (Jimmy Carter, speech, 100th anniversary of the Los Angeles County Bar Association, May 4th, 1978).

The Fisherman's Law. 90 percent of the fish are caught by 10 percent of the fishermen. *Corollary.* 90 percent of the fishermen are doing nothing 99 percent of the time; the others are doing nothing 98 percent of the time.

See also **Woody Allen's Observation, Pareto's Law** and **Sturgeon's Law.**

Mencken's Law of Social Reform

Whenever A annoys or injures B on the pretence of saving or improving X, A is a scoundrel (H. L. Mencken, *Newspaper Days: 1899-1906*, 1941).

Meyer's Law

If the facts don't fit the theory, discard the facts.

Cited by C. L. Sulzberger in the *New York Times* (August 20th, 1969), this law has mutated slightly over the years. Thus, a group of laws collected from the internet (January 8th, 1996) included a Maier's (sic) Law: "If the facts do not conform to the theory, they must be disposed of."

Aldous Huxley, not noted for his conventional views, would not have agreed. "Facts do not cease to exist because they are ignored," he wrote in a 'Note on Dogma' (in *Proper Studies*, 1927). The best analysis of the relationship between facts and theory comes from Charles Darwin: "False facts are highly injurious to the progress of science, for they often endure long; but false views, if supported by some evidence, do little harm, for everyone takes a salutary pleasure in proving their falseness" (quoted by Stephen Jay Gould, *Natural History*, July 1996).

Twains's Corollary. Get your facts first, and then you can distort 'em as much as you please (interview with Rudyard Kipling, Elmira, N.Y., summer of 1889, in Kipling's *From Sea to Sea*, 1899).

See **Holmes's Second Law** and **Michael's Law of Advocacy**.

Micawber's First Law

Annual income twenty pounds, annual expenditure nineteen six, result happiness. Annual income twenty pounds, annual expenditure twenty pounds ought and six, result misery.

This basic law of economics was propounded by Mr. Wilkins Micawber in Charles Dickens's *David Copperfield* (1849-1850).

To the American humorist Josh Billings (Henry Wheeler Shaw) is attributed the corollary: "Live within your income, even if you have to borrow to do it" (in Laurence J. Peter, *Peter's Quotations*, 1977).

See also the second of **Parkinson's Laws**.

Micawber's Second Law

Accidents will occur in the best regulated families.

This insight by Mr. Wilkins Micawber in Charles Dickens's *David Copperfield* (1849-1850) was inspired by a series of disasters at a dinner party that Copperfield held for Mr. and Mrs. Micawber and a former classmate, Tommie Traddles. The mutton was covered with grit because the cook had dropped it in the fireplace ashes, the young serving 'gal' spilled all the gravy on the stairs, and the crust of the pigeon-pie was lumpy and bumpy with nothing particular underneath. But the guests took all of this in good grace, as evidenced by Mr. Micawber's consoling remark about accidents. Indeed, he went on to say that unless families are regulated "by the influence of a woman, in the lofty character of a wife" accidents will not only occur but "may be expected with confidence, and must be borne with philosophy" – a clear anticipation of **Murphy's Law**.

Michael's Law of Advocacy

If you have the facts on your side, hammer the facts. If you have the law on your side, hammer the law. If you have neither the facts nor the law, hammer the table (attributed to Columbia Law School professor Jerome Michael).

A variant, credited to a Judge Joe Baldwin is "If you have a strong case in law, talk to the judge. If you have a strong case in fact, talk to the jury. But if you have no case in law or fact, talk to the wild elements and bellow like a bull" (in William Safire and Leonard Safir, *Good Advice*, 1982).

Midas's Law

Possession diminishes perception of value, immediately (John Updike, *New Yorker*, November 3rd, 1975).

This is essentially a modern reformulation of the old saw, 'Familiarity breeds contempt'; see **Aesop's Adages**. Midas, of course, was the legendary king of Phrygia, in Asia Minor, to whom Dionysus granted the power to turn everything he touched into gold. This included, as Midas found to his dismay, any food he tried to eat – a classic example of **Wilde's First Law**.

The Inverse Midas Touch is the power possessed by some unfortunate beings today to turn everything they touch into shit.

Miller's Law

The quality of food in restaurants is in inverse proportion to the number of signed celebrity photographs on the walls.

This law was handed down by *New York Times* food critic Bryan Miller in the course of a review on March 24th, 1989. "Where do all these black-and-white glossies come from?" he wondered. "Are they actually tokens of gratitude from stage and screen stars, or does some photo lab simply churn them out and peddle them by mail? . . . if one believes these are authentic testimonies – 'To Moe, a great host!' – then Joey Heatherton must be the greatest roving gastronome since Escoffier."

Calkin's Corollary. The number of adjectives and verbs that are added to the description of a menu item is in inverse proportion to the quality of the dish (in Louis D. Rubin, Jr., ed., with Jerry Leath Mills, *A Writer's Companion*, 1995).

Hewes's Corollary. The less you offer, the more you have to say about it (Clarence Hewes, on restaurant menu writing, *Time*, December 12th, 1968). Mr. Hewes gained his knowledge of menus professionally as head of Bell Printing Co. in Chicago. The same *Time* piece went on to suggest two additional rules as guidance for people who dine out:

1. The quality of food is in inverse proportion to the number of semicolons and exclamation marks on the menu, and conversely –

2. The better the restaurant, the less likely it is to play the word game.

Mitchell's Law

When the going gets tough, the tough get going.

This bit of folk wisdom was popularised by John N. Mitchell, attorney general in the first Nixon administration and chairman of the Committee to Re-elect the President (CRP, pronounced 'creep'). A former Nixon speechwriter recast Mitchell's Law this way: "When duty calls, that is when character counts" (William Safire, *New York Times*, May 23rd, 1986).

n.b. The 'creep' pronunciation of the Nixon's committee's name was not the inspiration of some devilish Democrat but of the man who then headed the Republican National Committee, Robert Dole, whose senatorial feathers had been ruffled by some of Nixon's smarty-pants young aides.

Waitley-Witt's Antithesis. The trouble with most of us is that we stop trying in trying times (Denis Waitley and Remi L. Witt, *The Joy of Working*, 1985).

Mizner's Law of Research

If you steal from one author it's plagiarism; if you steal from many it's research.

Wilson Mizner, writer, restaurateur (part owner of the Brown Derby in Hollywood), gambler, miner, prizefighter, con man, and all-round wit, may actually have delivered some of the lines attributed to him. (This one is credited to him in John Burke's *Rogue's Progress*, 1975) For other reputed Miznerisms, see **Barnum's Law** and **Cheshire's Law of the Social Jungle.**

Most writers, even the greatest, follow Mizner's Law religiously. Thus, discussing the formulaic expressions (e.g. 'wine-dark sea') employed by Homer and other minstrels, Dr. Robert E. D. Cattley, a former classics professor at the University of New Brunswick in Canada, cited "the old principle that 'He writeth best who stealeth best all things both great and small, for the great mind that used them first from nature stole them all'" (*New York Times*, December 20th, 1983). Or as the Reverend Joseph E. Lowery, president of the Southern Christian Leadership Conference, said concerning allegations that Martin Luther King had plagiarised parts of his doctoral dissertation: "Preachers have an old saying. The first time they use somebody else's work, they give credit. The second time they say some thinker said it. The third time they just say it" (*New York Times*, November 10th, 1990). Seneca, writing in the first century A.D., and well before authors and publishers dreamed up the concept of copyright, was of much the same opinion, noting in one of his *Moral Essays*: "Whatever is well said by anyone is mine."

For particular examples of great poets who have lifted lines from the works of others – 'sampled' in the vernacular of modern rap musicians – see **Eliot's Observation.**

Molière's Law

Things are only worth what you make them worth (Jean Baptiste Poquelin, a.k.a. Molière, *Les Précieuses Ridicules*, 1690)

The law is exhibited most forcefully in the stock market, where the price of a security (the word 'security' bears thinking about in this context) typically has little, if any, relationship to its intrinsic value.

Mom's Law

See **Zahner's Law.**

Montagu's Motto

General notions are generally wrong.

Lady Mary Wortley Montagu (1689-1762) produced this insight at the tender age of twenty-one, when she was still Mary Pierrepont, in a letter of March 28th, 1710, to her future husband, Edward Wortley Montagu.

Her insight was not twenty-twenty, however, as she went on to tell Wortley Montagu, "I don't enjoin you to burn this letter; I know you will. 'Tis the first I ever writ to one of your sex and shall be the last. You must never expect another. I resolve against all correspondence of this kind. My resolutions are seldom made and never broken." On both counts, she proved wrong. Wortley Montagu not only kept the letter but made a careful copy of it. Meanwhile, Lady Mary broke her resolution by writing again to him the following month. And once started, she hardly let up, going on to write many more letters to a great many people, both men and women, with the result that she is remembered today mainly for her dazzling lifelong correspondence.

Similar laws about generalisations include "All

generalisations are dangerous, even this one," attributed to Alexander Dumas, *fils*, and "No generalisation is wholly true, not even this one," credited both to Benjamin Disraeli and Oliver Wendell Holmes, Jr.

See also **Burton's Rule, Macaulay's Maxim** and **Russell's Conclusion.**

Montaigne's Law

Nothing is so firmly believed as what is least known (Michel Eyquem de Montaigne, *Essays*, 1580). See also **Osler's Law** and **Papagiannis's Law.**

Morrow's Law

The candidate who takes the credit for the rain gets the blame for the drought.

This basic law of politics generally is attributed to Dwight W. Morrow, lawyer, banker, diplomat, and father of Anne Morrow Linbergh. Of course a fortunate candidate may get away with the claim if water keeps falling from the sky. Thus, Frank Mankiewicz, manager of George McGovern's 1972 presidential campaign, cited Morrow's Law as a warning to Republicans of the dangers of taking too much credit for an improving economy. Nevertheless, his candidate was trounced by Republican Richard M. Nixon.

Morton's Fork

Rich or poor, the government will get your money.

If HM Revenue & Customs had an escutcheon, Morton's Fork would be emblazoned upon it. The Fork (formerly also known as Morton's Crotch) is named for John Morton, statesman, prelate, and principal adviser for many years to Henry VII, though some say he has been improperly credited for the work of another, either an earlier functionary or a subordinate, Bishop Richard Fox. (See **The Matthew Effect** for more about crediting, or not crediting, subordinates.) Morton, however, had a very high public profile. He even has a walk-on part in Shakespeare's *Richard III*, thanks to a famous incident, apparently founded on fact, in which the king joked with Morton about the fine strawberries in his garden – all the while planning to arrest him and throw him into the Tower. After Henry took the throne from Richard, Morton was rewarded with appointments to the two greatest offices in the land, Lord Chancellor and Archbishop of Canterbury.

The principle of Morton's Fork was that people who displayed their wealth can afford to pay taxes – or, in Morton's time, make forced loans to the king – while those who did not appear to be rich must be saving their money and, hence, also could be required to make loans to the king. In an extended sense, Morton's Fork can be used to characterise any no-win situation, e.g. "A fine Morton's fork this – those who went were conspirators and those who stayed away were cowards" (*Times Literary Supplement*, August 17th, 1973).

Thus, Morton's Fork is a precursor of *Catch-22*, devised by Joseph Heller in his 1961 novel of that name to characterise a paradoxical situation to which the only logical response is deemed illogical. (Catch-22 would have been Catch-18 but for the appearance that same year of Leon Uris's *Mila 18*, which led Mr. Heller to change his title shortly before publication.) In the novel, the Catch applies to pilots who are regarded as crazy if they want to continue flying combat missions but who, if they asked to be relieved, then are deemed by the Air Force to have demonstrated sufficient sanity to keep on flying. Mr. Heller described the double-bind in his mind-bending fashion:

There was only one catch and that was Catch-22, which specified that a concern for one's own safety in the face of dangers that were real and immediate was the process of a rational mind. Orr was crazy and could be grounded. All he had to do was ask; and as soon as he did he would no longer be crazy and would have to fly more missions. Orr would be crazy to fly more missions and sane if he didn't, but if he was sane he had to fly them. If he flew them he was crazy and didn't have to; but if he didn't want to he was sane and had to.

Murphy's Law

If anything can go wrong, it will.

Undoubtedly the most frequently cited of all laws, and a remarkably fecund one, too, having inspired a host of related rules, Murphy's Law is of surprisingly recent vintage. The earliest reference to it in the *Oxford English Dictionary*, the usual benchmark for dating the origins of words and phrases, comes only from 1958. And despite its apparent newness, the authorship of the law was a mystery for some years. The most common assumption at first was that Murphy was a mythical character, similar to the author of the parallel Finagle's Law. A cartoon character, the anti-hero of a series of Navy training films, was suggested as the source of the law by John Glenn, the astronaut who became a senator, in *Into Orbit* (1962). The theory had some logic to it since the Murphy of the films was a careless mechanic, apt to turn bolts the wrong way and install propellors backwards. Still another candidate for the honour was an actual person, William Lawrence Murphy (1876-1959), inventor of the Murphy bed that folds out of a closet. But there was no real evidence for this attribution aside from occasional reports of beds collapsing or retracting at especially awkward moments.

Best evidence now is that the true progenitor was Captain Edward A. Murphy, Jr. a development engineer from Wright Field (Ohio) Aircraft Laboratory. He is said to have produced the law in a moment of exasperation while working at Edwards Air Force Base in California in 1949. Captain Murphy was helping to conduct a series of tests in which Colonel John P. Stapp was strapped onto a rocket-powered sled mounted on a track, accelerated quickly to high speed, and then abruptly halted. The object of the exercise was to improve airplane and flightsuit design by determining just what the human body could tolerate in the way of G-forces.

Present at the creation – and godfather, in effect – was George E. Nichols, an engineer at the Jet Propulsion Laboratory at Pasedena. As Mr. Nichols tells the story: "I was project manager at Edwards Air Force Base during Colonel J. P. Stapp's experimental crash research testing on the track at North Base. The law's namesake was Captain Ed Murphy . . . Frustration with a strap transducer which was malfunctioning due to an error by a lab technician in the wiring of the strain gauge bridges caused Murphy to remark: 'If there's any way to do it wrong, he will!' I assigned Murphy's Law to the statement and the associated variations" (*Listener*, February 16th, 1984).

Slightly longer versions of Murphy's original complaint also have been recorded, e.g. "If there is a wrong way to do something, then someone will do it" (Robert L. Forward, 'Murphy Lives!', *Science 83*, January-February 1983) and "If there's more than one way to do a job and one of those ways will end in disaster, then somebody will do it that way" (*People*, January 31st, 1983).

While the name of the technician has been forgotten, mercifully, the basic law has been elaborated in many ways.

The law and many of its variations are paralleled by laws attributed to other individuals, both in general (see **Fetridge's**

Law) and sometimes in word-for-word detail (see **Chisholm's Law of Human Interaction**). Precedence in such cases is impossible to determine. The folk may have assigned other people's laws to Murphy, or others may have drawn upon the pool wisdom credited to him.

Still another possibility is that great minds have stumbled onto the same truths independently – something that happens fairly frequently in the history of ideas. Thus, key elements of Murphy's Laws were foreshadowed in the eighteenth and nineteenth centuries; see **Robert Burns's Law, Disraeli's Second Law**, and **Micawber's Second Law**. Or consider the following ad from ca. 1916 for subscriptions to *House Beautiful*: "The one number you neglect getting is sure to be the one you wouldn't have missed for the world. Don't take the chance!" (This was when the magazine cost thirty-five cents a copy and the 'special introductory' don't-take-a-chance rates ranged from $1 for five months to $2 for two years.)

Prestidigitators also have long all too familiar with the Murphy effect since the beginning of the twentieth century, if not earlier. The May 1913 issue of *The Magic Wand* magazine quoted David Devant (stage name of David Wighton, 1868-1941), brilliant performer and ingenious deviser of new tricks, as remarking: "There is an old saying among conjurers that it is impossible for a performer to know a trick thoroughly well until everything that can possibly go wrong with it has gone wrong – in front of an audience."

Murphy's Law also is known as Sod's Law. As elucidated in the *New Statesman*: "Sod's Law . . . is the force in nature which causes it to rain mostly at weekends, which makes you get flu when you are on holiday, and which makes the phone ring just as you got into the bath" (October 9th, 1970). ('Sod' is short for the abominable 'sodomite', but in extended use, as in the name of this law, the term is generic for a male person, especially one who is to be pitied.)

Most remarkably, Murphy's Law also constitutes one of the few links between the everyday world that we perceive with our normal senses and the counter-intuitive world of quantum mechanics, with Murphy's promise of inevitability meshing nicely with the subatomic rule that "Whatever isn't forbidden is required"; see **Gell-Mann's Dictum.**

The following list of Murphy's laws does not pretend to be complete but it is representative of those ascribed to him and casts them in a more or less logical order.

First Corollary to Murphy's First Law. Of the things that can't go wrong, some will.

Second Corollary to Murphy's First Law. If everything seems to be going well, you've obviously overlooked something. See also **Kerr's Law.**

Third Corollary to Murphy's First Law. If two or more things can go wrong, the one that will go wrong first is the one that will cause the most damage. See also **Koppett's First Law** and **Rudin's Law.**

Fourth Corollary to Murphy's First Law. It is impossible to make anything foolproof because fools are so ingenious.

Fifth Corollary to Murphy's First Law. No matter what goes wrong, there's always someone who will say he knew it would.

Murphy's Second Law

Everything takes longer than you expect.

See also **Cheops's Law, DeCaprio's Law,** and **Hofstadter's Law.**

Corollary to Murphy's Second Law. Everything takes longer than it should except sex.

Murphy's Third Law

Nothing is as simple as it looks.

See **Agnes Allen's Law** for her husband's version of the Third Law.

Murphy's Fourth Law

If you play with anything long enough, it will break.

See also **Zahner's Law**.

Corollary to the Murphy's Fourth Law. It wll always break just when you need it the most.

Murphy's Fifth Law

Left to themselves, things tend to go from bad to worse.

First Amendment to Murphy's Fifth Law. The difference between Murphy's Law and the Laws of Nature is that with the Laws of Nature you can count on things screwing up the same way every time.

Rider to the First Amendment to the Fifth Law. But Nature always sides with the hidden flaw.

Corollary to the Rider to the Second Amendment to the Fifth Law. Mother Nature is a bitch; see **Haldane's Observation** for details.

Murphy's Law of Auto Repair

Any tool dropped while repairing an automobile will roll beneath the vehicle to its exact centre.

See also **Anthony's Law of the Workshop** and **Theodore Bernstein's First Law**.

Murphy's First Military Law (a.k.a. The Army Law)

Any order that can be misunderstood will be misunderstood.

Murphy's Second Military Law

Friendly fire isn't.

Murphy's Third Military Law

The most dangerous thing in a combat zone is an officer with a map.

Murphy's Fourth Military Law

If you really need an officer in a hurry, take a nap.

Murphy's First Law of Biology

Under any given set of environmental conditions an experimental animal will behave as it damn well pleases.

Murphy's Law of Botany

When visiting a botanical garden, the one plant that you have never seen before and admire the most is the only one that lacks an identifying label.

Murphy's Law of Research

Enough research will tend to support your theory.

Murphy's Law of Thermodynamics

Things get worse under pressure.

And finally, in the interest of equality, we have:

Mrs. Murphy's First Law (a.k.a. The Law of Perversity)

You cannot tell for certain ahead of time which side of the bread to put the butter on. See also **Payn's Law**.

Mrs. Murphy's Second Law

Anything that can go wrong will go wrong while Mr. Murphy, or the man of the house, whomever he may be, is out of town.

N

Napoleon's Law

From the sublime to the ridiculous there is only one step.

This was the emperor's summation in 1812 to the Polish ambassador to France, the Abbe du Pradt, of the campaign he had just completed – his retreat from Moscow. He may have picked up the thought from Thomas Paine: "The sublime and the ridiculous are often so nearly related, that it is difficult to class them separately. One step above the sublime makes the ridiculous; and one step above the ridiculous makes the sublime again" (*The Age of Reason, Part II*, 1795).

Other observations of Napoleon that have the force of law, from his *Maximes et Pensées*:

> If you want a thing done well, do it yourself.

> Men are more easily governed through their vices than their virtues.

> The greatest general is he who makes the fewest mistakes.

> In war, the moral is to the physical as three to one.

> In war as in love, one must meet at close quarters to get things over with.

Neely's Laws

1. If the project works, you must be using the wrong equipment.

2. The accessibility, during recovery, of small parts which fall from the workbench, varies directly with the size of the part and inversely with its importance to the completion of the work in progress.

3. The nearest living relative of the football player you are criticising is sitting directly in front of you in the football stadium (Gerald Neely, Billings, Mont., in *Harper's*, August, 1974).

Neely's Second Law also is credited frequently to the great Anthony; see **Anthony's Law of the Workshop**.

Nehru's Law

Even in politics, an evil action has evil consequences. That, I believe, is the law of Nature as precise as any law of physics or chemistry (Jawaharlal Nehru, quoted in Laurence Peter, *The Peter Prescription*, 1972).

Newton's Laws of Motion

1. Every body continues in its state of rest, or of uniform motion in a right line, unless it is compelled to change that state by forces impressed upon it.

2. The change of motion [acceleration] is proportional to the motive force impressed; and is made in the direction of the right line in which that force is impressed.

3. To every action there is opposed an equal reaction: or the mutual actions of two bodies upon each other are always equal, and directed to contrary parts

      (Sir Isaac Newton, *Principia Mathematica*, 1687).

Newton devised these laws to explain the motions of physical objects such as planets and cannonballs, but they have a wider application. For example:

1. A body in a state of rest (on a couch, say) will remain there until compelled into motion by an outside force (such as its wife or significant other).

2. The change of motion [acceleration] of the body from the resting position will be proportional to motive force impressed (as by a punch in the ribs).

3. The action and reaction of the body and its wife or significant other are always equal and directed to contrary parts.

See also **Ohm's Law**.

Nies's Law

The effort expended by a bureaucracy in defending any error is in direct proportion to the size of the error (John Nies, quoted by Alan L. Otten, *Wall Street Journal*, December 23rd, 1973).

It seems hardly coincidental that this law was proposed as wagons were being drawn up around the White House, where President Nixon was frantically resisting subpoenas that had been issued by the Senate Watergate committee just four days previously for almost five hundred tapes and documents.

Nixon's Law

When the President does it, that means that it is not illegal (Richard M. Nixon, in David Frost, *I Gave Them a Sword*, 1978).

This was Mr. Nixon's reply to a question by Mr. Frost about the president's approval in 1970 of a plan for domestic spying. The plan, authored by an aid, Tom Charles Huston, entailed such criminal activities as break-ins, wiretaps, and secret opening of mail. It never went into effect, thanks to the objections of FBI director J. Edgar Hoover, who feared the bureau would get a black eye if one of his agents were nabbed in one of these operations. Subsequently, the White House went ahead on its own, creating a special unit to conduct criminal operations, the so-called plumbers (their first mission was to stop leaks), thus setting in motion the train of events that led to the Watergate break-in and, in due course, to Mr. Nixon's resignation.

Norris's Law

If you know the answer, then you don't know the question (Anne Norris, Spokane, Washington, *Harper's*, August, 1974).

Norris's Law harks back to Gertrude Stein's last words as recorded by her companion Alice B. Toklas: "What is the answer?" [I was silent.] "In that case what is the question?" (*What Is Remembered*, 1963).

See also **Publilius's Maxims** (no. 596).

Nowlan's Deduction

Following the path of least resistance is what makes men and rivers crooked (in John Peers, *1,001 Logical Laws . . .*, 1979).

O

Ockham's Razor

Do not assume more causes for any phenomenon than are absolutely necessary to explain it.

Also called the Principle of Parsimony, this rule often appears as "Entities are not to be multiplied without necessity." William of Ockham (or Occam, a village in Surrey) lived in the first half of the fourteenth century. He never seems to have stated the law in precisely these words. Rather, he tended to express it in such forms as "Plurality is not to be assumed without necessity" and "What can be done with fewer [assumptions] is done in vain with more," i.e. when given a choice of theories or explanations, pick the simplest. William of Ockham used his razor to cut away medieval metaphysical abstractions and pseudo explanations that obscured the fundamentals of Christian faith. Formerly a student of the great scholastic theologian Duns Scotus, William became his rival. Scotus was known as *Doctor Subtilis* and William as *Doctor Invincibilis*. (Poor Scotus: his followers later were attacked by rising humanists and reformers of the sixteenth century as 'Duns men' or – the source of the modern word – *dunces*.)

Sir Isaac Newton applied Ockham's Razor to the physical world, stating it in the process more clearly than had William himself. "We are to admit no more causes of natural things than such as are both true and sufficient to explain their appearances," wrote Newton in the *Principia Mathematica*

(1687). "To this purpose the philosophers say that Nature does nothing in vain, and more is in vain when less will serve; for Nature is pleased with simplicity, and affects not the pomp of superfluous causes." (Or, as Henry David Thoreau put it, even more simply in *Walden* (1854): "Simplify, simplify.")

The Scottish philosopher David Hume further adapted Ockham's Razor in *Of Miracles* (1748), producing a principle, sometimes called Hume's Razor, which is as useful for evaluating claims for the existence of flying saucers, big-footed creatures, ghosts, and so on, as it is for miracles of a more traditional sort. In Hume's words: "No testimony is sufficient to establish a miracle unless that testimony be of such kind that its falsehood would be more miraculous than the fact which it endeavours to establish."

A twentieth-century update of Ockham's Razor is Wald's Principle of Scientific Parsimony: "If you have one explanation for a phenomenon, there is no need to seek a second explanation: (biochemist George Wald, *New York Times*, February 29th, 1976). A less reverent variant is called The KISS Principle, where the acronym stands for Keep It Simple, Stupid! At the same time, it is worth remembering Albert Einstein's advice: "Everything should be made as simple as possible, but not simpler" (*Reader's Digest*, October 1977).

See also **Koppett's Observation** and **Ulmann's Razor**.

Ohm's Law

The electric current in any circuit is directly proportional to the voltage and inversely proportional to the resistance.

The law, named for the German physicist Georg Simon Ohm, has wider applications than one might think. Thus, from a review of the British novelist Alan (*Loneliness of the Long Distance Runner*) Sillitoe's memoir, *Life without Armour*:

"Applying himself both to work and to women, he lived by Ohm's law, which he learned in his air force radio job as a flight controller: 'The current in a conductor is directly proportional to the applied voltage'" (*Publishers Weekly*, August 12th, 1996).

See also *Newton's Laws of Motion*.

O'Malley's Observation

When there is a choice of two evils, most men take both.

This observation by Austin O'Malley in *Keystones of Thought* is essentially an updating of Aristotle's recommendation, "Of evils we must choose the least" (*Nicomachean Ethics*), as rephrased, in turn, by Thomas à Kempis, "Of two evils we should always choose the less" (*Imitation of Christ*). Or as Ambrose Bierce said, putting some reverse English on the basic expression: "Of two evils choose to be the least" (*The Devil's Dictionary*).

Examination of the the female mind provides an entirely different slant on the problem of evil (no surprise here). Thus, Talullah Bankhead advised in her autobiography, *Talullah*, "Never practise two vices at once," while Mae West explained in *Klondike Annie* (1936), "Between two evils, I always like to take the one I've never tried before."

See also **Aspin's Axiom, Bierce's Law,** and **Thomas's Law.**

O'Neill's Rule

All politics is local.

Former speaker of the house Tip O'Neill used this saying in the title of a memoir that he wrote with the help of Gary Hymel, *All Politics Is Local: And Other Rules of the Game* (1993).

Among O'Neill's other rules:

1. No contribution is too small.
2. Avoid bunk.
3. To be a successful public speaker, memorise poetry.
4. Never be introduced at a sporting event; the crowd will only boo.
5. Remember names.
6. Tip well.

See also **Clinton's Laws of Politics**.

Oppenheimer's Observation

The optimist thinks this is the best of all possible worlds, and the pessimist knows it.

J. Robert Oppenheimer, the nuclear physicist who headed the Manhattan Project to build the atomic bomb during World War II, made this observation in *The Bulletin of Atomic Scientists* in February, 1951. (This was some two years before he was declared a security risk on account of his left-wing associations and his alleged 'defects of character,' including, apparently, his opposition to building the H-bomb.) Other people, before and after Oppenheimer, have expressed the essential thought, as in:

Cabell's Rule. The optimist proclaims that we live in the best of all possible worlds; and the pessimist fears this is true. (This is from *The Silver Stallion*, 1926, one of a series of eighteen novels by James Branch Cabell that recount the history, from 1234 to 1750, of the mythical French province of Poictesme.)

Ustinov's Ukase. An optimist is one who knows exactly how bad a place the world can be; a pessimist is one who finds out anew every morning. (The Ustinov here is the great Peter, actor, director, playwright, and novelist, as quoted in 1968 in the *Illustrated London News*.)

Oppenheimer, Cabell, and Ustinov all are indebted, of course, to **Voltaire's Law.**

Orwell's Law of Language

The great enemy of clear language is insincerity. When there is a gap between one's real and one's declared aims, one turns as it were instinctively to long words and exhausted idioms, like a cuttlefish squirting out ink.

George Orwell (Eric Blair) was thinking of political discourse in particular when he wrote these lines, as evidenced by the title that he gave to the essay in which they appear 'Politics and the English Language' (1946). The principle applies across the board, however. For example, Wall Street analysts commonly avoid the offputting word 'drop' when prices are falling and instead pontificate about the market making a 'technical correction'; corporate spokespersons speak of 'managing down' or 'reducing duplication' in workforces, not 'firing' people; generals who never 'retreat' will admit to making 'adjustments of the front' or 'breaking off contact with the enemy', and 'funeral directors' (not 'undertakers') refer solemnly to the 'deceased', the 'departed', or 'the loved one' – anything but the 'corpse'. Or, taking one of Orwell's examples from the political sphere: "Defenceless villages are bombarded from the air, the inhabitants are driven out into the countryside, the huts set on fire with incendiary bullets: this is called *pacification*."

Orwell suggested six rules to improve one's writing:

1. Never use a metaphor, simile or other figure of speech which you are used to seeing in print.
2. Never use a long word where a short one will do.
3. If it is possible to cut a word out, always cut it out.
4. Never use the passive where you can use the active.

5. Never use a foreign phrase, a scientific word or a jargon word if you can think of an everyday English equivalent.

6. Break any of these rules sooner than say anything outright barbarous.

n.b. Orwell wrote this essay twenty years before the United States started conducting 'pacification' and 'accelerated pacification' programs in Vietnam with bombs, defoliants, and so on. See also **Kahn's Law, McNaughton's Rule,** and **Rosten's Other Laws (no. 3)**

Osler's Law

The greater the ignorance, the greater the dogmatism (Sir William Osler, *Montreal Medical Journal*, September, 1902).

A Canadian doctor, teacher, and medical historian, Sir William also produced some pithy rules, e.g. "Failure to examine the throat is a glaring sin of omission, especially in children. One finger in the throat and one in the rectum makes a good diagnostician," and "One of the first duties of the physician is to educate the masses not to take medicine" (*Aphorisms from his Bedside Teachings*, 1961).

See also **Montaigne's Law.**

Ovid's Observation

Whether a pretty woman grants or withholds her favours, she always likes to be asked for them (Ovid [Publius Ovidus Naso], *Art of Love*, ca. 2 B.C.).

The *Art of Love*, in which Ovid sets forth the rules of the mating game, sufficiently scandalised the emperor Augustus that it was cited as the reason for exiling him for the rest of his life to Tomi, a bleak fishing village on the Black Sea, near the mouth of the Danube. Ovid said in a letter to a friend that there also was another, undeclared reason for his banishment. No one knows what it was, but it probably involved a scandal that touched the imperial family. One guess is that Ovid was one of the many lovers of Augustus's daughter Julia.

To the statesman Talleyrand (in full, Charles Maurice de Talleyrand-Périgord) is attributed the following amendment to Ovid's Observation: "Women sometimes forgive a man who forces the opportunity, but never a man who misses one." He was French, of course.

See also **Addison's Law,** and **Rowland's Law.**

P

Paige's Rules for Living

1. Avoid fried meats, which angry up the blood.

2. If your stomach disputes you, lie down and pacify it with cool thoughts.

3. Keep the juices flowing by jangling around gently as you move.

4. Go very light on the vices, such as carrying on in society. The social ramble ain't restful.

5. Avoid running at all times.

6. Don't look back. Something might be gaining on you.

Baseball pitcher Leroy 'Satchel' Paige didn't actually write these rules. They were set down by Richard Donovan, who was asked by the editor of *Collier's* magazine for some typical Paige quotes to accompany a 1953 profile of the seemingly ageless player. (Paige became a veritable legend for his feats in black baseball years before so-called major league baseball was integrated. He was forty-two when he pitched his first game in the majors for the Cleveland Indians in 1948 and he made his last appearance – three scoreless innings – for the Kansas City A's in 1965 at age fifty-nine. He was the first African-American named to baseball's Hall of Fame.) The sentiments were true to Paige's way of thinking, however, and he adopted the rules as his own, including them in his 1953 autobiography, *How to Stay Young*.

Gilmer's Law of Political Leadership (amending Paige's sixth rule). Look over your shoulder now and then to be sure someone's following you (Henry Gilmer, Virginia State Treasurer, ca. 1948, in Paul Dickson, *The Official Rules*, 1978).

See also **Brooks's Law.**

(Babe) Paley's Law

You can never be too skinny or too rich.

The law also has been attributed to Gloria Vanderbilt and the Duchess of Windsor, but the beautiful and witty Mrs. Paley, wife of William S., who ran the Columbia Broadcasting System for fifty-five years (1928-83), usually gets the credit for it.

(William) Paley's Law

White lies always introduce others of a darker complexion (William Paley, *The Principles of Moral and Political Philosophy*, 1785).

A cleric, philosopher, and teacher, the *Principles* was derived from Paley's lectures and was used as a textbook at Cambridge University for many years.

Papagiannis's Law

The absence of evidence is not evidence of absence.

Michael Papagiannis, professor of astronomy at Boston University, offered this law as a defence for the possibility of the existence of UFOs at an Abduction Study Conference held at Massachusetts Institute of Technology in 1992. According to this law, then, just because no one has found a piece of a UFO doesn't mean that there are no UFOs. (The Roswell incident, famed in UFO circles and mentioned in the 1996 movie *Independence Day*, does not count; the wreckage found on the New Mexican desert floor was of a high-altitude balloon for detecting Russian atomic tests.)

Papagiannis's Law is useful as a way of persuading people to suspend overwhelming doubts in many fields. For example: Just because no one has brought home the skin of a Himalayan Yeti or a domestic Bigfoot does not mean that either creature does not exist. Or again: Just because no self-professed clairvoyant has ever survived scientific scrutiny (and the Pentagon did sponsor remote-viewing tests of psychics) does not mean that someone somewhere does not possess the ability to see things that are not within eyesight. Same goes for water dowsers, who show only chance results under test conditions.

Appeals to Papagiannis's Law are not limited to paranormal phenomena. For example, Marcia Clark, lead prosecutor in the O. J. Simpson trial, cited this law when rebutting a defense contention that O.J. couldn't have committed the double murder because he was not completely covered with blood. "Absence of evidence is not evidence of absence," she argued. "This makes sense. If you're standing behind somebody cutting their throat, they're bleeding out and not bleeding on you. So you'll get a little bit of spatter but you're not going to be covered with blood" (Los Angeles, September 29th, 1995).

Secretary of Defense Donald Rumsfeld also invoked this law at a Pentagon press conference on February 12th, 2002. Fending off a question regarding the lack of evidence that Iraq had attempted to, or was willing to, supply weapons of mass destruction to terrorist organisations, Mr. Rumsfeld replied: "I could have said that the absence of evidence is not evidence of absence, or vice versa." As it turned out, of course, the absence of evidence in this instance did prove, after much fruitless searching, to be evidence of absence.

See also **Holmes's First Law, Montaigne's Law** and **Wittgenstein's Law.**

Pareto's Law

Twenty percent of the customers account for eighty percent of the turnover; twenty percent of the components account for eighty percent of the cost, etc.

Also known as the 20/80 law, this rule is attributed to the Italian economist Vilfredo Pareto. A case in point was noted by Robert Townsend in *Up the Organization* (1970): "Twenty percent of any given group of salesmen will always produce eighty per cent of the sales."

See also **Woody Allen's Law, Mencken's Second Law,** and **Sturgeon's Law.**

Parker's Observation

Men seldom make passes / At girls who wear glasses (Dorothy Parker, 'News Item', in *Enough Rope*, 1927).

Pogrebin's Amendment. Boys don't make passes at female smartasses (Lenny Pogrebin, in Jon Winokur, *Friendly Advice,* 1990).

Parkinson's Law

Work expands so as to fill the time available for its completion.

Like a voice calling from the wilderness, C. (for Cyril) Northcote Parkinson, Raffles Professor of History at the University of Malaya, caught the world's attention with this profound insight, initially published in the *Economist* (November 19th, 1955) and then developed into a book entitled, naturally enough, *Parkinson's Law* (1957).

Professor Parkinson showed that his law applied on individual as well as institutional levels. "Thus, an elderly lady of leisure," he wrote, "can spend the entire day in writing and dispatching a postcard to her niece at Bognor Regis. An hour will be spent in finding the postcard, another in hunting spectacles, half an hour in search of the address, an hour and a quarter in composition, and twenty minutes in deciding whether or not to take an umbrella when going to the mailbox in the next street."

On the institutional level, Professor Parkinson showed that the law operated in terms of two motive forces:

1. An official wants to multiply subordinates, not rivals;
2. Officials make work for each other.

The professor adduced a number of examples to prove his case, the clincher being the Royal Navy, the number of whose capital ships declined 67.74 percent from 1914 to 1928, while dockyard officials and clerks rose 40.28 percent and admiralty officials increased by a truly remarkable 78.45 percent.

With this, the hitherto unknown professor was off and running. He expanded upon his first law in a series of articles and bestselling books, developed a flourishing new career as a lecturer and visiting professor, and removed himself from Malaya to the tax-sheltered Channel Island of Guernsey. Of his later laws, the most significant are:

Parkinson's Second Law

Expenditure rises to meet income (The Law and the Profits, 1960). See also **Micawber's First Law**.

Parkinson's Third Law

Expansion means complexity and complexity, decay; or to put it even more plainly – the more complex, the sooner dead (Inlaws and Outlaws, 1962).

This law often is glossed: Growth leads to complexity, and complexity to decay.

Parkinson's Fourth Law

Delay is the deadliest form of denial (The Law of Delay, 1971).

Parkinson's Law of Medical Research

Successful research attracts the bigger grant which makes further research impossible (The New Scientist, Jan 25th, 1962).

Professor P. elucidated: "In accordance with this law, we mostly end as administrators. We should have ended administering, in any event, remember, had we never done any research."

Parkinson's Law of Triviality

The time spent on any item of the [meeting] *agenda will be in inverse proportion to the sum involved* (Parkinson's Law).

Thus a $10 million-project may be approved in two-and-one-half minutes, while an expenditure of $2,350 – a much easier sum to comprehend for a much smaller item, something easier to visualise – will be debated for an hour and a quarter, then deferred for decision to the next meeting pending the gathering of more information. See also **Kirkland's Law**.

Parkinson's Telephone Law

The effectiveness of a telephone conversation is in inverse proportion to the time spent on it (New York Times Magazine, April 12th, 1974).

Mrs. Parkinson's Law

Heat produced by pressure expands to fill the mind available from which it can pass only to a cooler mind (Mrs. Parkinson's Law, 1968).

This is another version of the second law of thermodynamics, also implicit in **Friedman's Law**.

Parkinson also inspired many other great minds to develop similar laws. Among them:

Brown's Extension of Parkinson's Law. The volume of paper expands to fill the available briefcases (quondam California governor Edmund G. Brown, Jr., quoted by Alan L. Otten, *Wall Street Journal*, February 26th, 1976).

Einstein's Extension of Parkinson's Law. A work project expands to fill the space available. *Corollary.* No matter how large the work space, if two projects must be done at the same time they will require the use of the same part of the work space (in Arthur Bloch, *The Complete Murphy's Law*, 1991).

Ryan's Extension to Parkinson's Law. Objects expand to fill the space available (Patrick Ryan, in *Smithsonian*, May 1978).

Finally, Professor Parkinson also deserves credit for the keen insight, contained in *Parkinson's Law*, which, though not strictly a law, probably has a more universal application that he himself suggested, i.e. "It is now known . . . that men enter local politics solely as a result of being unhappily married."

See also **Conran's Law of Housework** and **Riggs's Hypothesis.**

Pascal's Law

The greater the intellect one has, the more originality one finds in men. Ordinary persons find no differences between men.

This is only one of many remarkable thoughts in Blaise Pascal's posthumously published *Pensées* (1670), e.g. "Cleopatra's nose, had it been shorter, the whole face of the world would have been changed," "The heart has its reasons, which reasons knows nothing of," and "Evil is easy, and has infinite forms."

A true polymath, Pascal was an inventor (he devised a calculator that could add eight columns of numbers while still in his teens) a mathematician, and a pioneer in physics. He probably is best remembered today, however, for his religious and philosophical writings, especially his justification, known as Pascal's Wager, for believing in God. Assuming that God's existence could not be categorically proved or disproved, Pascal argued in the *Pensées* that the reasonable person would make the leap of faith and believe, since belief promised eternal life. If God existed, and the leap of faith were not made, eternal damnation would result. On the other hand, if God did not exist, the gambler would have lost nothing. Pascal's Wager, then, represented by far the safest bet. The gambler may win everything while risking nothing.

Given this turn of mind, it should come as no surprise to learn that Pascal's work in mathematics included contributions to probability theory. His researches in this field, developed mainly in correspondence with Pierre de Fermat, were inspired by a question posed by a dice hustler who couldn't understand why he was losing when he bet even money that double sixes would turn up at least once on average in every twenty-four rolls of two dice. (Once in 24.6 rolls is the true answer, which means, since dice can't be rolled a fractional number of times, that the hustler could only win this bet at even-money if the dice were rolled at least 25 times.) Probability theory has since developed in directions that Pascal could not have foreseen; see **Heisenberg's Uncertainty Principle** and **Spencer's Law**.

Pasteur's Observation

In the field of observation, chance favours only the prepared mind (Louis Pasteur, address, December 7th, 1854).

Pasteur was still a young man, just thirty-two, when he made this observation in his inaugural address as professor of chemistry and dean of the faculty of sciences at the university in Lille. He already had done important work in explaining the differences between isomers – compounds with identical compositions and molecular weights but different chemical or physical properties – and he had a long and productive career ahead of him, including development of the process named for him, pasteurisation. (Being French, Pasteur naturally had wine and beer in mind, not milk, when he devised it.) Pasteur himself left little to chance, however, supplementing his powers of keen observation with long hours in the lab. "Work, always work" was his motto. His dying words were *Il faut travailler*, It is necessary to work.

The prepared mind that makes a discovery by chance, or accident, usually is said to do so through *serendipity*, a word coined by Horace Walpole. He explained in a letter of January 28th, 1754, that he based the term on a children's story, The *Three Princes of Serendip*, whose protagonists "were always making discoveries, by accidents and sagacity, of things they were not in quest of." (Serendip is an old word for Ceylon, itself an old word for Sri Lanka.)

The classic example of serendipity is that of Alexander Fleming, who was slightly dismayed one morning in 1928 to find that something had contaminated an experiment with staphylococcus cultures, killing some of the bacteria overnight. Instead of tossing out the petri dishes with the ruined specimens, and proceeding with his experiment, Fleming investigated to see what had destroyed the bacteria. It turned out to be penicillin.

Whitehead's Amendment. Familiar things happen, and mankind does not bother much about them. It requires a very unusual mind to undertake the analysis of the obvious (Alfred North Whitehead, *Science and the Modern World*, 1925).

See also **Euripides' Third Law** and **Rickey's Law.**

The Paul Principle

People become progressively less competent for jobs they once were well equipped to handle.

The principle, set forth by Paul Armer in *The Futurist* (June 1970), supplements **The Peter Principle**, given to the world the preceding year.

Payn's Law

If a piece of buttered toast falls, it will land face down.

This variant of Murphy's Law (see especially **Mrs. Murphy's First Law**) has been discovered independently by a great many people, to their chagrin, but no one has stated it as elegantly did James Payn, the English novelist, editor, and light versifier, back in 1884:

> *I've never had a piece of toast*
> *Particularly long and wide,*
> *But fell upon the sanded floor*
> *And always on the butter side.*

Some nay-sayers have doubted the universality of this law. Folklorist Roger L. Welch has contended that "Sometimes, maybe as often as one out of every hundred or so droppings, the toast will fall dry side down. No one knows why. Well, if it isn't always true, it isn't a universal law. I'd be willing to go to the Supreme Court with that one" (*Natural History*, March 1992).

And Henry Kissinger has opined that "If you drop a piece of buttered bread on the carpet, the chances of its falling with the buttered side down are in direct relationship with the cost of the carpet" (in Marvin Kalb and Bernard Kalb, *Kissinger*, 1974). (I am indebted to an English correspondent, Michael Swan, for pointing out that Mr. Kissinger appears to have summarised, knowingly or not, the Clark-Trimble experiments of 1935, originally described by British humorist

Paul Jennings in a 'Report on Resistentialism' in the *Spectator* in 1948. In this series of experiments, so Mr. Jennings said, pieces of toast with marmalade were dropped on four hundred pieces of carpet, ranging in quality from coarse matting to priceless Chinese silk. Surprise! The toast fell marmalade side up on cheap carpet every time and marmalade side down every time on Chinese silk. The only exception was when the cheap carpet was screened, in which case the toast didn't know what to do. Most remarkably, according to Mr. Jennings, and as Mr. Kissinger noted, "the marmalade-downwards incidence for the intermediate grades was found to vary exactly with the quality of the carpet.")

Payn's law was put to a scientific test for the first time on the BBC's *QED* program in 1991. In 300 tosses of buttered toast under various conditions, no statistical difference was found in which side landed face down, according to a report on this epic series of experiments by Ian Stewart in *Scientic American* ('Mathematical Recreations', December, 1995). But deeper analysis by Robert Matthews, a British journalist, showed that the BBC tests were flawed: Toast is not normally tossed in the air at the breakfast table (except when children are present); rather, it is knocked sideways off the table edge. And when this happens, given the normal height of tables, the laws of physics ordain that the toast will rotate at least 180 degrees, but less than 360, while falling. Consequently, the buttered side must land face down.

Exceptions to this law, as analysed by Mr. Matthews, occur only under extremely abnormal conditions. According to his calculations, as summarised in Mr. Stewart's *Scientific American* column, the toast would have to be shoved horizontally with a force of at least 1.6 meters per second, or else the table would have to be some ten feet high, in order for the toast to undergo a full revolution during its descent, thus allowing it to land buttered side up.

In other words, if the folklorist, Mr. Welch, took this one to the Supreme Court, he would lose. Of course, another possibility – not considered by Messrs. Welch, Matthews, Jennings, Kissinger, or the BBC, is that the buttered side would not land face down if only people didn't start by buttering, or marmalading, the wrong side of the toast.

Peers's Law

The solution to a problem changes the nature of the problem.

John Peers, president of Logical Machine Corp, was thinking of the way in which many solutions to computer problems tend to create greater problems, according to the introduction to his collection of 1978 collection of sayings, *1,001 Logical Laws, Accurate Axioms . . .* , 1979. In fact, though, it applies universally. For example, considering our manifold social problems, Martin Luther King, Jr., came to much the same conclusion: "All progress is precarious, and the solution of one problem brings us face to face with another problem" (*The Strength to Love*, 1963).

The implications of Peers's Law are good or bad, depending on one's cast of mind. Thus, of four corollaries, two are positive and two negative:

Krishnamurti's Corollary. If we can really understand the problem, the answer will come out of it, because the answer is not separate from the problem (Jiddu Krishnamurti, *The Penguin Krishnamurti Reader*).

Gould's Corollary. The pleasure of discovery in science derives not only from the satisfaction of new explanations but also, if not more so, from fresh (and often more difficult) puzzles that the novel solutions generate (Stephen Jay Gould, *Natural History*, January 1991).

And on the down side:

Kissinger's Corollary. Each success only buys an admission ticket to a more difficult problem (Henry A. Kissinger, *Wilson Library Bulletin*, March, 1979).

Baker's Corollary. A solved problem creates two new problems, and the best prescription for happy living is not to solve any more problems than you have to (Russell Baker, in Jon Winokur, *Friendly Advice*, 1990).

See also **Cleaver's Law** and **Spencer's Law.**

The Peter Principle

In a hierarchy every employee tends to rise to his level of incompetence.

This insight is the key to the science of hierarchiology – that is, the study of hierachies – introduced to the world in 1969 by Dr. Laurence J. Peter in *The Peter Principle: Why Things Always Go Wrong* (with Raymond Hull). Pursuing this principle, Dr. Peter made the depressing discovery that "In time, every post tends to be occupied by an employee who is incompetent to carry out his duties." He also offered several other insights into the workings of hierarchies, the first two of which class as corollaries and the third as prescription for action:

1. Incompetence knows no barriers of time or place.
2. Work is accomplished by those employees who have not yet reached the level of their incompetence.
3. If at first you don't succeed, try something else.

In addition, Dr. Peter introduced a number of subsidiary rules in this work, including:

Peter's Inversion. Internal consistency is valued more highly than efficiency.

Peter's Paradox. Employees in a hierarchy do not really object to the incompetence of their colleagues.

Peter's Placebo. An ounce of image is worth a pound of performance.

Peter's Theorum. Incompetence plus incompetence equals incompetence.

Dr. Peter termed his basic concept a 'principle' rather than a 'law' because it describes a tendency rather than a universal, immutable progression. As exceptions, he noted that on occasion a good teacher will choose to remain a teacher instead of becoming a poor administrator, a successful sales representative may decline a promotion to sales manager, a competent mayor may decide not to run for governor or president, and so on. In general, though, the principle holds, and exceptions to it are more apparent than real. Among the apparent exceptions:

1. *The Percussive Sublimation*, i.e. being kicked upstairs, which is not, as might first appear a move from a position of incompetence to one of competence, but a pseudo-promotion from one unproductive job to another. The object of the Percussive Sublimation usually is to deceive the outside world. It camouflages the flaws in the employer's promotion policy, supports staff morale, and maintains the hierarchy (in lieu of firing the incompetent person, in which case he might actually get another job with a competitor where, despite his incompetence, his knowledge could be dangerous).

2. *The Lateral Arabesque*, another pseudo-promotion in which the incompetent person is not really raised in rank (and perhaps not in pay either), but is given a longer title and a new office in a remote part of the building. (See also **McGovern's Law** for another take on the length of titles.) Dr. Peter also pointed out that the larger the hierarchy, the easier The Lateral Arabesque, citing as an example

one corporation that had banished no less than twenty-five senior executives to the provinces as regional vice presidents.

3. *The Eichmann Exception*, also known as *Peter's Invert* or *the professional automaton*. This 'exceptional' person shows obsessive concern with filling out forms correctly, permits no deviations from established routine, has little or no capacity for independent judgment, always obeys, and never, never decides. "To the professional automaton, it is clear that means are more important than ends; the paperwork is more important than the purpose for which it was originally designed," wrote Dr. Peter. The automaton "no longer sees himself as existing to serve the public; he sees the public as the raw material that serves to maintain him, the forms, the rituals, and the hierarchy!" Unfortunately for the public, the automaton appears to be competent from the hierarchy's point of view. As a result, he remains eligible for promotion until, by some mischance, he is elevated into a position where he absolutely has to make a decision. It is at that point that he reaches his level of incompetence.

Dr. Peter confessed that his book was intended more as satire than actual fact, but a great many people took his message to heart, particularly middle managers, who looked around them at their peers – above them at their bosses – and saw much truth in what he said. As a result, *The Peter Principle* became an immediate bestseller, putting Dr. Peter in the same league as a lawgiver with the authors of Murphy's Law and Parkinson's Law. Success begetting success, it also led to additional books, all of which sold well, including *The Peter Prescription* (1972), *Peter's Quotations* (1977), and *The Peter Pyramid* (1986). The latter works introduced such additional rules as:

Peter's Law. The unexpected always happens.

Mrs. (Irene) Peter's Law. Today, if you are not confused, you're just not thinking clearly. (See also **Kerr's Law**.)

Peter's Statement of Objectives. If you don't know where you are going, you will end up somewhere else (which has a Yogi-esque ring to it; see **Berra's Law**).

For would-be authors, this tale also has a pleasing moral: The manuscript of *The Peter Principle* was turned down by thirty book publishers over a five-year period before it was accepted by William Morrow. The first rejection, from an editor at McGraw-Hill, which had previously published a textbook by Dr. Peter, was fairly typical: "I can foresee no commercial possibilities for such a book and consequently can offer no encouragement." Even Morrow, which paid the author a less-than-princely advance against royalties of $2500, was bowled over by its success – 200,000 copies sold in the first year alone, followed by translations into 38 languages. So much for the prescience of publishing hierarchies.

See also **Dumas's Law, The Paul Principle, Riggs's Hypothesis,** and **Ustinov's Ukase.**

Pindar's Law

Custom is king over all.

The law is a fragment from one of the odes of the Theban poet. He lived in the fifth century B.C. Compare **Catt's Law**.

Plimpton's Small Ball Theory

The smaller the ball used in a sport, the better the book.

George Plimpton, who tried his hand at a lot of sports as well as writing about them (e.g. *Paper Lion*, *Shadow Box*, and *The Bogey Man*) proposed this theory to explain why books about

American football do not sell as well as those about baseball, tennis, or golf (*New York Times*, September 25th, 1986). The underlying reason, he argued, is that smaller balls bring out better writing. Thus, superb books have been written about golf, very good ones about baseball, not so many good ones about American football (where the ball is not only large but misshapen), only a few good ones about basketball, and none at all about beach ball. He capped his theory with one of the best known of all sports stories, Mark Twain's *The Celebrated Jumping Frog of Calaveras County*, which involves the nefarious use of bird shot – extremely small balls, indeed.

Five years later, in another *Times* article (March 31st, 1991) Plimpton proposed a second theory governing books about sports that are not played with balls: "The literary quality of sports without balls seems connected with the danger involved – the higher the risk, the more memorable the literature." Thus, there are good books about motor racing, mountain climbing, the more dangerous kinds of big-game hunting, and boxing, "but less good books about the 100-yard dash, swimming, canoeing, the tug-of-war and so on in which danger does not figure." Noting that most of the great accounts in this category "have someone teetering on the edge, if not to the point of tragedy", Plimpton suggested that this second theory might be called the 'Look Out!' or 'Uh-Oh' theory.

Pogo's Observation

We have met the enemy and it is us.

This comment by Walt Kelly's immortal possum in the 'Pogo' cartoon strip has been recorded in various forms. On the 1971 Earth Day poster it was rendered as "We have met the enemy and he is us." What apparently is the Ur version of text comes from the foreword to *The Pogo Papers* (1953): "Resolve then, that on this very ground, with small flags waving and tinny blasts on tiny trumpets, we shall meet the enemy, and not only may he be ours, he may be us." Ultimately, of course, the observation, whatever the precise wording, derives from Oliver Hazard Perry's dispatch following the Battle of Lake Erie in the War of 1812: "We have met the enemy and they are ours – two ships, two brigs, one schooner."

Powell's Rules

1. It ain't as bad as you think. It will look better in the morning.
2. Get mad, then get over it.
3. Avoid having your ego so close to your position that, when your position falls, your ego goes with it.
4. It can be done!
5. Be careful what you choose. You may get it.
6. Don't let adverse facts stand in the way of a good decision.
7. You can't make someone else's choices. You shouldn't let someone else make yours.
8. Check small things.
9. Share credit.
10. Remain calm. Be kind.
11. Have a vision. Be demanding.
12. Don't take counsel of your fears or naysayers.
13. Perpetual optimism is a force multiplier.

Former Secretary of State Colin Powell reported in his memoir *My American Journey* (1995) that he kept these rules on his desk in the Pentagon when he was chairman of the joint chiefs of staff. Powell also offered a rule for making decisions: "The key is not to make quick decisions but to make timely decisions," he wrote. To do this, he developed a formula, $P = 40$ to 70, where P stands for probability of success and the numbers represent the percentage of information acquired. "I don't act if I only have enough information to give me a less than 40 percent chance of being right," he continued. "And I don't wait until I have enough facts to be 100 percent sure of being right, because by then it is almost always too late." Just how one determines what percentage of the available information one has in hand, Powell did not explain.

Price's Law

If everybody doesn't want it, nobody gets it (R. Price, quoted in *The Peter Prescription*, 1972).

The law relates specifically to mass production for general consumers, as evidenced by its follow-up: "Mass man must be served by mass means." But see also **Publilius's Maxims**.

Prior's Precept

The end must justify the means.

This is Matthew Prior's happy distillation in his poem 'Hans Carvel' (1700) of a time-honoured thought. Thus, St. Jerome (ca. 342-420) referred in a letter to "The line, often adopted by strong men in controversy, of justifying the means by the end." And much closer to Prior's time, William Penn held that "A good End cannot sanctifie evil Means; nor must we ever do Evil, that Good may come of it" (maxim 537 in *Some Fruits of Solitude*, 1693). Both St. Jerome and Penn seemed to have assumed that good could come from evil. Aldous Huxley disagreed. "The end cannot justify the means," he contended, "for the simple and obvious reason that the means employed determine the nature of the ends produced" (*Ends and Means*, 1937).

Getting back to 'Hans Carvel': Prior's poem enjoyed considerably popularity in liberated circles in the eighteenth century but more for its risqué story line, based on an old tale, than for Prior's wisdom. Captain Francis Grose, one of the first collectors of slang, summarised the plot line this way in his *Classical Dictionary of the Vulgar Tongue* (1796): "Hans Carvel, a jealous old doctor, being in bed with his wife, dreamed that the Devil gave him a ring, which, so long as he had it on his finger, would prevent his being made a cuckhold: waking, he found he had got his finger the Lord knows where." Thanks to Prior's popularisation of the tale, 'Carvel's ring' was employed for a hundred years or so afterward as euphemistic slang for what Grose delicately referred to as "the Lord knows where."

See also **St. Augustine's Law to End all Laws**.

Publilius's Maxims

Publilius Syrus was a celebrated mime of the first century B.C. Brought to Rome as a slave from Syria, he was later freed. More than a thousand maxims attributed to him have been preserved. Supposedly taken from plays that he wrote, these wise sayings probably were not composed until after his death. Many appear to be proverbs that already were time-honoured in his own time. Among them:

> *He doubly benefits the needy who gives quickly* (Maxim 6). Modern politicians – and wise donors – appreciate this. Early contributions are vital to getting campaigns underway; hence the name of the political fundraising organisation, EMILY'S List, the EMILY being an acronym for Early Money Is Like Yeast.

> *There are some remedies worse than the disease* (Maxim 301). A partial dissent from **Hippocrates's First Law**.

> *Practice is the best of all instructors* (Maxim 439). Or, as the more familiar prover, has it: Practice makes perfect.

> *He who is bent on doing evil can never want occasion* (Maxim 459).

It is a bad plan that admits of no modification (Maxim 469). Military strategists are very well aware of this; see the sixth of **Liddell Hart's Maxims.**

A rolling stone gathers no moss (Maxim 524). For an update, see **Gordon's Rule of Evolving Bryographic Systems.**

Never promise more than you can perform (Maxim 528). A corollary, in effect, to the first maxim cited here.

No one should be judge in his own case (Maxim 545).

We desire nothing so much as what we ought not to have (Maxim 559). See also the last of *Aesop's Adages.*

It is not every question that deserves an answer (Maxim 581). See also **Norris's Law.**

You cannot put the same shoe on every foot (Maxim 596).

Money sets all the world in motion (Maxim 656).

It is a very hard undertaking to seek to please everybody (Maxim 675).

No one knows what he can do until he tries (Maxim 786).

Everything is worth what its purchaser will pay for it (Maxim 847).

Better be ignorant of a matter than half know it (Maxim 865).

Whom Fortune wishes to destroy she first makes mad (Maxim 911).

I have often regretted my speech, never my silence (Maxim 1070). See also **Horace's Law.**

Pym's Law

Actions speak louder than words.

John Pym, a leader of the House of Commons in its struggles with Charles I, is credited with the earliest known expression of this basic law of behaviour in *A Dictionary of American Proverbs* (1992). He uttered it in 1628 during a debate on a message from the king.

The observation probably was already proverbial in Pym's time. A half century earlier, and across the Channel, Montaigne brushed up against it in one of his *Essays* (1580): "Saying is one thing and doing is another." Shakespeare, meanwhile, approached it from another angle: "Talkers are no good doers" (*Richard III*, 1592-93). He also advised in *Hamlet* (1600-01): "Suit the action to the word, the word to the action." In their wisdom, the folk have embroidered the thought in different ways, e.g. "Actions lie louder than words" and "Actions speak louder than words – but not so often." Other emendations include:

Singer's Amplification. We know what a person thinks not when he tells us what he thinks, but by his actions (Isaac Bashevis Singer, interview in the *New York Times Magazine*, November 26th, 1978).

Lebowitz's Prescription. If you are of the opinion that the contemplation of suicide is sufficient evidence of a poetic nature, do not forget that actions speak louder than words. (Fran Lebowitz, in Jonathon Green, *The Cynic's Lexicon*, 1984).

Q

Quincy's Law

Man passes away; generations are but shadows; there is nothing stable but truth.

Josiah Quincy, Jr., president of Harvard, articulated this law in a speech in Boston on September 17th, 1830. An all-around politician (previously minority leader of the U.S. House of Representatives, speaker of the Massachusetts House of Representatives, and mayor of Boston), the groves of academe presumably held no surprises for him.

Quintilian's Law

A liar should have a good memory.

Quintilian – Marcus Fabius Quintilianus, in full – was a teacher of rhetoric. He himself identified this statement as a proverb, in his *Institutio oratoria*, a twelve-book program for training orators, composed in the last decades of the first century A.D. Many of his pupils became politicians or played other prominent public roles; they included Pliny the Younger and the future emperor Hadrian. Quintilian's remarks on educating children also have withstood the test of time (and probably should be made required reading in teacher-training courses). For example:

> Above all things we must take care that the child, who is not yet old enough to love his studies, does not come to hate them and dread the bitterness which he once

tasted, even when the years of infancy are left behind. His studies must be made an amusement.

Study depends on the goodwill of the student, a quality that cannot be secured by compulsion.

It is easier to do many things than to do one thing for a long time continuously.

Exuberance is easily remedied, but barrenness is incurable, be your efforts what they may.

While they [dull teachers] are content that their work should be devoid of faults they fall into the fault of being devoid of merit.

The Qwerty Factor

See **David's Qwerty Factor**.

R

Ravitch's Rule

The person who knows 'how' will always have a job. The person who knows 'why' will always be his boss (Diane Ravitch, *Time*, June 17th, 1985).

The 'how' part was severely tested in the 1990s, as downsizing corporations dehired, delayered, deselected, and outplaced legions of middle managers, who hardly knew 'why.'

Rawson's First Law

As soon as you dispose of a book, even one that has gathered dust for years, a pressing need to refer to it will arise.

First Corollary. Never loan a book, not even to your very best friend, if you really want to get it back.

Second Corollary. No matter how much bookshelf space you have, it is never enough.

The first corollary was anticipated in part by Isaac D'Israeli, father of Benjamin, who pointed out that "Great collections of books are subject to certain accidents besides the damp, worms, and the rats; one not less common is that of the borrowers, not to say a word of the purloiners" (*Curiosities of Literature*, 1791-1834).

Rawson's Second Law

Never throw away anything unless you know what it came from.

This law applies especially to such items as small screws and other bits of hardware that appear mysteriously on kitchen floors. Only after being thrown away will it be discovered that the item in question forms an essential part of a refrigerator or another appliance – and that it cannot be replaced because the item is non-standard and the product itself is no longer manufactured.

Rawson's Third Law

A malfunctioning car will stop displaying symptoms of imminent breakdown when driven to within one-quarter mile of a garage.

This law parallels Fetridge's Law, but was independently discovered – and rediscovered more than once – by this author. The same principle applies to people with pains en route to doctors and dentists.

Mrs. Rawson's Law for Sharing Desserts

The child that divides gets last pick.

This rule ensures that pie, cake, fudge, and all other delectables are apportioned with exquisite precision into equal shares. It probably is too much to expect that my mother was the first to adopt this method of maintaining peace and harmony among brothers and sisters, but I am crediting her for it. She certainly used it often enough.

Rayburn's First Law

When you get too big a majority, you're immediately in trouble.

This law grew out of Texas Democrat Sam Rayburn's difficulties in helping to keep fellow party members in line during Roosevelt's second administration, according to *Safire's Political Dictionary* (2008). Rayburn's experience led him to believe, William Safire explained, "that lopsided majorities had a way of producing splinter parties and factions along regional, ethnic, or economic lines."

Variously known as 'Mr. Democrat' and 'Mr. Sam,' Rayburn went on to serve longer than any other person as Speaker of the House of Representatives – seventeen years in three terms between 1940 and 1961. In this capacity, he popularised Rayburn's Second Law.

Rayburn's Second Law

To get along, go along.

Generally attributed to Speaker of the House Sam Rayburn, this motto was foreshadowed early in the twentieth century by the humorist Philander Chase Johnson, who advised, with tongue only slightly in cheek, that "The politician who looks for a fight is the man who attracts attention. But the one who looks for a compromise is the man who gets ahead" *Senator Sorghum's Primer of Politics* (1906).

Reagan's Rule

Never sleep with a girl if you're going to be embarrassed to be seen on the street with her the next day.

Ronald Reagan's fatherly advice to his son Ron (*Playboy*, January 1984). Added young Ron: "I think that was more for the girl's benefit than mine. He didn't want me jumping on some girl and then leaving her in the lurch." See also **Algren's Laws.**

Rench's Law

While the people who run political campaigns complain most about their shortage of money, the first thing they run out of is time . . . to listen and to think.

J. F. Rench, a longtime Republican strategist – "an old (very experienced) precinct hack" in his own words – offered this law in a letter to the *New York Times* (March 26th, 1996). His communication was a rebuttal to one of Senator Bob Dole's handlers, who asserted, as the Kansas Republican marched toward his party's presidential nomination, that "Old style campaigning is what's needed, not new vision." In theory this is true in low-turn-out elections, said Mr. Rench, but "the mood and patience of the electorate have shifted." Remembering his own experiences in George Bush's campaign for the presidential nomination in 1991-92, Mr. Rench (no monkey, he) urged that Senator Dole and his staff develop before it was too late what Mr. Bush himself called "the vision thing."

Reston's Observation

All politics, however, are based on the indifference of the majority (James Reston, *New York Times*, December 16th, 1964).

Restaurants, Laws of

See **Miller's Law.**

Reuther's Law

If it walks like a duck and quacks like a duck, then it just may be a duck.

Labor leader Walter Reuther used this rule for telling whether or not a person was a Communist, but it can be applied as a litmus test for determining the true nature of things generally. For example: "Dan Rather defended the accusations linking a doctor to an insurance-fraud scheme in a controversial segment of '60 Minutes,' testifying today in a slander suit against CBS that 'if it looks like a duck, walks like a duck, and quacks like a duck, you've got a duck'" (*New York Times*, June 1st, 1983). Then there was the Reagan-era Task Force on Regulatory Relief, chaired by Vice President George Bush, which was taken to court after refusing to reply to a Freedom of Information Act on the grounds that it wasn't a government agency: "With if-it-quacks-like-a-duck-it-is-a-duck reasoning, the judge ruled that a Government entity is judged by the work that it does, not where it sits, even in the case of the Vice President's office" (*New York Times*, November 29th, 1991). See also **Thoreau's Ruling**.

Rice's Rule

It's not important whether you win or lose but how you play the game.

This is the popular version of the last two lines of Grantland Rice's poem *Alumnus Football* (1930):

> *For when the one Great Scorer comes to mark against your name,*
> *He writes – not that you won or lost – but how you played the game.*

Rice was by all accounts an exceedingly decent man and a wonderful companion as well as a great sportswriter. Most other people have taken a more jaundiced view of winning and losing. See, for example, **Durocher's Law** and **Lombardi's Law**. Then there is:

Sheetz's Amendment. It's not whether you win or lose, but how you place the blame (in John Peers, *1,001 Logical Laws . . . , 1979*)

Rickey's Law

Luck is the residue of design.

This was the title of a lecture delivered by Branch Rickey in about 1950, when he was president of the Brooklyn Dodgers. Rickey himself did not leave a great deal to chance. Best remembered today for integrating professional baseball by signing Jackie Robinson in 1947 to a Dodger contract, he had already revolutionised baseball once before: While running the St. Louis Cardinals, he had established, starting in 1919, the farm system for developing players. The products of his system brought St. Louis six pennants and four world championships during his tenure, and made that team the most profitable in baseball. (In the process, he also popularised the phrase 'Addition by subtraction,' referring to the way a team sometimes can be improved by trading away a player.) As for luck, other great minds have come to similar conclusions. For example:

Cervantes's Saying. Diligence is the mother of good fortune (Miguel de Cervantes, *Don Quixote, Part IV*, 1615).

Dickinson's Extrapolation. Luck is not chance / It's toil / Fortune's expensive smile is earned (Emily Dickinson, poem no. 1350, ca. 1876).

Leacock's Tenet. I am a great believer in luck, and I find the harder I work the more I have of it (Stephen Leacock, in Robert W. Kent, *Money Talks*, 1985).

Carville's Distillation of Leacock's Tenet. The harder you work, the luckier you are (James Carville, in the film documentary of the 1992 Clinton presidential campaign, *The War Room*, 1993).

Stengel's Summation. You make your own luck. Some people have bad luck all their lives (Casey Stengel, in Geoffrey C. Ward, *Baseball*, 1994, based on the television series of the same name by Ward and Ken Burns).

Kowalski's Dissent. You know what luck is? Luck is believing you're lucky. Take at Salerno. I believed I was lucky. I figured that four out of five would not come through but I would . . . and I did. I put that down as a rule. To hold front position in this rat-race you've got to believe you are lucky (Stanley Kowalski, in Tennessee Williams, *A Streetcar Named Desire*, 1947).

See also **Euripides' Third Law, Pasteur's Observation,** and **Webster's Axiom.**

Riggs's Hypothesis

Incompetence tends to increase with the level of work performed. And, naturally, the individual's staff needs will increase as his level of incompetence increases (Arthur J. Riggs, 'Parkinson's Law, the Peter Principle, and the Riggs Hypothesis – A Synthesis,' *Michigan Business Review*, March 1971).

Riley's Law

The ripest peach is highest on the tree (James Whitcom, Riley, *The Ripest Peach*, 1892).

The observation is essentially proverbial. The 1678 edition of John Ray's *English Proverbs* includes the similar "The fairest apple hangs on the highest bough." See also **Erasmus's Law.**

Ringer's Rule

The results a person obtains are inversely proportional to the degree to which the person is intimidated (Robert J. Ringer, *Winning Through Intimidation*, 1979).

Robinson's Law

The guy you beat out of a prime parking space is the one you have to see for a job interview (Cal Robinson, Edinboro, Pa., in *Harper's*, August 1974).

The Rockefeller Principle

Never do anything you wouldn't be caught dead doing.

The principle is named for Nelson A. Rockefeller, who passed away in 1979, age 70, not while working late in his Rockefeller Center office, as a family spokesman initially asserted, but while visiting the nearby apartment of a twenty-five-year-old woman aide. A former governor of New York State, a former vice president of the United States, and a presidential aspirant, Rockefeller enjoyed a long and largely successful public career, but it could also be said, in Shakespeare's words, that "Nothing in his life became him like the leaving of it" (*Macbeth*, 1605-06).

Rogers's Laws

Will Rogers was one America's best-loved humorists of the 1920s and 1930s. In 1934, the year before he died with aviator Wiley Post in a plane crash near Point Barrow, Alaska, he was the nation's most popular newspaper columnist as well as the top box-office film attraction. And unlike many wits of the past, his humour holds up exceedingly well after several generations because he addressed timeless topics with homespun wisdom. Among the memorable remarks by Rogers that have – or should have – the force of law:

> Everything is funny as long as it is happening to someone else (*Illiterate Digest*, a collection of his newspaper columns, 1924).

> The more you read and observe about this Politics thing, you got to admit that each party is worse than the other. The one that's out always looks the best (*Illiterate Digest*).

> The Income Tax has made more Liars out of the American people than Golf has. Even when you make out on the

level, you don't know when it's through if you are a Crook or a Martyr (*Illiterate Digest*).

When you straddle a thing it takes a long time to explain it (*Convention Articles*, June 29th, 1924).

You know everybody is ignorant, only on different subjects (*Weekly Articles*, August 31st, 1924).

Heroing is one of the shortest lived professions there is (*Weekly Articles*, July 17th, 1928).

The more ignorant you are, the quicker you fight (*Daily Telegrams*, August 11th, 1929).

Don't gamble; take all your savings and buy some good stock, and hold it till it goes up, then sell it. If it don't go up, don't buy it (*Daily Telegrams*, October 31st, 1929). Note the date: this was the Thursday after Black Tuesday, the day of the great Wall Street crash that presaged the Depression of the 1930s.

You can't say civilization don't advance, however, for in every war they kill you in a new way (*Daily Telegrams*, December 22nd, 1929).

Half our life is spent trying to find something to do with the time we have rushed through life trying to save (letter, *New York Times*, April 29th, 1930).

Politics has got so expensive that it takes lots of money to even get beat with nowadays (*Daily Telegrams*, June 28th, 1931).

You can't make a dollar without taking it from somebody (*Weekly Articles*, October 2nd, 1932).

If I don't see things your way, well, why should I? (*Weekly Articles*, December 18th, 1932). See also **Sterne's Law**.

(Eleanor) Roosevelt's First Law

No one can make you feel inferior without your consent (Eleanor Roosevelt, *This Is My Story*, 1937).

(Eleanor) Roosevelt's Second Law

When you cease to make a contribution, you begin to die (letter to Mr. Horne, February 19th, 1960).

See also **Gibbon's Law**.

(Teddy) Roosevelt's Law

Speak softly and carry a big stick; you will go far.

Vice President Theodore Roosevelt identified this as an adage when he included it in a speech on September 2nd, 1901 – just twelve days before he came president following the assassination of President William McKinley. It has been identified variously as a proverb from Africa and from Spain. It has also inspired the corollary:

Dave's Rule of Street Survival. Speak softly and own a big, mean Doberman (Dave Miliman, Baltimore, Md., in Paul Dickson, *The Official Rules*, 1978).

See also **Capone's Law**.

Rose's Rule

Never invest your money in anything that eats or needs repainting.

Showman Billy Rose – *née* William Samuel Rosenberg – knew what he was talking about (*New York Post*, October 26th, 1957). He had learned from a good source, millionaire Bernard Baruch, for whom he worked as chief stenographer when Baruch headed the War Industries Board during World War I. Rose went on to a fine career as a songwriter ('That

Old Gang of Mine,' among other hits), Broadway producer, and nightclub owner, but he was also – getting to the point of Rose's Rule – a shrewd investor and a noted collector of the kind of timeless art that does not need repainting.

Rosenfield's Regret

The most delicate component will be dropped (internet collection of laws, January 8th, 1996).

Rosten's First Law

*Second-rate people hire third-rate people (*Leo Rosten, in John Peers, *1,001 Logical Laws . . . , 1979).*

Rosten's Other Laws

1. Thinking is harder work than hard work.
2. The love of money is the source of an enormous amount of good; the fact that the good is a by-product of the selfish pursuit of riches has nothing to do with its indisputable value.
3. Most people confuse complexity with profundity; an opaque prose with deep meaning. But the greatest ideas have been expressed clearly.
4. Most men never mature; they simply grow taller (quoted in *Saturday Review*, April 4th, 1970).

Leo Rosten was a Renaissance man – or 'Renaissance mensch,' as he has also been termed. Holder of a Ph.D. in economics from the University of Chicago, Rosten taught at the London School of Economics, Columbia, and Yale. He also wrote scores of stories, articles, and columns; ten movies; and thirty-four books, including such modern day classics as *The Education of H*Y*M*A*N K*A*P*L*A*N, Captain Newman, M.D.,* and *The Joys of Yiddish.*

To Rosten's credit also goes the popularisation of a famous saying that often is attributed mistakenly to W. C. Fields: "Any man who hates dogs and babies can't be all bad." Unexpectedly called upon to speak at a roast for Fields at the Masquer's Club in Hollywood on February 16th, 1939, and with nothing prepared to say, Rosten arose, delivered a single sentence, and sat down again to tremendous applause. Said Rosten: "The only thing I can say about W. C. Fields, whom I have admired since the day he advanced upon Baby LeRoy with an ice pick, is this: Any man who hates dogs and babies can't be all bad."

Similar versions of the remark had been employed earlier. One of *New York Times* columnist William Safire's correspondents reported finding "No man who hates dogs and children can be all bad" in a 1937 article by Cedric Worth in *Harper's*. Worth, in turn, attributed the bon mot to a *Times* reporter, Byron Darton, who supposedly made it in 1930 in an elevator, having just left a party where the conversation was dominated by a man who hated dogs.

Rousseau's Law of Laws

Good laws lead to the making of better ones; bad ones bring about worse (Jean-Jacques Rousseau, *The Social Contract*, 1762).

Rowland's Law

The follies which a man regrets most, in his life, are those which he didn't commit when he had the opportunity.

A syndicated columnist and author of a number of books, Helen Rowland's epigrams were once widely quoted. This one is from *A Guide to Men* (1922), which also contains her famous description of the male-female bond: "Love, the quest; marriage, the conquest; divorce, the inquest." Another zinger from Rowland: "When you see what some girls marry, you realise how they must hate to work for a living" (*Reflections of a Bachelor Girl*, 1909).

Twain's Corollary. The first half of life consists of the capacity to enjoy without the chance; the last half consists of the chance without the capacity (Mark Twain, letter to Edward L. Dimmit, July 19th, 1901).

See also **Ovid's Observation.**

Rubin's Laws

1. (literature) All writers are neurotics, but not all neurotics are writers.

2. (fishing) Whenever two fishing lines are contiguous, they will become continuous (Louis D. Rubin, Jr., in *A Writer's Companion*, with Jerry Leath Mills, 1995).

Rudin's Law

In a crisis that forces a choice to be made among alternative courses of action, most people will choose the worst one possible (S. A. Rudin, letter to *The New Republic*, 1961, in Harold Faber, *The Book of Laws*, 1979).

Much the same thought also has been attributed to others, including the American novelist and essayist Edward Dahlberg and the British writer and critic Cyril Connolly. Thus, we have:

Dahlberg's Declaration. Every decision you make is a mistake (in Frank Muir, *An Irreverent and Thoroughly Incomplete Social History of Almost Everything*, 1976).

Connolly's English Law. Where there are two alternatives: one intelligent, one stupid; one attractive, one vulgar; one noble, one ape-like; one serious and sincere, one undignified and false; one far-sighted, one short; EVERYBODY WILL

INVARIABLY choose the latter (in Jonathon Green, *The Cynic's Lexicon*, 1984).

West's Solution. Between two evils, I always pick the one I've never tried before (Mae West, *Klondike Annie*, 1936).

Runyon's First Law

All life is 6 to 5 against.

In full, as Damon Runyon put it in 'A Nice Price': "'In fact,' Sam the Gonoph says, 'I long ago came to the conclusion that all life is 6 to 5 against'" (*Collier's*, September 8th, 1934). The point here is that 6 to 5 are not bad odds. The bettor risks £6 against the house's £5. He wins just often enough to be enticed into staying in the game. In the long run, of course, he goes broke.

See also **Lowell's Law**.

Runyon's Second Law

The race is not always to the swift nor the battle to the strong – but that's the way to bet (Damon Runyon, *More Than Somewhat* 1937).

The reference is to the biblical verse: "The race is not to the swift, nor the battle to the strong, neither yet bread to the wise, nor yet riches to men of understanding, nor yet favour to men of skill; but time and chance happeneth to them all" (Ecclesiastes 9:11).

Memorable advice on betting also was included in Runyon's *The Idyll of Miss Sarah Brown* (1933), the short story that formed the basis of the 1952 musical *Guys and Dolls*: "Someday, somewhere, a guy is going to come up to you and show you a nice brand-new deck of cards on which the seal is never broken, and this guy is going to offer to bet you that the jack of spades will jump out of this deck and squirt cider in your ear. But, son, do not bet him, for as sure as you stand there, you are going to get an ear full of cider."

See also **Algren's Laws** and **Sweet P's Rule**.

Russell's Conclusion

The fact that an opinion has been widely held is no evidence whatsoever that it is not utterly absurd; indeed in view of the silliness of the majority of mankind a widespread belief is more likely to be foolish than sensible.

Bertrand Russell, a.k.a. Bertrand Arthur William, third Earl Russell, made this comment in passing in *Marriage and Morals* (1929) a work whose liberal views on divorce, adultery, and homosexuality so outraged widely held public opinion, especially in the United States, that his appointment in 1940 to teach philosophy at the City University of New York was canceled, following a campaign of abuse by religious leaders, politicians, and the press.

The attacks on Russell culminated in a taxpayer's suit in Brooklyn demanding that his appointment be revoked. The plaintiff's lawyer characterised Russell as "lecherous, libidinous, lustful, venerous, erotomaniac, aphrodisiac, irreverent, narrow-minded, untruthful, and bereft of moral fibre." (Another shocking example of immorality from this same work: "Marriage is for women the commonest mode of livelihood, and the total amount of undesired sex endured by women is probably greater in marriage than in prostitution.") The judge ruled in favour of the plaintiff, voiding Russell's appointment because, among other things, it would create "a chair of indecency," tend to bring students "and in some cases their parents and guardians into conflict with Penal Law," and even lead in some way (the judge did not explain exactly how) to "abduction" and rape. This strange decision was never appealed because Mayor Fiorello La Guardia did not want to pursue a case that had become a political hot potato. Meantime, the Barnes Foundation in Philadelphia got the city off the hook by offering Russell another appointment.

Ten years later, in 1950, Russell received the Nobel Prize for Literature for his significant writings "as the champion of humanity and freedom of thought." When he returned to New York later that year to lecture at Columbia University, he was greeted with thunderous acclaim by the students. The minions of public morality chose to remain silent, but it would be too much to hope that they did so out of any real embarrassment.

See also **Montagu's Motto, Thoreau's First Law, Udall's Law, and Valery's Law.**

S

Sagan's Standard

Extraordinary claims require extraordinary proof.

Cornell astronomer Carl Sagan was credited with originating this high standard of proof by William Schopf at the news conference at which NASA announced the discovery of microfossils of apparently primitive organic forms in a meteorite that had come to Earth from Mars (*New York Times*, August 8th, 1996). Schopf, a paleobiologist at the University of California at Los Angeles, had doubts about the analysis of the meteorite, as indicated by his appeal to Sagan's Standard. Before accepting the claim of life on Mars, he wanted to see more evidence, including the presence of a population of organisms, with traces of cell walls and cell divisions, showing their life cycle.

Sagan's Standard is a distillation, in effect, of Scottish philosopher David Hume's rule for judging miracles: "No testimony is sufficient to establish a miracle, unless the testimony be of such kind that its falsehood would be more miraculous than the fact which it endeavors to establish" (*An Enquiry Concerning Human Understanding 'Of Miracles'*, 1748).

Saki's First Law

Women and elephants never forget an injury.

This profound revelation by H. H. Munro, who wrote under the pen name of Saki, is from one of his many short stories,

'Reginald on Besetting Sins,' in *Reginald* (1904). The same story also contains the wonderful line, "The cook was a good cook, as cooks go; and as good cooks go, she went."

Saki's Second Law

A little inaccuracy sometimes saves tons of explanation.

Another dollop of wisdom from H. H. Munro, this is from 'Clovis on the Alleged Romance of Business,' a short story in *The Square Egg*, a collection published in 1924, eight years after the author's death in action in World War I.

Sandburg's Law

The customer is always right.

This is the motto of Selfridges department store in London but the earliest known example of the law in writing comes not from a retailer, as one would expect, but from a poet, Carl Sandburg, who worked it into 'The Proverbs of a People,' in *Good Morning, America* (1928). He led up to it this way:

> Aye, behold the proverbs of a people:
> The big word is Service.
> Service – first, last and always.
> Business is business.
> What you don't know won't hurt you.
> Courtesy pays.
> Fair enough.
> The voice with a smile.
> Say it with flowers.
> Let one hand wash the other.
> The customer is always right.

Santayana's Law

Those who cannot remember the past are condemned to repeat it.

George Santayana, philosopher, poet, novelist, and critic, produced this gem in the first of the five volumes of *The Life of Reason* (1905-06). Of course, the idea that history is repetitive is not particularly new. Already, in the fifth century B.C., Thucydides asserted in his *History of the Peloponesian War* that events tended to repeat themselves. He would be content, Thucydides told his readers at the outset, if his work were to be "judged useful by those inquirers who desire an exact knowledge of the past as an aid to the interpretation of the future, which in the course of human things must resemble if it does not reflect it."

See also **Thucydides's Law**. A number of variations on Santayana's Law have been produced, including:

Darrow's Observation. History repeats itself. That's one of the things wrong with history (attributed to Clarence Darrow in Paul Dickson, *The Official Rules*, 1978).

Huxley's Amendment. That men do not learn very much from the lessons of history is the most important of all the lessons that history has to teach (Aldous Huxley, 'Case of Voluntary Ignorance,' *Collected Essays*, 1959). Here, Huxley may also have been partly inspired by Hegel's assertion: "What experience and history teach is this – that peoples and governments have never learned anything from history, or acted on principles deduced from it" (*Philosophy of History*, 1832).

Wolf's Law of Historical Lessons. Those who don't study the past will repeat its errors; those who do study it will find other ways to err (Charles Wolf, Jr., quoted by Alan L. Otten, in the *Wall Street Journal*, February 26th, 1976).

McKernan's Maxim. Those who are unable to learn from past meetings are condemned to repeat them (in Arthur Block, *The Complete Murphy's Law*, 1991).

Hollywood's Rewrite of Santayana's Law. Unless you remember the past, you can't possibly repeat it at the box office (film review of *The Two Jakes*, a belated sequel to *Chinatown*, in the *New York Times*, April 10th, 1990).

Not everyone agrees that history has much value, of course. Notable dissents from the opinions of Santayana, Thucydides, et. al., include those of Henry Ford, who asserted that "History is more or less bunk" (interview, *Chicago Tribune*, May 25th, 1916), and Carl Sandburg, who took, if anything a dimmer view, declaring that "the past is a bucket of ashes" ('Prairie,' in *Cornhuskers*, 1918).

See also **Eban's Law, Karr's Amendment to Heraclitus's Law,** and **Marx's Second Law.**

Sattinger's Law

It works better if you plug it in (internet collection of laws, January 8th, 1996).

Sattler's Law

The grapefruit juice will always hit you in the eye.

As reported by H. Allen Smith: "There are thirty-two points in the compass, meaning that there are thirty-two directions in which a spoon can squirt grapefruit, yet a professor of chemistry named Louis Sattler has found that the juice invariably flies straight to the human eye" (*A Short History of Fingers*, 1963).

Sattler's Law is more or less the reverse of (**Theodore**) **Bernstein's First Law,** which ensures that desired objects always fly as a far as possible away from you, and both are particular examples of the universal tendency of unwanted things to happen (and wanted things to not happen). For example: Take an umbrella when you go out, and the sun will surely shine; forget the umbrella, and you will be caught in the rain. To ensure a truly torrential rain, it is best to neglect the umbrella and wear a freshly pressed suit.

See also **Fetridge's Law**.

Say's Law

Supply creates its own demand.

This law of economics, named for Jean Baptiste Say, economist and populariser of Adam Smith's theories in France at the end of the eighteenth century, has broader, not-strictly-economic ramifications. Put a box of chocolates on a cupboard shelf, and they will disappear one by one, or by the handful if children are around. Open a clinic in an area that lacks medical services, and sick people will show up. The law was epitomised in the 1989 movie *Field of Dreams*, leading to:

Kinsella's Corollary. If you build it, they will come (after W. P. Kinsella, author of *Shoeless Joe*, the book on which the movie was based). This is how moviegoers usually remember the line in the film, spoken to an Iowa farmer by a mysterious voice that urges him to construct a baseball diamond in one of his fields instead of using it to grow corn. Actually, the voice says "If you build it, he will come," the 'he' being 'Shoeless' Joe Jackson, the great hitter (.356 lifetime average), banished from professional baseball because of his involvement in fixing the 1919 world series. But the voice also promises "People will come," meaning tourists whose money will save the family farm. And they do. The baseball diamond – the supply – has created its own demand.

Schiller's Dictum

Anyone taken as an individual is tolerably sensible and reasonable – as a member of a crowd, he at once becomes a blockhead (attributed to Friedrich von Schiller by Bernard Baruch in his 1932 foreword to a classic study of mass manias, Charles Mackay's *Extraordinary Popular Delusions and the Madness of Crowds*).

Schonberg's Law

Anybody who gets away with something will come back to get away with a little more (Harold Schonberg, *New York Times*, October 8th, 1972). See also **Kipling's Law of Blackmail**.

Scott's Law

In order to win 24 games, you have to win 18.

The law was propounded by Houston Astro's pitcher Mike Scott in the summer of 1989, shortly before taking the mound in quest of his 18th win. (He wound 20-10 that year.)

Scott's law is a play on another baseball truism: In order to sweep a doubleheader, you have to win the first game.

Searle's Sage Sample

The cussedness of inanimate objects is beyond understanding (in John Peers, *1,001 Logical Laws . . . , 1979*).

Rawson's First Corollary. Never let an inanimate object know that you are in a hurry.

Rawson's Second Corollary. Never let an inanimate object know that you are losing your temper, or its cussedness will just get worse.

See also **Baker's Law of Inanimation**.

Segal's Law

A man with a watch knows what time it is. A man with two watches is never sure (in Arthur Bloch, *The Complete Murphy's Law*, 1991).

The technologically sophisticated, who want to be very sure of themselves, can get around this problem by having three watches, or whatever. Thus, some twenty years before democracy came to Russia, Wernher von Braun was interested to see that a Russian SST at the Paris air show had three gyroscopes. When he asked why, the pilot explained that three were needed in case of disagreement. "Ah, I see," said von Braun, "sometimes you *do* go by majority opinion!" (personal communication, 1975).

Zanuck's Corollary. If two men on the same job agree all the time, then one of them is useless. If they disagree all the time, then both are useless (movie mogul Darryl Zanuck, in the *Observer*, 'Sayings of the Week', October 23rd, 1949).

Seits's Law of Higher Education

The one course you must take to graduate will not be offered during your last semester (in Louis D. Rubin, Jr., with Jerry Leath Mills, *The Writer's Companion*, 1995).

Selden's Law

Ignorance of the law is no excuse.

This is the popular, slightly amended version of a comment by John Selden, English jurist and scholar, from *Table Talk*, edited by his amanuensis Richard Milward, and published in 1689, thirty-five years after his death. The passage reads in full: "Ignorance of the law excuses no man; not that all men know the law, but because 'tis an excuse every man will plead, and no man can tell how to refute him."

Other wise scraps from *Table Talk*:

> Humility is a virtue all preach, none practice; and yet everybody is content to hear.
>
> 'Tis not the drinking that is to be blamed, but the excess.
>
> Few men make themselves masters of the things they write and speak.
>
> Marriage is a desperate thing. (Note: After the death of his patron, the earl of Kent, Selden lived, as the *Encyclopedia Britannica* delicately put it, "under the same roof with his widow." If they actually got married, this was never publicly acknowledged.)
>
> Wise men say nothing in dangerous times. (This is something Selden apparently learned from experience, his political views having resulted in two tours in the Tower of London.)
>
> Pleasure is nothing else than the intermission of pain, the enjoying of something I am in great trouble for till I have it.
>
> Preachers say, Do as I say, not as I do. (See **Tilton's Law** for picturesque details.)

Seneca's Standard

It is quality rather than quantity that matters.

Lucius Annaeus Seneca, lawyer, playwright, philosopher, and tutor to Nero, made this observation in a letter some time prior to A.D. 65 when, following his implication in a conspiracy against the emperor, he committed suicide as instructed by his former pupil.

Service's Law

It's later than you think.

A good law from a not-so-good poet (and novelist), Robert W. Service. In context: "Ah! the clock is always slow; / It's later than you think." The verse is from *Songs of the Sourdough* (1907), later retitled *The Spell of the Yukon*, which contains Service's best known ballad, 'The Shooting of Dan McGrew'. Service's popularity periodically waxes and wanes, with sales of his works being especially strong, for some reason unknown to his publishers, during time of war.

Shadwell's Law

Every man loves what he is good at.

The thought is from *A True Widow* (1679) by Thomas Shadwell, who is best remembered today (to the extent that he is remembered by anyone except students of English literature) as the subject of John Dryden's attacks in *MacFlecknoe* and *Absolam and Achitophel*. Though now lost in the shadows of literary history, Shadwell had his revenge at the time. After the Glorious Revolution of 1688, when William and Mary assumed the throne, Dryden lost his post as poet laureate to Shadwell. Variations on Shadwell's theme include:

Colette's Corollary. We only do well the things we love doing (attributed to the French novelist Sidonie-Gabrielle Colette, who was referring to cooking in this instance, in a *New York Times* column by Mimi Sheraton, whose date I neglected to note.)

Ashleigh's First Law. If you can't do it well, you should learn to do it badly (internet collection of laws, January 8th, 1996).

Shakespeare's First Law

There's small choice in rotten apples (The Taming of the Shrew, 1593-94).

The law has been promulgated in many forms by many people over the years, e.g. "There is little choice in a barrel of rotten apples" and "Taint no choice in rotten apples," but Shakespeare's version is the earliest recorded in *A Dictionary of American Proverbs* (1992). See also **Hobson's Choice**.

Shakespeare's Second Law

Some men are born great, some achieve greatness, and some have greatness thrust upon 'em (Twelfth Night, 1599-1600).

Heller's Amendment. Some men are born mediocre, some men achieve mediocrity, and some men have mediocrity thrust upon them. With Major Major it had been all three (Joseph Heller, *Catch-22*, 1961).

Shakespeare's Third Law

Brevity is the soul of wit (Hamlet, 1600-01).

Parker's Amendment. Brevity is the soul of lingerie (Dorothy Parker, in Alexander Woollcott, *While Rome Burns*, 1934).

Shakespeare's Fourth Law

All's well that ends well.

The saying was proverbial for some hundreds of years (it appears in a collection of proverbs dating from ca. 1300) before Shakespeare used it in his play of this title (1602-04): "All's well that ends well; still the fine's the crown. / Whate'er the course, the end is the renown."

Buffett's Amendment. All's well that ends (Warren E. Buffett, interim chairman of Salomon, Inc., quoted in the *New York Times*, May 21st, 1992, after the Wall Street firm agreed to pay a $290-million fine in order to settle charges that it had violated U. S. Treasury auction rules.

p.s. The 'crown' in Shakespeare's line alludes to a Latin proverb that was better known in his time than our own: *Finis coronat opus*, the end crowns the work.

Shakespeare's Fifth Law

Misery acquaints a man with strange bedfellows (The Tempest, 1611-12).

The felicitous phrasing, if not the thought, may well have been original to Shakespeare. Variants include "Misfortunes cause queer bedfellows," "Wealth and content are not always bedfellows," and most commonly today, "Politics makes strange bedfellows."

Shanahan's Law

The length of a meeting rises with the square of the number of people present, and the productiveness of the meeting falls with the square of the number of people present (financial writer Eileen Shanahan, as quoted in *Timestalk*, house organ of the *New York Times*, in 1963, and recorded in Harold Faber, *The Book of Laws*, 1978). See also **Kirkland's Law**.

Shannon's Law of Administration

What is actually happening is often less important that what appears to be happening (William V. Shannon, *The Dallas Morning News*, July 2nd, 1972).

See also **Gilbert's Law of Appearances**.

Shaw's Conclusion

If all economists were laid end to end, they would not reach a conclusion (George Bernard Shaw, attributed, in John Peers, *1,001 Logical Laws . . .* , 1979).

Parker's Amendment. If all the girls attending it [the Yale junior prom] were laid end to end – I wouldn't be surprised (in Alexander Woollcott, *While Rome Burns*, 1934).

Shaw's Maxims

George Bernard Shaw graced the 'epistle dedicatory' to *Man and Superman* (1903) with a number of 'Maxims for Revolutionists'. Many of them have the force of law. For example:

The golden rule is that there are no golden rules. See also **Confucius's Law.**

He who can, does. He who cannot, teaches. (H. L. Mencken may well have said much the same thing. Arthur Block credits him with the genderless "Those who can do. Those who cannot, teach" in *The Complete Murphy's Law* [1991]. Bloch also cites, without further details, a corollary that he terms 'Martin's Extension': Those who cannot teach, administrate.)

Marriage is popular because it combines the maximum of temptation with the maximum of opportunity.

The reasonable man adapts himself to the world: the unreasonable one persists in trying to adapt the world to himself. Therefore all progress depends on unreasonable men.

Decency is Indecency's conspiracy of silence.

Every man over forty is a scoundrel. See also **Weinberg's Laws.**

Shaw's Quandary

There are two tragedies in life. One is not to get your heart's desire. The other is to get it (George Bernard Shaw, *Man and Superman*, 1903).

The basic thought has been around for a while. Aesop, back in the seventh century B.C., concluded his fable of 'The Old Man and Death' with the moral, "We would often be sorry if our wishes were gratified." Rather closer to our time, the American essayist Logan Pearsall Smith observed, "How many of our daydreams would darken into nightmares if there seemed any danger of their coming true!" ('Life and Human Nature', in *Afterthoughts*, 1931). See also **Kristol's Law** and **Wilde's First Law**.

Simmons's Law

The desire for racial integration increases with the square of the distance from the actual event (in Louis D. Rubin, Jr., ed., with Jerry Leath Mills, *A Writer's Companion*, 1995). See also **Alinsky's Law**.

Slim's Rule

Look around the table. If you don't see a sucker, get up, because you're the sucker (poker champion Thomas Austin Preston, Jr., a.k.a. Amarillo Slim, in Jon Winokur, *Friendly Advice*, 1991).

Financial wizard Warren E. Buffett, chairman of Berkshire Hathaway, Inc., cited another version of this rule in a letter to shareholders: "As they say in poker, 'If you've been in the game thirty minutes, and don't know who the patsy is, you're the patsy'" (*New York Times*, August 17th, 1991). He used the rule to illustrate his contention that investors who base their decisions on movements of stockmarket prices rather than analysis of fundamental values are likely to get in trouble. Note: Berkshire Hathaway shares have the highest list price of any stock on the Wall Street exchange.

Poker players may also want to consider another tidbit of Amarillo Slim's wisdom: "If you're going to bluff, make it a big one" (in Winokur, op. cit.).

(Adam) Smith's Observation

People of the same trade seldom meet together, even for merriment and diversion, but the conversation ends in a conspiracy against the public to raise prices (The Wealth of Nations, 1776).

Continuing a famous metaphor of Smith's, it could be said that 'the invisible hand' operates beneath the table as well as above it. For more about that hand, see **Spencer's Law**.

(Sydney) Smith's Secret

Digestion is the great secret of life (Reverend Sydney Smith, letter to Arthur Kinglake, September 30th, 1837).

Reverend Smith, a founder of the *Edinburgh Review*, was a very witty man, so much so that his reputation as a humorist was largely responsible for his never becoming a bishop. His daughter, Lady Holland, preserved many of his sayings in her *Memoir*, including one that is, in effect, a corollary to Smith's Secret, i.e. "Praise is the best diet for us, after all."

A sampling of other Smith-isms:

> It requires a surgical operation to get a joke well into Scotch understanding. Their only idea of wit . . . is laughing immoderately at stated intervals.

> Take short views, hope for the best, and trust in God.

> How can a bishop marry? How can he flirt? The most he can say is "I will see you in the vestry after service."

> I have, alas, only one illusion left, and that is the Archbishop of Canterbury.

> He was a one-book man. Some men have only one book in them; others a library.

> Marriage . . . resembles a pair of shears, so joined that they

cannot be separated; often moving in opposite directions, yet always punishing anyone who comes between them.

Voltaire's Caveat to Smith's Secret. Thought depends absolutely on the stomach, but in spite of that, those who have the best stomachs are not the best thinkers (letter to D'Alembert, August 20th, 1770).

Socrates's Law

The life which is unexamined is not worth living.

This law was attributed to Socrates (ca. 469-399 B.C.) by Plato in the *Apology*, a dialogue centering around his teacher's trial and execution for 'impiety' (especially for 'corrupting' the youth of Athens by teaching them how to think).

It took more than two thousand years, but Socrates's Law finally has been updated to suit modern sensibilities. Thus, in a review of Zsa Zsa Gabor's memoir, *One Lifetime Is Not Enough*, Gerri Hirshey pointed out: "Her book is a grisly specimen of the celeb-opportunist's maxim: The unexamined life may not be worth living, but it can be worth selling" (*Gentlemen's Quarterly*, November, 1991).

Sophocles's First Law

The greatest griefs are those we cause ourselves.

The line is spoken in *Oedipus Rex* (ca. 430 B.C.) by a messenger who brings the terrible news that Jocasta, queen of Thebes, has hanged herself and that Oedipus, her husband but also – the essence of the tragedy – her son, has blinded himself with her golden brooches.

See also **Emerson's Third Law.**

Sophocles's Second Law

Time eases all things.

The line comes toward the conclusion of *Oedipus Rex*. It is delivered by Jocasta's brother Creon to Oedipus, his brother-in-law/nephew, as the latter prepares to go into exile. The play ends with the chorus reciting a familiar Greek maxim that has continuing relevance: "Judge no man happy until his whole life has been lived."

The common English version of Sophocles's Second Law is "Time heals all wounds," which has been updated in our time to the equally optimistic "Time wounds all heels." The latter crops up in *The Marx Brothers Go West* (1940), but Goodman Ace credited it in *The Fine Art of Hypochondria; or, How Are You?* (1966) to his wife Jane, who co-starred with him on their long-running radio show (1930-45) radioshow, *The Easy Aces*. Ms. Ace specialised in malapropisms, e.g. "Congress is still in season" and "I'm really in a quarry."

Sophocles's Third Law

Nobody likes the man who brings bad news.

Long before people began beating up on the press ("Why do newspapers only print the bad things?"), messengers were well aware of the danger of bearing bad tidings. This line comes from *Antigone* (ca. 422 B.C.), the last of the three plays in the Oedipus cycle. It is spoken by the sentry who has come to tell Creon, now king of Thebes, that someone has disobeyed him by giving a token burial to Oedipus's son Polyneices, slain by his own brother while assaulting the city. The sentry is half-scared out of his wits. The guards had rolled dice to see who would bring the bad news to the king, and he was the one who lost. The messenger escapes with this life, but not before an angry Creon has threatened him with torture and death. As the scene ends, and with king out of earshot, the sentry promises "You have seen the last of me here. At any rate, I am safe!"

Senator Sorghum's Laws of Politics

The sayings of Senator Sorghum, the prototypical southern senator, created by Philander Chase Johnson, enjoyed considerable popularity in the early 1900s but have been unjustly forgotten. In the interest of rehabilitating the distinguished gentleman's reputation, here are some nuggets of wisdom from *Senator Sorghum's Primer of Politics or, Helpful Hints on the Science of Not Getting the Worst of It* (1906):

Politics is the art of turning influence into affluence.

Every practical politician should frankly confess to a profound respect for money; for he is a bad workman who quarrels with his tools. (See also **Bacon's Law** and **Clinton's Law of Politics**.)

A good memory is often a great help; but knowing just when to forget things sometimes counts for more.

Anybody can keep a promise, but it sometimes requires an artist to break one.

Never do anything that popular opinion and your own sense of right do not approve. Hire someone else to do it.

Occasionally a reputation for great wisdom is obtained by doing absolutely nothing and thereby avoiding mistakes. *Corollary*: It is safer to be criticised for not doing anything, than it is to be blamed for doing something badly. (See also **Jefferson's Ukase** and **Byron Johnson's Laws of Bureaucratic Success**.)

Don't complain that you are not getting what you deserve. Your impressions in such matters may be misleading. If you saw what you deserve coming, maybe you would dodge. (See also **De Maistre's Law.**)

When in doubt for an argument, turn to statistics. They sound wise and very few people will do the arithmetic necessary to contradict you. (See also the last of the epigrams under **Disraeli's Second Law.**)

Spencer's Law

Every cause produces more than one effect.

Herbert Spencer included this law, as profound as it is obvious (when you stop to think about it), in an essay, 'On Progress: Its Law and Cause' (*Essays on Education*, 1861). The insight was one of the keys to his forty-year effort, encompassed in the ten volumes of *Synthetic Philosophy* (from 1862), to provide a philosophical underpinning for the theory of evolution and other scientific advances of the nineteenth century. (In passing, he provided Darwin with the phrase 'survival of the fittest'; see **Charles Darwin's Law.**)

In our own time, Garrett Hardin, a biologist who helped found the new discipline of human ecology, restated this law in a more active, more personal form: "You can never do merely one thing." Commenting on Hardin's statement at the time, *Fortune* asserted in an editorial (February, 1973) that "If a prize were to be awarded for the most illuminating single sentence authored in the past ten years, one of the candidates would surely be Hardin's law."

Because all the effects of any one cause are rarely, if ever, foreseen (even the most sophisticated computer models have their limits), Spencer's Law can also be described as the Law, or Doctrine, of Unintended Consequences. By whatever name, it applies with as much or greater force than the more famous

Murphy's Law to human activities of all kinds. It reminds us – and we often do need reminding – that every action has many results, both immediate and in the future as each effect causes additional effects in an unending ripple through time. As the naturalist John Muir explained: "Whenever we try to pick out anything by itself, we find it hitched to everything else in the universe" (as quoted by John T. Nichols in *Natural History*, November, 1992).

The history of science and technology is rife with examples of such unintended consequences. A dice hustler, the Chevalier de Mere, posed a question to Blaise Pascal, and Pascal helped him out by developing probability theory (see **Pascal's Law**). Guglielmo Marconi thought radio would be used mainly where wires could not be run, as between ships at sea; hence the name of his corporation, the Marconi Wireless Telegraph Co. The Wright brothers could not foresee the Flying Fortress, the SST, and an international travel industry. Henry Ford did not mean to create suburbs or change the nation's courting customs when he began assembly-line production of the Model T but these were among the results of mass availability of the automobile. The shortage of lifeboats on the Titanic led the owners of an excursion steamer, the Eastland, to add enough boats to accommodate all passengers; the extra weight also helped make the Eastland top-heavy and 812 people were killed when it capsized in the Chicago River in 1915. On a more mundane level: In the interest of protecting cab drivers, the New York City Taxi Commission ordered that bulletproof panels be installed between the front and back seats of yellow cabs in 1994; this resulted in an unexpected epidemic of broken noses and other facial injuries as riders in braking cabs crashed into the unforgiving barriers.

Unintended consequences also are part and parcel of most other aspects of life. Adam Smith, prophet of capitalism, clearly sensed this, asserting in a famous passage of *The*

Wealth of Nations (1776) that "Every individual . . . intends only his own gain, and he is in this, as in many other cases, led by an invisible hand to promote an end which was no part of his intention. . . . By pursuing his own interest he frequently promotes that of society more effectively than when he really intends to promote it."

Smith saw the 'invisible hand' as justifying private as opposed to public enterprise. ("I have never known much good done by those who affect to trade for the public good," he continued.) And today the operations of the law in the social sphere are seen most clearly when examining the unintended consequences of well-intentioned efforts to regulate human behavior. For example, laws prohibiting drugs were not intended to increase crime, but that is what they have done. By driving up the prices of banned drugs, they lead users to commit crimes to get the cash for obtaining substances that otherwise would be available at little cost. Again, one of the unintended results of the government's crackdown on synthetic drugs was an increase in use of cocaine (crack from a crackdown, so to speak). Meanwhile, laws that restrict smoking of cigarettes have had the unintended consequence of adding to the litter on city pavements because office workers must go outdoors for their periodic nicotine rushes. In New York City, the head of the Times Square Business Improvement District estimated that the B.I.D.'s workers were sweeping up 12,272 butts per day in 1996. That's quite a mess, as well as a lot of lost work time – another unintended consequence of the anti-smoking laws.

Efforts to control crime may also lead to unexpected results. Thus, long prison sentences for teenage offenders may be counterproductive, cutting them off from the opportunities to start families and obtain jobs – the two factors that appear to be most important in turning young criminals away from lifelong careers in crime. Then there is the move to reduce crime by enacting tough three-strikes-and-you're-out laws. California passed such a law in March of 1994; it mandated sentences of twenty-five years to life for a third felony conviction. A year later, the state's crime index was down, which might or might not have been due to the law. More certain were the law's unintended consequences: People with two felony convictions stopped plea-bargaining because sentences were so harsh, court calendars in some places were so clogged with criminal cases that civil trials were halted, and county jails became so overcrowded that non-violent inmates had to be given early releases.

California also passed a term-limits law in 1990 that was intended to reshape the political scene by forcing long-entrenched members of the assembly and senate in Sacramento out of office. Instead, the law signaled the beginning of a game of musical chairs. Assembly members scrambled for senate seats, while senators looked for statewide offices. One of the chief targets of the term-limits law was assembly speaker Willie L. Brown, Jr. He did have to give up his assembly seat but hardly faded from the political scene, getting himself a new job right away as mayor of San Francisco.

On the international scene, governmental efforts to halt smuggling of looted antiquities have resulted in a huge increase in production of forged antiquities. In Japan, an attempt to curb the crime-ridden pachinko gambling industry by encouraging players to use magnetic cards instead of cash has led to a new form of crime – the forging of magnetic cards. Then there are the Canadian lawmakers who sought to reduce illegal immigration by passing an act to fine ship operators about $5,000 per stowaway. The law does seem to have reduced the number of illegal immigrants but in an unexpected manner: When three Romanian stowaways were found aboard a Taiwanese vessel en route to Halifax, Nova

Scotia, in the spring of 1996, the captain and officers of ship were reported by other crew members to have avoided the fines by putting two of the stowaways onto an oil-drum raft and tossing the third into the sea.

And so it goes. Former Defense Secretary Robert S. McNamara, in *In Retrospect* (1995), his apologia for his role in managing the Vietnam war, assigned some of the blame for that debacle to the unforeseen effects of particular decisions. The chain of events went like this: the decision to start bombing North Vietnam (the first raids took place on February 7th, 1965) led to the need to defend airbases in South Vietnam (Marines arrived at Da Nang with Hawk air defense missiles on February 7th), which led to the need to deploy troops to protect the missile batteries (two battalions of Marines were deployed at Da Nang airfield on March 9th), which led just three weeks later to offensive operations (the Marines couldn't just sit around as targets waiting to be attacked), which led to the need for still more combat troops (General William C. Westmoreland asked for 44 battalions on June 7th and the request was approved at the end of the following month). By the end of 1965, American forces in Vietnam totaled 184,314, and the U.S. was up to its neck in an Asian land war – an unintended consequence of monumental proportions.

See also **Robert Burns's Law, Cleaver's Law, Emerson's Third Law, Forrester's Laws, Heisenberg's Uncertainty Principle,** and **Marx's Third Law.**

Spock's Law

Trust yourself. You know more than you think you do.

This is the opening line in a book that besides being a bestseller has also been carefully read (the two do not always go together) – *Baby and Child Care* (1946), by Benjamin Spock.

de Staël's Law

To understand everything is to forgive everything.

This is how the law usually is quoted, but it isn't exactly what Madame de Staël, better remembered today for her literary salons than for her own literary production, wrote in *Corinne, or Italy* (1807). In the original, the statement is the slightly less forceful *Tout comprendre rend très indulgent*, i.e. To understand everything makes one very tolerant.

Stalin's Law

You can't make an omelet without breaking eggs.

Though frequently credited to the Soviet dictator, as well as to the equally unappetising Nazi Reichsmarshall Hermann Goering, either of whom may well have justified the policies of their regimes in this manner, the phrase actually is much older. William Howard Taft used a close variation of it – "We cannot make omelets without breaking eggs" – in a speech during his presidency (1909-13), according to *They Never Said It* (1989), by Paul F. Boller, Jr. and John George. The rather more radical revolutionary Robespierre, who sought to establish a 'Reign of Virtue' by marching all of France's internal enemies to the guillotine, also is reported to have employed this extenuation. Most likely, the phrase is a French proverb.

See also **Baker's Laws of Progress** and, for more about cooking, **Longworth's Law**.

Staples's First Law of the Universe

Evil and stupidity are randomly distributed.

Reviewing the autobiography of Native American activist Russell Means, *Where White Men Fear to Tread*, Brent Staples noted in the *New York Times Book Review* (October

15th, 1995) that Mr. Means blamed either racist bosses or "the dictates of the Indian Way" for his past truancy, boozing, drug dealing, indolence, and irresponsibility (e.g. working only half-heartedly despite having a wife and two children, then leaving town when he could no longer feed them). Mr. Staples (whose own memoir is entitled *Parallel Time: Growing Up in Black and White*) reacted negatively to Mr. Means's claims:

> His repeated assertion that Native American culture is cosmologically superior to Europe's seems patronising, even coming from an Indian. The first law of the universe, after all, is that evil and stupidity are randomly distributed. Had the Lakota and others been the seers Mr. Means seems to think they were, they would have avoided at least some of the disasters that befell them.

See also **Ulmann's Razor.**

Steinbeck's Law of Traveling

When you need towns they are very far apart.

John Steinbeck characterised this as an "ancient law" in *Travels with Charley in Search of America* (1962) but he gets credit here for distilling it in this form. He was in Oregon at the time.

See also **Ettore's Law of Lines.**

Stengel's Laws

Charles Dillon 'Casey' Stengel, legendary baseball manager, and a pretty good ball player before that (.284 lifetime average), was celebrated for his wise but often mangled thoughts. For example:

> Good pitching will always stop good hitting, and vice versa.

The secret of managing is to keep the guys who hate you away from the guys who are undecided.

You make your own luck. (See **Rickey's Law** for more.)

[Re ball players breaking curfew] It ain't getting it that hurts them, it's staying up all night looking for it. They gotta learn that if you don't get it by midnight, you ain't going to get it, and if you do it ain't worth it.

I'll never make the mistake of being seventy again. (Upon being fired by the New York Yankees in 1960, after having won ten American League pennants and seven world series in the preceding dozen years.)

See also **Berra's Laws**.

Sterne's Law

The desire of knowledge, like the thirst of riches, increases ever with the acquisition of it.

Thus, the narrator of Laurence Sterne's *The Life and Opinions of Tristram Shandy* (1760-67) tells how his Uncle Toby, having been given a map of Namur, where he had been wounded in King William's War (a.k.a. the War of the Grand Alliance), began to delve ever deeper into military matters, accumulating maps of other fortified towns, books on military strategy and architecture, and so on, until this one pursuit took over his entire life.

What became Uncle Toby's 'Hobby-Horse', as Tristram termed it, was a bit odd, perhaps, but not as peculiar as that of Dr. Kunastrokius (a name to be conjured with), who delighted in spending his leisure hours "in combing asses tails, and plucking the dead hairs out with his teeth, though he had tweezers always in his pocket." Tristram regards such foibles equably (collecting coins, cockle-shells, maggots, and butterflies also are mentioned), however, and he produces a classic defence for nonconformists of all stripes: "So long as a man rides his Hobby-Horse peaceably and quietly along the King's highway, and neither compels you or me to get up behind him, – pray, Sir, what have either you or I to do with it?" (See also the last of **Roger's Laws**.)

Uncle Toby himself had much the same generous spirit. Catching a fly that had been buzzing about his nose at dinner one day, he took it in his cupped hand to the window and let it escape. "Go, poor devil, get thee gone," he said. "Why should I hurt thee? – This world surely is wide enough to hold both thee and me."

It is to be hoped that the reader of this book also will agree with another of Tristram's pronouncements: "Digressions, incontestably, are the sunshine; – they are the life, the soul of reading – take them out of this book, for instance, – you might as well take the book along with them – one cold eternal winter would reign in every page of it."

Stilwell's Observation

The higher a monkey climbs, the more you can see of his ass.

The saying generally is credited to General Joseph Stilwell, who commanded American and Chinese forces in Burma, India, and China during World War II. It certainly is in keeping with 'Vinegar Joe's' reputation for brutally honest, frequently acid appraisals of friend and foe. Stilwell's character also is indicated by personal motto, *illegitimi non carborundum,* a fake-Latin phrase (the last word is the made-up trade name of an abrasive substance), which he translated as "Don't let the bastards grind you down."

Stolley's Law

Younger is better than older, pretty is better than ugly, TV is better than music, music is better than movies, movies is better than sports, anything is better than politics and p.s., nothing is better than a dead celebrity.

Dick Stolley, managing editor of *People* during its first eight years of existence, devised this law as an aid to determining whose face to put on the magazine's cover each week (interview, *Chicago Tribune*, March 4th, 1994, on the occasion of *People's* twentieth anniversary). The bestselling cover: The December 1980 tribute to John Lennon, with a newsstand sale of 2,644,000 copies.

Sturgeon's Law

Ninety percent of everything is crud.

This law generally is assigned to science fiction writer Theodore Sturgeon, but in different forms. This version appeared in *Playboy* in February 1984. The stated percentage varies from source to source (the figure of 99 percent is often given) as does the composition of 'everything'. Depending, apparently, on the fastidiousness of individual editors, it is said to be *junk*, *bullshit*, or *crap*. See also **Woody Allen's Observation**.

Sullivan's Law

Form ever follows function.

This is the key tenet of modern architecture, as propounded by a pioneer in the field, Louis Henri Sullivan, in an article 'The Tall Office Building Artistically Considered' (*Lippincott's Magazine*, March 1896). It became a motto, along with 'Less is more', of the influential Bauhaus school of design and architecture in Germany in the 1920s. See also **Browning's Observation** and **John Yardley's Law**.

Sutton's Law

[In answer to the question, "Why do you rob banks?"] *That's where the money is.*

Despite Willie Sutton's denials (he maintained that the words were dreamed up by some reporter "who felt a need to fill out his copy"), this explanation of why the bank robber pursued his trade has become firmly entrenched in American lore. Sutton himself is partly responsible for this, since he (or his publishers) could not resist drawing on the quote for the title of his 1976 autobiography, *Where the Money Was*. Leo Durocher faced the same problem and 'solved' it the same way. See also **Brecht's Law** and **Durocher's Law**.

Swanson's Law

When the water reaches the upper deck, follow the rats.

Claude Swanson, a cabinet member under Franklin D. Roosevelt, generally gets credit for devising this law, perhaps because he was secretary of the navy.

Sweet P's Rule

Nobody plays nobody for big stakes.

A New York City chess hustler, identified only as Sweet P, cited this as a cardinal rule of hustling in an interview with the *New York Times* (September 8th, 1988). A good player himself, with an expert rating of 1,800 (compared to 2,500 for grandmasters), Sweet P and his fellow hustlers can never be sure of who they are facing across the board. The unknown might be the champion of Montana, who intentionally blunders away a couple of games, asks for increased stakes, and then cleans up. Sweet P's limit was $10 a game. See also **Runyon's Second Law**.

Swift's First Law

When a true genius appears in the world, you may know him by this sign, that the dunces are all in confederacy against him.

Good news for late starters: Jonathan Swift was nearing forty when he included this observation in *Thoughts on Various Subjects* (1706). He had just completed 'The Tale of a Tub' (1704), but still had most of his most important work ahead of him, including *Gulliver's Travels* (1726) and such significant political and satirical pieces as 'An Argument Against Abolishing Christianity' (1708), *The Drapier's Letters* (1724-25), and 'A Modest Proposal for Preventing the Children of Ireland from being a Burden to their Parents or Country' (1729).

Swift's Law of Laws

Laws are like cobwebs, which may catch small flies, but let wasps and hornets break through (Jonathan Swift, 'A Critical Essay Upon the Faculties of the Mind', 1707).

As noted in Bartlett's *Familiar Quotations*, the thought here is essentially the same as that passed along in Plutarch's *Life of Solon*, where it is credited to Anacharsis, a Sythian sage who lived, according to Herodotus, in the sixth century B.C. In Plutarch's account: "[Anacharsis] laughed at him [Solon] for imagining the dishonesty and covetousness of his countrymen could be restrained by written laws, which were like spiders' webs, and would catch, it is true, the weak and poor, but easily be broken by the mighty and rich."

Swift's Maxim

Those to whom everybody allows the second place, have an undoubted title to the first (Jonathan Swift, 'The Tale of a Tub', 1704).

Szasz's Rules

1. Two wrongs don't make a right, but they make a good excuse.

2. If you talk to God you are praying; if God talks to you, you have schizophrenia (Thomas Szasz, *The Second Sin*, 1973).

T

Tacitus's Laws

Cornelius Tacitus held a series of high public offices in Rome and its dominions, married well (to the daughter of Agricola, governor of Britain), and enjoyed the reputation of being a fine orator. His enduring fame comes from his writings, however, principally the *Histories*, covering events of his own time, from A.D. 69 to 96; the *Annales*, a history of Rome from the death of Augustus in A.D. 14 through the year 69; the *Life of Agricola*, his biography of his father-in-law; and *De Germania*, an account of the manners and customs of the German tribes. A keen student of human nature, he searched for the causes of events, and distilled his observations in epigrammatic prose replete with many observations that bear repeating nearly two thousand years later. For example:

The unknown always passes for the marvelous (*Agricola*).

It is human nature to hate the man whom you have injured (*Agricola*).

It has been thought more pious and reverential to believe in the actions of the gods than to inquire about them (*Germania*).

The desire for glory clings even to the best men longer than any other passion (*Histories*).

The gods are on the side of the stronger (*Histories*).

Wrongs done to the gods are the gods' concern (*Annals*).

Laws were most numerous when the commonwealth was most corrupt (*Annals*).

There is some injustice in every great precedent, which though injurious to individuals, has its compensation in the public advantage (*Annals*).

More faults are often committed while we are trying to oblige than while we are giving offence (*Annals*).

Temple's Law

No body should make love after forty, nor bee in business after fifety (Sir William Temple, in Richard Faber, *The Brave Courtier: Sir William Temple*, 1983).

History does not reveal whether Sir William took the first part of his own advice but he came very close with second. Chiefly known for his triumphs as a diplomat during the reign of Charles II (he arranged the marriage of William of Orange to Mary, daughter of James II, in 1677), Sir William retired from public life early in 1681 at about age fifty-two.

Joseph Addison quoted another of Temple's precepts, a rule for drinking, in the the *Spectator* (October 13th, 1711): "The first glass for myself, the second for my friends, the third for good humor, and the fourth for mine enemies." Two weeks later, Addison was corrected by a 'Robin Goodfellow', who said that he had got Temple's words wrong – that 'bottle' should be substituted for 'glass.' And again, history does not reveal the true answer.

See also **Weinberg's Laws.**

Tennyson's First Law

'Tis better to have loved and lost / Than never to have loved at all (Alfred, Lord Tennyson, *In Memoriam*, 1850).

Butler's Amendment. 'Tis better to have loved and lost than never to have lost at all (Samuel Butler, *The Way of All Flesh*, 1903).

Clough's Antithesis. 'Tis better to have fought and lost, / Than never to have fought at all (Arthur Hugh Clough, *Peschiera*, 1865).

Thurber's Conclusion. It is better to have loafed and lost than never to have loafed at all (James Thurber, 'The Courtship of Arthur and Al', *Fables for Our Time*, 1940).

Tennyson's Second Law

In the spring a young man's fancy lightly turns to thoughts of love.

This is a famous law (from *Locksley Hall*, 1842) but not, as recent scientific research has disclosed, a valid one. Tennyson to the contrary, it appears that testosterone levels of young men (and older ones, too!) are higher in the fall than in the spring. How the seasonal cycle evolved is not clear. Perhaps children born in the spring and summer, when food is plentiful, once had a better chance of living than those born in later in the year, thus creating a genetic bias in favour of males who did their procreating in the fall. Whatever the reason for the cycle, Lord Tennyson got the time of year wrong.

Terence's Law

The law at its most rigorous is often injustice at its worst.

Terence (Publius Terentius Afer) was born in Carthage, the son of a Libyan slave, given a good education and brought to Rome by his owner, a senator, and then freed. He wrote six plays within his short life (185-159 B.C.). His observation about the law (sometimes translated as "extreme law is often extreme injustice") is from *The Self-Tormentor*. Romans repeated the statement so often, regarding it as a truism, that in the next century Cicero characterised it as "a stale proverb."

Other lines by Terence that continue to reverberate:

I am a man: nothing human is alien to me (*The Self-Tormentor*).

While there's life, there's hope (*The Self-Tormentor*).

Moderation in all things (*The Lady of Andros*).

Nowadays flattery wins friends, truth begets hatred (*The Lady of Andros*).

Charity begins at home (*The Lady of Andros*).

How unfair that poor people should always be adding to the wealth of the rich (*Phormio*).

Fortune helps the brave (*Phormio*).

I know women's ways: when you will, they won't, and when you won't, they're dying for it (*Eunuchus*).

Thatcher's Law

In politics, if you want anything said, ask a man; if you want anything done, ask a woman (Margaret Thatcher, quoted in Anthony Sampson, *The Changing Anatomy of Britain*, 1983).

See also **Austen's Second Law**.

Thomas's Law

Out of sight, out of mind.

This grim reminder of the shortness of the attention span of most human beings comes from *On the Imitation of Christ* (ca. 1420), most likely written by the Augustinian friar, Thomas Hemerken von Kempen, better known as Thomas à Kempis (ca. 1380-1471). As originally written, the thought was expressed in more roundabout form: "And when he is out of sight, quickly is he out of mind."

Other perceptive observers of human nature have noted the same phenomenon, e.g. from George Gordon Lord Byron's *Don Juan*:

Wives in their husbands' absences grow subtler [sneakier], *And daughters sometimes run off with the butler.*

Not all law-givers agree on the effects of absence, of course.

See also **Bayly's Observation** and, for another general observation by Thomas à Kempis, **O'Malley's Observation**.

Thoreau's First Law

Any man more right than his neighbors constitutes a majority of one (Henry David Thoreau, *The Maine Woods*, 1848).

Gandhi's Amendment. In matters of conscience, the law of the majority has no place (Mohandus K. Gandhi, quoted in Laurence J. Peter, *The Peter Prescription*, 1972).

See also **Russell's Conclusion** and, for the dark side of this principle, **Torquemada's Law**.

Thoreau's Second Law

In the long run men only hit what they aim at ('Economy', in *Walden*, 1854).

Waitley and Witt's Corollary. Those who aim low usually hit their target (Denis Waitly and Remi L. Witt, *The Joy of Working*, 1985).

But see also the next to last of **Berra's Laws**.

Thoreau's Third Law

The man who goes alone can start today; but he who travels with another must wait till that other is ready, and it may be a long time before they get off ('Economy', in *Walden*, 1854).

Thoreau's Ruling

Some circumstantial evidence is very strong, as when you find a trout in the milk (Journal, *November 11th, 1854*).

Thoreau's simile referred to a common nineteenth-century consumer fraud: selling milk that had been adulterated with water.

See also **Reuther's Law.**

Thucydides' Law of Peace and War

In times of peace and prosperity cities and individuals alike follow higher standards because they are not forced into a situation where they have to do what they do not want to do. But war is a stern teacher; in depriving them of the power of easily satisfying their wants, it brings most people's minds down to the level of their actual circumstances.

Exiled from Athens in 424 B.C. for his failure as a general to save a colony from Spartan attacks, Thucydides used most of the last twenty years of his life to compose his *History of the Peloponnesian War*. No mere chronicler of events, he attempted, as evidenced by this passage from his account of civil war in Corcyra (modern Corfu) to understand causes and effects. He well fulfilled the goal that he set himself: "My work is not a piece of writing designed to meet the taste of an immediate public, but was done to last for ever."

See also **Santayana's Law** and **Vegetius's Maxim.**

Thurber's Morals

A number of James Thurber's wise and witty observations are scattered through this book; see, for example, **Addison's Law, Lincoln's First Law,** and **Tennyson's First Law**. Other timeless morals from his *Fables for Our Time* (1940) include:

> It is better to ask some of the questions than to know all the answers ('The Scotty Who Knew Too Much').

> You might as well fall flat on your face as lean over too far backward ('The Bear Who Let It Alone').

> Early to rise and early to bed makes a male healthy and wealthy and dead ('The Shrike and the Chipmunks').

> There is no safety in numbers, or in anything else ('The Fairly Intelligent Fly').

Tierny's Law

Never kibitz and play in the same place.

In an article on kibitzing, or the annoying practice of inflicting players of games with unwanted advice, occasioned by the opening of a world chess championship series between Gary Kasparov and Anatoly Karpov, John Tierny explained that ignorance of this law has ended many promising careers of kibitzers who had hoped to pass themselves off as experts. "If challenged to a game," he advised would-be kibitzers, "you might try pleading fatigue: 'Karpov's team needed some help trying to repair the Flohr-Zaitsev [opening] for today's game. We were up all night working on it'" (*New York Times*, October 15th, 1990).

'Kibitz', by the way, comes from *kiebitz*, the German name of a bird, the lapwing, that is regarded as being especially bold.

Tilton's Law

Even this shall pass away.

Theodore Tilton may have had his own tumultuous private life in mind when he penned *The King's Ring*. This is the context of the line in the poem:

Once in Persia reigned a king
Who upon his signet ring
Graved a maxim true and wise,
Solemn words, and these are they,
"Even this shall pass away."

The personal context was much more complicated, Tilton having been at the centre of one of the most delicious scandals of the nineteenth century. In 1874 Tilton formally accused Henry Ward Beecher, pastor of Plymouth Church in Brooklyn, the most famous preacher of the era, and Tilton's own friend and mentor, of having had an affair with his wife Elizabeth. The scandal had been simmering for some time. Tilton's wife had confessed all to her husband in 1870. He, in turn, had confided the details to the fascinating Victoria Woodhull, the first woman to run for president (1872), who had already heard reports of the liaison. (Details here are from Lois Beachy Underhill's *The Woman Who Ran for President*, 1995.) Woodhull, in due course, proceeded to blow the lid off Beecher's secret life, publishing the story in the November 2nd, 1872, issue of her *Woodhull and Claflin's Weekly*. As if all this were not enough, Woodhull and Tilton knew each other very well, almost certainly in the biblical sense. Chances are that Woodhull had a fling with Beecher, too. She was consistent, at least, openly advocating free love in public lectures while Beecher did not practise what he preached.

But the pastor had many powerful friends. The censorious Anthony Comstock caused Woodhull and her sister Tennessee Claflin to be arrested and tried on obscenity charges because copies of the newspaper with the article about Beecher had sullied the United States mails. (Comstock himself mailed several copies.) The sisters spent more than a month in jail but the case against them collapsed when it finally went to court; even Comstock, on the witness stand, could not point to anything in the article that was actually obscene.

Beecher, meanwhile, never had the nerve to accuse Woodhull or her sister of libel. He managed to get Mrs. Tilton to retract her confession, however, and was exonerated at a church hearing. Tilton, who had been expelled from the church for slandering the minister, then proceeded to sue Beecher for alienation of his wife's affections (an 'Action for Criminal Conversation' as it was called in official documents). Following a six-month trial in 1875, the jury split 9-3 in Beecher's favour. His reputation was left sadly frayed, however, Mrs. Tilton did not help matters by reversing herself again, writing a letter to the *New York Times* in 1878 in which she said she had committed adultery with Beecher after all.

Having lost his case, Theodore Tilton spent most of the rest of his life in exile, living in genteel poverty in Paris, where he had plenty of time to reflect on the theme of "this, too, shall pass away." He died in 1907.

Toffler's Law

The Law of Raspberry Jam: The wider any culture is spread, the thinner it gets (Alvin Toffler, *The Culture Consumers*, 1964). See also **Galbraith's First Law**.

Tolstoy's Family Law

Happy families are all alike; every unhappy family is unhappy in its own way (Leo Tolstoy, *Anna Karenina*, 1873-76).

The first sentence of the novel: one of the most famous opening salvos in literature.

Torquemada's Law

When you are right, you have a moral duty to impose your will upon anyone who disagrees with you (quoted by Alan L. Otten, *Wall Street Journal*, September 18th, 1977).

It is just a coincidence that the surname of Thomas de Torquemada, who presided over the torture of some thousands – probably hundreds of thousands – of people during his eighteen years as inquistor-general of Spain (1481-98) derives from the Latin *torquere*, to twist.

See also **Thoreau's First Law** and **Van der Post's Observation**.

The Trollope Ploy

To interpret – or willfully misinterpret – a message in the most favourable manner to oneself.

The Trollope Ploy was popularised by a critical diplomatic manoeuvre during the Cuban missile crisis of 1962. On October 26th, President Kennedy received a long, rambling, but basically conciliatory private letter from Premier Nikita Khrushchev. The next day, however, the Russians publicly released a second letter, which took a much harder line. This left Kennedy and his advisers in a quandary. Had Khrushchev changed his mind? Was he really in control of events on the Soviet side? Or had the second letter perhaps been composed first but delayed in transmission as it passed through different levels of approval in the Russian foreign office?

At this point the president's brother and attorney general, Robert F. Kennedy, came up with what Arthur Schlesinger, Jr., called "a thought of breathtaking simplicity and ingenuity: why not ignore the second Khrushchev message and reply to the first?" (*A Thousand Days*, 1965). The president delegated his brother and his special counsel, Theodore C. Sorenson, to prepare a reply to the first letter. The terms of the American reply were accepted by Khrushchev on October 28th and the two nations backed away from the brink of nuclear war.

The manoeuvre was not characterised as the Trollope Ploy in the heat of the moment; the name came later, after the participants in the crisis had time to analyse what had happened. As Sorenson reported: "Much misinformation has been written about – who said what, and about such terms as 'hawks and doves,' 'think tank,' 'Ex Comm' and 'Trollope ploy' which I never heard used at the time" (*Kennedy*, 1965).

The 'Trollope' here comes from the novelist Anthony Trollope, whose Victorian heroines were inclined to interpret a slight squeeze of the hand as a proposal of marriage. The 'Ploy' part – the gambit or manoeuvre – was popularised in this sense by Stephen Potter, wiley author of *Gamesmanship or The Art of Winning Games without Actually Cheating* (1947) and several sequels in which he showed how the principles explained in the first, breakthrough work about games could be applied to the smaller world of life.

Trollope's Rule

Three hours a day will produce as much as a man ought to write.

Trollope rigorously followed his own rule, given in his 1883 *Autobiography*. What separates him from almost all other writers is that he put in three hours at his writing desk every single day. At his height, he turned out 250 words every fifteen minutes with clocklike regularity. The result was an astonishing literary output of well over fifty novels, biographies, travel books, and volumes of short stories – while all the time holding down a job as inspector in Her Majesty's Post Office, hunting three times a week in the season, playing much whist, and generally socialising. In the *Autobiography*, he added: "A small daily task, if it be really daily, will beat the labours of a spasmodic Hercules."

Truman's First Law

The buck stops here.

President Harry S. Truman popularised this admonition as his personal motto. "When the decision is up before you – and on my desk I have a motto which says 'The buck stops here' – the decision has to be made" (speech, National War College (December 19th, 1952.) David McCullough reported in *Truman* (1992) that the sign was given to the president by his longtime friend Fred Canfil. It was a copy of a sign that Canfil had spotted on the desk of the warden at the federal reformatory in El Reno, Oklahoma. The motto derives from poker as played in the west in the nineteenth century, where the buck was a marker to indicate the upcoming dealer. 'To pass the buck' was to ante and hand over the responsibility of dealing to the next player. No one is sure what the original 'buck' was. It might have been a silver dollar, but pencils, knives, and other objects also were used as markers. Many westerners carried knives with handles of buck horn, which may also explain the origin of the term.

Truman's Second Law

If you can't stand the heat, get out of the kitchen.

President Harry S. Truman frequently repeated this saying over the years, orally and in writing. It appears in his book *Mr. Citizen* (1960), for example. According to David McCullough's 1992 biography *Truman*, this is an old Missouri saying that Truman first heard in the 1930s.

Truman's Third Law

Nobody, not even the President of the United States, can approach too close to a skunk in skunk territory, and expect to get anything out of it except a bad smell.

The skunk in this instance was Senator Joseph McCarthy (R., Wisc.), who was seeing Communists under every bed, even in the White House. Truman himself was being guided by a "larger conspiracy, the worldwide web of which has been spun in Moscow." This attack, made in a three-hour senate speech in mid-June 1951, occasioned a meeting of the president and his chief political advisers at which it was suggested that McCarthy could be stopped in his tracks by leaking personally damaging material about him to the press. Truman angrily refused to listen to such talk. John Hersey, who was there, having been granted unprecedented permission to follow the president through several working days in order to prepare a *New Yorker* profile of him, recalled the skunk comment in his *Aspects of the Presidency* (1980). Two other "pungent comments" by Truman at this meeting also stuck in Hersey's mind. Their gist, in Hersey's words, was this:

1. You must not ask the President of the United States to get down in the gutter with a guttersnipe.

2. If you think somebody is telling a big lie about you, the only way to answer is with the whole truth.

Twain's First Law

In order to make a man or boy covet a thing, it is only necessary to make the thing difficult to attain.

Tom Sawyer discovered this "great law of human action, without knowing it" toward the beginning of his *Adventures* (1876), while allowing – with a great show of reluctance – the other boys in town to whitewash Aunt Polly's fence for him. Mark Twain went on to note that if Tom "had been a great and wise philosopher, like the writer of this book," he also would have comprehended a second important law, i.e. "that Work consists of whatever a body is obliged to do, and that Play consists of whatever a body is not obliged to do."

The law of Work and Play is by no means limited to the doings of youngsters, as Twain proceeded to illustrate with the example of "wealthy gentlemen in England who drive four-horse passenger-coaches twenty or thirty miles on a daily line, in the summer, because the privilege costs them considerable money; but if they were offered wages for the same service, that would turn it into work and then they would resign."

Twain's Second Law

To promise not to do a thing is the surest way in the world to make a body want to go and do that very thing.

The Second Law is practically a mirror image of the First. Tom Sawyer discovered the second law after joining the Cadets of Temperance and promising to abstain from smoking, chewing tobacco, and using profanity as long as he remained a member. Soon he found himself tormented with the desire to drink and swear. Not until after he resigned did he discover the law's corollary: "Tom was a free boy again – He could drink and swear, now – but found to his surprise that he did not want to. The simple fact that he could took the desire away, and the charm of it."

Twain's Rules for Pleasing Authors

There are three infallible ways of pleasing an author and the three form a rising scale of compliment; 1, to tell him that you have read one of his books; 2, to tell him that you have read all of his books; 3, to ask him to let you read the manuscript of his forthcoming book. No. 1 admits you to his respect; No. 2 admits you to his admiration; No. 3 carries you clear into his heart (Mark Twain, *Pudd'nhead Wilson*, 1894).

Tyler's Washington Multiplier Effect

The flunky always wears the big man's shoes. If he's a White House flunky he rules by right of the President of the United States.

The Multiplier Effect was first described as such by W. T. Tyler in a novel, *The Shadow Cabinet* (1984). W. T. Tyler is the pseudonym of Samuel J. Hamrick, who spent twenty years as an officer in the Foreign Service before making use of his bureaucratic expertise in a literary way.

U

Udall's Law

If you can find something everyone agrees on, it's wrong (Representative Morris K. Udall, D., Ariz., *New York Times*, April 4th, 1975).

See also **Russell's Conclusion** and **Valéry's Law**.

Ulmann's Razor

When stupidity is a sufficient explanation, there is no need to have recourse to any other (Mitchell Ulmann, quoted by Alan L. Otten, in the *Wall Street Journal*, February 26th, 1976).

A variant of this, known as Hanlon's Razor, is "Never attribute to malice that which is adequately explained by stupidity" (internet collection of laws, January 8th, 1996).

Schiller's Amendment. With stupidity the gods themselves struggle in vain (Friedrich von Schiller, *Die Jungfrau von Orleans*, i.e. Joan of Arc, 1801).

See also **Ockham's Razor** and **Staples's First Law of the Universe**.

Urquhart's Rule of Diplomacy

Don't dive into an empty pool.

This rule for conducting diplomatic negotiations, which applies in business and other fields (besides backyards), was credited to United Nations peacekeeper Sir Brian Urquhart by another U.N. official, Alvaro de Soto, in the *New York Times Magazine* (September 10th, 1989). Speaking in Washington, D.C., in 1983, Sir Brian included this rule in a list of 'don'ts for workers for peace.' Said Sir Brian: "Don't dive into an empty pool. This may create a temporary sensation, but it will leave you stunned and incapable of further action. It is equally inadvisable to dive into a pool of boiling water."

Within the office of the U. N. Secretary General, this became the rule to follow in determining if and when to intervene in international disputes, said Mr. de Soto, then serving as executive assistant to Secretary General Javier Pérez de Cuéllar. The 'empty pool category' became in turn, he said, "shorthand for cases in which it would not be advisable, or might be counterproductive, to attempt to assist in resolving a given dispute or conflict."

Updike's Observation

One out of three hundred and twelve Americans is a bore, for instance, and a healthy male adult bore consumes each year one and a half times his own weight in other people's patience (John Updike, 'Confessions of a Wild Bore', in *Assorted Prose*, 1965).

Upton's Implacable Principle

Stop Look Listen. (Ralph R. Upton, notice devised for American railroad crossings, 1912).

Ustinov's Ukase

Those who rise to executive positions lack the qualifications for anything lower (Sir Peter Ustinov, quoted by Dick Cavett, *New York Times*, August 10th, 1990).

See also **The Peter Principle**.

V

Valéry's Law

That which has always been accepted by everyone, everywhere, is almost certain to be false (Paul Valéry, *Tel Quel*, 1943). See also **Russell's Conclusion** and **Udall's Law**.

The French poet, essayist, and cultural affairs official (for the French Academy, the League of Nations, and various universities) also deserves much credit for his elucidation of the essence of female intelligence: "An intelligent woman is a woman with whom one can be as stupid as one wants" (*Mauvais Pensées et Aurtres*, 1941).

Vanbrugh's First Law

Once a woman has given you her heart you can never get rid of the rest of her.

Sir John Vanbrugh was an architect, the designer of Blenheim Palace among other structures, as well as a playwright. This line is from *The Relapse* (1697).

Vanbrugh's Second Law

He laughs best who laughs last.

An immortal line, proverbial now if it wasn't then, from Sir John's *The Country House* (1706).

Bocklage's Amendment. He who laughs last – probably didn't get the joke (an otherwise unidentified Bocklage, in Arthur Bloch, *The Complete Murphy's Law*, 1991).

Van der Post's Observation

Human beings are perhaps never more frightening than when they are convinced beyond doubt that they are right (Laurens van der Post, *Lost World of the Kalahari*, 1958).

See also **Torquemada's Law.**

Veblen's Law

Conspicuous consumption of valuable goods is a means of respectability to the gentleman of leisure (Thorstein Veblen, *The Theory of the Leisure Class*, 1899).

See also **Galbraith's First Law.**

Vegetius's Maxim

He therefore, who desires peace, should prepare for war.

This is the most frequently quoted of the maxims in the third book of *De Rei Militari* by the fourth-century writer Flavius Vegetius Renatus, about whom nothing is known except that he left this book behind him. Other typical maxims include "No man is to be employed in the field who is not trained and tested in discipline" and "All that is advantageous to the enemy is disadvantageous to you, and all that is useful to you damages the enemy."

De Rei Militari was translated widely (into English by Caxton in 1489) and served as a handbook for the commanders of many armies up into the eighteenth century. George Washington was familiar with his work and paraphrased this maxim, telling Congress in his first annual address to that body, "To be prepared for war is one of the most effectual means of preserving peace" (January 8th, 1790).

See also **Thucydides's Law of Peace and War.**

Vertosick's Rules for Neurosurgeons

1. You ain't never the same when the air hits your brain.

2. The only minor operation is one that someone else is doing.

3. If the patient isn't dead, you can always make him worse if you try hard enough.

4. One look at the patient is better than a thousand phone calls from the nurse.

5. Operating on the wrong patient or doing the wrong side of the body makes for a very bad day.

(Frank T. Vertosick, Jr., *When the Air Hits Your Brain: Tales of Neurosurgery*, 1996).

Vidal's Law

It is not enough to succeed. Others must fail (Gore Vidal, in G. Irvine, *Antipanegyris for Tom Driberg*, December 8th, 1976). See also **Bierce's Law** and **La Rochefoucauld's Rule**.

Virgil's Law

Fear Greeks even when they bring gifts.

Virgil – Publius Vergilius Maro – spent the last ten or twelve years of his life working on the *Aeneid*, from which this line comes. It refers, of course, to the wooden horse that the Greeks left before the gates of Troy, and which the Trojans took inside their walls, not knowing that Greek soldiers were hidden inside. Virgil never completed the *Aeneid* and apparently didn't think it was ready to be read by other people since he asked his friends and literary executors, Varius and Tucca, to burn the manuscript after his death. The emperor Augustus countermanded the poet's wish. The executors did some minor editing and published the work, which was recognised immediately as the great Roman epic.

Voltaire's Law

It is better to risk saving a guilty person than to condemn an innocent one (François Marie Arouet, a. k. a., Voltaire, *Zadig ou la Destinée*, 1747).

An unwritten law that is being honoured increasingly in the breach, even by the Supreme Court of the United States in its eagerness to limit appeals by people who have been condemned to death.

W

Walpole's Law

Every man has his price.

The observation was made initially by Sir Robert Walpole, while surveying the distinguished members of the House of Commons in 1734: "I know the price of every man in this House." He later included the remark in his *Memoirs* in a slightly different form: "All those men have their price."

A corollary to Walpole's Law, attributed to Simon Cameron, Lincoln's first secretary of war, is: "An honest politician is one who, when he is bought, will stay bought." Or as Jesse M. Unruh, who wielded national influence as speaker of the California Assembly in the 1960s observed: "Money is the mother's milk of politics."

See also **Cameron's Rule of Etiquette.**

Walton's First Law

That which is everybody's business is nobody's business.

Izaak Walton credited this observation to "a wise friend of mine" in *The Compleat Angler* (1653-55). Since he did not give the friend's name, he himself gets credit for it here. Most likely, the unnamed friend probably picked it up from someone else. The saying has been dated in writing to 1611.

Walton's Second Law

No man can lose what he never had.

Walton was referring here to a trout. "Oh me! he has broke all! there's half a line and a good hook lost," exclaims Piscator, the fisherman. "Ay, and a good trout, too," chimes in Venator, the hunter who is learning how to be an angler. "Nay, the trout is not lost," replies Piscator, "for pray take notice, no man can lose what he never had."

Walton's Second Law extends far beyond the science of angling – which is worth remembering when charges are made that somebody is responsible for losing, say, China.

Warhol's Law

In the future, everyone will be famous for fifteen minutes.

Of all the wit and wisdom that emanated from Andy Warhol (*née* Warhola), this is the line that is likely to last the longest. It was included in *Andy Warhol's Exposures*, the catalogue for an exhibition of his photographs in Stockholm, Sweden, in 1968.

Warshawski's Rule

Rule number something or other – never tell anybody anything unless you're going to get something better in return (V. I. Warshawski, private detective, in Sara Paretsky, *Deadlock*, 1984).

Washington's Maxim

I hold the maxim no less applicable to public than to private affairs that honesty is the best policy.

Optimists have held that 'honesty is the best policy' since at least the early 1600s. For example, Cervantes employed the phrase in *Don Quixote* (1605-15). George Washington recommended the maxim as a public policy in his *Farewell Address* (September 17th, 1796). He cited it in connection with his advice that the new nation "steer clear of permanent alliances, with any portion of the foreign world." Existing engagements with other nations should be observed, he said – that was the honest thing to do – but he thought it unnecessary and unwise to extend them.

Watson's Law

If you can't lick 'em, jine 'em

This was described as one of the 'favourite sayings' of James E. Watson in an article by Frank R. Kent about the Indiana Republican, who served as Senate majority leader during Hoover's administration (*Atlantic Monthly*, February 1932). The line has an old-time western ring to it and perhaps dates to when Indiana was in the west, not the midwest. Variants include "If you can't beat 'em, join 'em" and "If you can't whip 'em, join 'em." (The latter appears in Niven Busch's 1944 novel *Duel in the Sun*, remembered today mainly as the basis of the 1946 film with the same title.)

Watts's Law

Idle hands make mischief.

This is the common rendering of two lines from a poem by Issac Watts: "For Satan finds some mischief still / For idle hands to do" ('Against Idleness and Mischief' in *Divine Songs for Children*, 1720). This same poem also includes "How doth the little busy bee / Improve each shining hour," lines that are famous in their own right as well as through Lewis Carroll's parody, "How doth the little crocodile / Improve each shining hour." Watts is best known, however, as the writer of such famous hymns, still sung regularly, as 'Oh God,

Our Help in Ages Past' and 'Joy to the world! the Lord is Come.'

West's Corollary to Watts's Law. Give a man a free hand and he'll try to put it all over you (Mae West, **Klondike Annie**, 1936).

Webster's Axiom

'Tis better to be fortunate than wise.

The axiom is from John Webster's play, *The White Devil* (1612). In context:

> *Let all that do ill, take this precedent:*
> *Man may his fate foresee, but not prevent.*
> *And of all axioms this shall win the prize:*
> *'Tis better to be fortunate than wise.*

Webster may be right, but other thinkers have suggested strongly that luck can be improved by wisdom and elbow grease; see **Rickey's Law.**

Parson Weems's Law

Historical fancy is more persistent than historical fact.

The editors of *American Heritage* cited this law (April, 1971) as part of an abject apology for passing along an old but colourful error about a Supreme Court justice in the *American Heritage History of the 20's and 30's.* Describing President Franklin Roosevelt's effort to "pack" the Court with additional members that would be more friendly to New Deal programs, it was stated that Justice Pierce Butler "had failed in constitutional law at college." Pierce Butler's daughter saw red when she saw this in print, and sent the editors a transcript of her father's grades at Carleton College. It showed that in 1887-88, his senior year, he had received a 7.6 (on a scale of 10) in constitutional law – clearly a passing mark. The *American Heritage* editors took only small consolation from knowing that the old allegation had also been repeated in a recent, scholarly book on justices of the Court . . . which their fact checker had had the misfortune to consult.

Parson Weems's Law honours Mason Locke Weems, who was a book salesman, a deacon, and a preacher, but not actually a parson, and who, more to the point, also purveyed the myth of George Washington and the cherry tree, along with many other fanciful stories, in his immensely popular 'biographies' of Washington, Franklin, William Penn, and Francis ('the Swamp Fox') Marion.

Weiler's Law

Nothing is impossible for the man who doesn't have to do it himself (movie critic A. H. Weiler, *New York Times*, March 17th, 1968).

(Jack) Weinberg's Credo

Don't trust anybody over thirty.

Often credited by mistake to Jerry Rubin, Abbie Hoffman, or one of the other well known radicals of the 1960s, the slogan seems to have been articulated first in November of 1964 by Weinberg, then a student at the University of California at Berkeley, in an interview with a reporter from the *San Francisco Chronicle*. The reporter had come across the Bay to do a story on the free speech movement among students on the campus. Thinking that the newsman was trying to get him to say that the students were acting out a Communist-inspired conspiracy, Weinberg jabbed back with, "We have a saying in the movement that we don't trust anybody over thirty." A quarter of a century later, he told Ralph Keyes, author of *They Never Said It* (1992), that he believed the words were original to him. He had described them as a 'movement saying' merely to give them more zing.

Other high authorities have disagreed on the significance of reaching age thirty. Thus, we have:

Emerson's Corollary. After thirty a man wakes up sad every morning, except perhaps five or six, until the day of his death (*Journal*, 1834).

Catherine's Consolation. Men make love more intensely at twenty, but make love better, however, at thirty (Catherine the Great, letter to Voltaire, in *The Complete Works of Catherine II*, Evdokimov, ed.).

For more on the difficult subject of aging, see **Clarke's Laws**, the last of **Shaw's Maxims**, and **Temple's Law**.

Weinberg's Laws

1. Progress is made on alternate Fridays.
2. If builders built buildings the way programmers wrote programs, then the first woodpecker that came along would destroy civilization.

   (internet collection of laws, January 1st, 1996, with no further identification of Weinberg).

Wellington's Rule

My rule always was to do the business of the day in the day (Arthur Wellesley, Duke of Wellington, November 2nd, 1835, in Philip Henry, Earl of Stanhope, *Notes of Conversations with the Duke of Wellington*, 1888).

Wells's First Law

In the Country of the Blind the One-Eyed Man is King (H. G. Wells, 'The Country of the Blind', 1904).

Wells's Second Law

Adapt or perish, now as ever, is Nature's inexorable imperative (H. G. Wells, *Mind at the End of Its Tether*, 1946).

See also **Charles Darwin's Law.**

Wells's Virtual Law

The uglier a man's legs are, the better he plays golf. It's almost a law (H. G. Wells, *Bealby*, 1915).

The law is best appreciated in the home of golf, Scotland.

Wesley's Law

Cleanliness is next to godliness.

The prescription is from a sermon, 'On Dress', by one of the founders of Methodism, John Wesley. In full, the passage reads: "Let it be observed, that slovenliness is no part of religion; that neither this nor any text of Scripture condemns neatness of apparel. Certainly this is a duty, not a sin. 'Cleanliness is, indeed, next to godliness.'" Wesley put the phrase in quotes because, as noted in Bartlett's *Familiar Quotations*, he was paraphrasing closely a thought from the Talmud:

> The doctrines of religion are resolved into carefulness; carefulness into vigorousness; vigorousness into guiltlessness; guiltlessness into abstemiousness; abstemiousness into cleanliness; cleanliness into godliness.

Twain's Amendment. Soap and education are not as sudden as a massacre, but they are more deadly in the long run (Mark Twain, *The Facts Concerning the Recent Resignation*, 1867).

Wharton's Law

If you were forced to read the book in high school, you'll probably hate the movie, too.

This is one of a number of film-land laws collected by critic Roger Ebert in *Ebert's Little Movie Glossary* (1994). Some are Ebert originals, others were supplied to him by fellow critic Gene Siskel and by correspondents from the field. (Wharton's Law came from Andy Ihnatko, of Westwood, Massachusetts) The book's subtitle tells the tale: *A Compendium of Movie Clichés, Stereotypes, Obligatory Scenes, Hackneyed Formulations, Shopworn Conventions and Outdated Archetypes*. Other examples:

Bad-Smoker Rule. In any cop movie made since the mid-70s the bad guys smoke while the good guy is trying to quit.

Divine Dog Syndrome. In movies, humans are violently killed with impunity, but dogs are never killed. Thus, an alien race studying films would conclude that dogs are gods (Paul Cassel).

Law of Movie Brand Loyalty. Thanks to product placement, all characters in a movie, no matter how heterogeneous or geographically dispersed, drink one brand of beer, use one brand of sporting equipment, drive cars produced by one company, etc. (Paul A. Lee, Germantown, Wisconsin).

Myopia Rule. Little girls who wear glasses in movies always tell the truth. Little boys who wear glasses in movies always lie (Gene Siskel).

White's First Rule

If a man is in health, he doesn't need to take anyone else's temperature to know where he is going.

E. B. White proposed this rule in a letter to the editor of the *New York Herald Tribune* (November 29th, 1947). Gripped with Cold War fervour, the *Tribune* had suggested in a Thanksgiving Day editorial that employees be required to state their beliefs as a condition for holding their jobs. Reminding the *Trib* editors of first principles, White wrote: "The idea is inconsistent with our constitutional theory and has been stubbornly opposed by watchful men since the first days of the Republic . . . Security, for me, took a tumble not when I read that there were Communists in Hollywood but when I read your editorial in praise of loyalty testing and thought control. If a man is in health, etc."

White's Second Rule

Never hurry and never worry!

This is Charlotte's advice to Wilbur in E. B. White's *Charlotte's Web* (1952). Certified philosophers have reached much the same conclusion, e.g.:

Russell's Rider. To realise the unimportance of time is the gate of wisdom (Bertrand Russell, title essay, *Mysticism and Logic*, 1918).

See also **Young's Law.**

White's Rule for Rating Poets

All poets who, when reading from their own works, experience a choked feeling, are major. For that matter, all poets who read from their own works are major, whether they choke or not. All women poets, dead or alive, who smoke cigars are major . . . All poets named Edna St. Vincent Millay are major . . . a poet who, in a roomful of people, is noticeably keeping at a little distance and seeing into things is a major poet.

White admitted that there were many other ways of distinguishing among poets. These seemed to him to be the principal ones, however. "The truth is," he continued, "it is fairly easy to tell the two types apart; it is only when one sets about trying to decide whether what they write is any good or not that the thing really becomes complicated" ('How to Tell a Major Poet from a Minor One,' in *Quo Vadimus, or The Case for the Bicycle*, 1938).

Whitehead's Observation

If a dog jumps into your lap, it is because he is fond of you; if a cat does the same thing, it is because your lap is warmer.

A philosophical observation from a great philosopher and mathematician, Alfred North Whitehead (in *Dialogues of Alfred North Whitehead*, 1953).

Whitton's Law

Whatever women do, they must do it twice as well as men to be thought half as good.

Whitton's Corollary. Luckily, this is not difficult.

Charlotte Whitton was mayor of Ottawa at the time that she dispensed this law and its corollary (*Canada Month*, June 1963).

Much the same thought also was expressed by the American novelist and playwright Fannie Hurst: "A woman has to be twice as good as a man to go half as far" (in Laurence F. Peter, *The Peter Prescription*, 1972).

Wilcox's Law

Laugh, and the world laughs with you; / Weep, and you weep alone.

The opening of *Solitude*, by far the most famous lines of Ella Wheeler Wilcox, whose sentimental novels and poems enjoyed great popularity in the closing decades of the nineteenth century and the opening ones of the twentieth (in *Collected Poems*, 1917).

Wilde's First Law

In this world there are two tragedies. One is not getting what one wants, and the other is getting it (Oscar Wilde, *Lady Windermere's Fan*, 1892).

Corollary. When the gods wish to punish us they answer our prayers (*An Ideal Husband*, 1895).

See also the last of **Aesop's Adages, Connolly's Observation, Kristol's Law, Midas's Law,** and **Shaw's Quandary.**

Wilde's Other Laws

The great Oscar was a master of the epigram – and at lifting bon mots from others, as evidenced by his exchange with James McNeil Whistler, reported in L. C. Ingleby's *Oscar Wilde* (1907):

> *Wilde:* I wish I'd said that.
> *Whistler:* You will, Oscar, you will.

More wisdom from Wilde:

> A little sincerity is a dangerous thing and a great deal of it is absolutely fatal (*The Critic as Artist*, 1891).

> There is only one thing in the world worse than being talked about, and that is not being talked about (*The Picture of Dorian Gray*, 1891).

> A man cannot be too careful in his choice of enemies (Ibid.).

> The only way to get rid of a temptation is to yield to it (Ibid.).

If one tells the truth, one is sure, sooner or later, to be found out (*Phrases and Philosophies for the Use of the Young*, 1894).

All women become like their mothers. That is their tragedy. No man does. That's his (Ibid.).

In matters of great importance, style, not sincerity, is the vital thing (Ibid.).

See also **Gilbert's Law of Appearances.**

Wilder's Law

Hindsight is always twenty-twenty (director and scriptwriter Billy Wilder, in J. R. Columbo, *Wit and Wisdom of the Moviemakers*, 1979).

Williams's Law

There is more law in the end of a policeman's nightstick than in a decision of the Supreme Court.

This was the law as it was enforced from the 1860s through the 1880s by one of New York City's most famous policemen, Inspector Alexander S. 'Clubber' Williams. He started out as a patrolman on the beat, so to speak, in Hell's Kitchen on the westside, then became a captain of the eastside Gas House district, where he and his men cowed the local toughs by clubbing them regularly, often with little or no pretext. When some bleeding hearts complained about his strongarm methods shortly after he took over the eastside precinct in 1871, Williams invited reporters and concerned citizens to a demonstration of the extent to which street crime had been reduced. Leaving his watch and chain on a lamp post one night at Third Ave. and 35th St., he sauntered around the block. Returning to the lamp post, his valuables remained untouched.

Williams next was assigned to Manhattan's midtown district, which thereupon gained a new nickname when he announced to a friend, just before assuming his new command, "I've had nothing but chuck steak for a long time and now I'm going to get a little of the tenderloin." And he got more than a little, extorting enough money from gamblers and procurers to acquire a townhouse and other city property, a country estate in Connecticut, a yacht, and several large bank accounts. He told an investigating committee in 1894 that his wealth came from speculating in building lots in Japan. A year later he had the grace to retire and went into the insurance business, where he made even more money.

Wilson's Law

Never murder a man who is committing suicide.

Discussing strategy for his campaign for re-election in 1916, Woodrow Wilson said in a letter to Bernard Baruch: "I am inclined to follow the course suggested by a friend, who says that he has always followed the rule never to murder a man who is committing suicide." Wilson's Republican opponent was Charles Evans Hughes and the race, despite Wilson's clever hands-off approach, was quite close, the president winning by less than 600,000 votes out of almost 18 million cast. The victor wasn't known until three days after the polls closed.

Kelly's Amendment. Among professionals in politics, the reaction to a misfortune that befalls one's opponent is governed by a law of inverse proportions: the more minor the misfortune – a debate gaffe, or a revelation of some bit of hideous behaviour on the part of a campaign co-chairman, the louder one trumpets; the graver the wound, the quieter and more reticent the response (Michael Kelly, in the *New Yorker*, June 10th, 1996).

Dewey's Proviso. When you're leading, don't talk (Thomas E.

Dewey, characterising his 1948 presidential campaign strategy, in Richard Norton Smith, *Thomas E. Dewey*, 1982). The trouble here was that Dewey, his advisers, and the major pollsters of the day all misread public opinion. While he declined to do much talking, President Harry S. Truman went on a whistlestop tour around the country, talking to everybody in sight. Dewey's lead, whatever it had been, vanished, and Truman won the election.

Duke of Windsor's Rules

Never miss an opportunity to relieve yourself; never miss a chance to rest your feet (quoted in Jon Winokur, *Friendly Advice*, 1990).

The Duke helped popularise the rules but did not devise them. Characterising them as "perhaps . . . the only positive pieces of advice that I was ever given", he said that he had learned these rules from "an old courtier."

The first of the rules recalls the reply that the Duke of Wellington is said to have made when asked if he could supply some motto that had served him in all his campaigns. "Certainly, sir", said the Duke, drawing on a British euphemism of nautical origin, "never lose an opportunity to pump ship."

Wittgenstein's Law

Of that which nothing is known, nothing can be said. Corollary. *The limits of my language mean the limits of my world.*

The law and its corollary are from Ludwig Wittgenstein's *Tractatus Logico-Philosophicus*. The law has wide ramifications, and serves especially as a caution against constructing theories (including conspiracy theories) in the absence of evidence. See also **Papagiannis's Law**.

Wolfe's Law

You Can't Go Home Again (Thomas Wolfe, book title, 1940).

You can't go home again because you've changed – and it's changed. See **Heraclitus's Law**.

Woollcott's Law

Anything good is either immoral, illegal, or fattening.

Labeled Pardo's Postulate in some collections of laws (e.g. Paul Dickson's *The Official Rules*, 1978, and John Peers's *1,001 Logical Laws . . .* , 1979), this law stems from a lament by the rotund critic Alexander Woollcott, "All the things I really like to do are either immoral, illegal, or fattening" (in Howard Teichman, *George S. Kaufman*, 1972). Other postulates attributed to the otherwise unknown Pardo include "The three faithful things in life are money, a dog, and an old woman," and "Don't care if you're rich or not, as long as you can live comfortably and have everything you want."

Closely related to Woollcott's Law is: **The Dieter's Dilemma.** The food that tastes the best has the most calories. See also **Feuerbach's Law of Consumption**.

Wycherley's Law

Necessity, mother of invention.

This was a Latin proverb (*Mater artium necessitas*) before William Wycherly worked it into his first comedy, *Love in a Wood, or St. James's Park* (1671). See also **St. Augustine's Law to End All Laws**.

X

Xenophanes's Law

It takes a wise man to recognise a wise man.

This snippet from the writings of Xenophanes, a Greek poet and philosopher of the sixth century B.C., was included in the *Lives of Eminent Philosophers*, composed by Diogenes Laertius in the third century A.D. Not much is known about Xenophanes (only about forty fragments from his poems have been preserved) except that, unlike most Greeks of his time, he believed in one god instead of many. Another fragment reveals his own cast of mind: "If cattle and horses, or lions, had hands, or were able to draw with their feet and produce the works which men do, horses would draw the forms of gods like horses, and cattle like cattle, and they would make the gods' bodies the same shape as their own."

Y

(John) Yardley's Law

Pretty is what works.

Astronaut Michael Collins thought the Mercury space capsule "looked more like a trash basket," compared to the sleek supersonic fighters that he had flown as a test pilot. The planes were "beautiful, exquisite aluminum sculptures that – even parked – looked like they were going 1,000 mph." But as John Yardley, the McDonnell Aircraft Co. engineer in charge of building the Mercury, pointed out, "Pretty is what works" (in Michael Collins, *Liftoff: The Story of America's Adventure in Space*, 1989).

See also **Sullivan's Law**.

(Jonathan) Yardley's Restaurant Law

No matter how many good tables are free, you will always be given the worst available (*Washington Post* book critic Jonathan Yardley, quoted in *A Writer's Companion*, Louis D. Rubin, Jr., with Jerry Leath Mills, 1995).

Much book-publishing business is conducted over lunch – an occupational hazard for reviewers as well as editors, authors, and agents.

See also **Cohen's Rules of Book Publishing** and **Creasey's Law**.

Young's Law

Procrastination is the thief of time.

Edward Young, poet and playwright, had an inkling whereof he spoke, having frittered away a considerable amount of time in his youth. He was in his mid-forties before he took holy orders and pushing fifty before he got married. This line, from his most famous work, *Night Thoughts* (1742-45), expresses the conventional view, strongly seconded by Lord Chesterfield in one of his many letters to his son: "No idleness, no laziness, no procrastination; never put off till tomorrow what you can do today" (December 26th, 1749). Unconventional types may prefer the advice of the nineteenth-century versifier, William Brighty Rands (pen name of Matthew Browne): "Never do today what you can / Put off till tomorrow" ('Lilliput Levee').

See also **Jefferson's Ukase** and **White's Second Rule**.

Z

Zahner's Law

If you play with anything long enough, it will break.

Louis Zahner, a student of historian Frederick Lewis Allen, had this insight (sometimes called Mom's Law) during a law-making session with his teacher. But both were outshone by the professor's wife; see **Agnes Allen's Law**. J. F. McCleary, of San Diego, California, cast Zahner's Law (perhaps unknowingly) in a slightly different form in a communication to *Harper's* magazine: "If you don't quit tampering with it, you're going to bust something" (August, 1974).

Wyszkowski's Dissent. Anything can be made to work if you fiddle with it long enough (in Arthur Block, *The Complete Murphy's Law*, 1991).

See also **Lance's Law.**

Zeno's Law

The goal of life is living in agreement with nature.

Not to be confused with Zeno of Elea, producer of paradoxes, who lived about a century and a half earlier, this Zeno, who hailed from Citium in Cyprus, established the Stoic school of philosophy in about 300 B.C. The name of the school comes from the building in Athens where he taught, *Stoa Poikile*, the Painted Porch. This observation was included in Diogenes Laertius's summary of Zeno's life and work in *Lives of*

Eminent Philosophers (third century A.D.). It goes to the heart of the Stoic philosophy, which holds that the virtuous man must live in harmony with nature's laws. In doing so, he will become wise and happy, free of desires for money, power, or fame, while accepting of pain, grief, and misfortune as part of nature.

Zimmerman's Law of Complaints

Nobody notices when things go right (internet collection of laws, January 8th, 1996).

Acknowledgements

This is by no means the first collection of wise sayings to be assembled, and I am indebted to previous collectors. Their works are cited in the text, along with other sources. Even when not drawn upon directly, however, other compilations often were helpful in guiding my research. Books of particular use includes *The Complete Murphy's Law* (Arthur Bloch, Price Stern Sloan, 1990) *The Official Rules* (Paul Dickson, Delacorte Press, 1978), *The Book of Laws* (Harold Faber, Times Books, 1979), *The Cynic's Lexicon* (Jonathon Green, Routledge & Kegan Paul, 1984), *Malice in Blunderland* (Thomas L. Martin Jr., McGraw-Hill, 1973), *1,001 Logical Laws, Accurate Axioms, Profound Principles, Quotable Quotes, and Rambunctious Ruminations for All Walks of Life* (John Peers, Ballantine Books, 1979), *The Peter Prescription*, Dr. Laurence J. Peter, William Morrow & Company, 1972) and *Friendly Advice* (Jon Winokur, Dutton, 1991).

Many individuals also helped in my research and supplied editorial support. I am particularly indebted to my literary agent, Jane Jordan Browner; to Brandt Aymar and Shelly Perron, my editor and copyeditor; to my sister, Joanna Hammond, and my friends, Barbara Livesey and Maureen Kim Sing, each of whom supplied laws; and to Margaret Miner, my severest – and best – critic, as well as my wife.

Index

A

abilities, from each according to his a., 174

absence, common cure for love, 25
a. makes the heart grow fonder, 25
a. of evidence, 208

absinthe makes tart grow fonder, 25

accepted, [what] always a. almost certain to be false, 294

accessibility of small parts, 197

accident, do something once [and] people call it an a., 137

accidents in best regulated families, 182

action, suit a. to word, 228
to every a. an equal reaction, 197

actions lie louder than words, 228
a. speak louder than words, 228
know what person thinks by a., 228

active, never use passive where active, 204

activity, any new a. will cause trouble, 40

adapt or perish, 304

administrators, we mostly end as a., 212

advance [against royalties] for book, 75
all must retrograde if does not a., 115

advertising, can fool people if a. right, 163
first law in a., 75

agree, if two men a. all of time, 253
no two people [in publishing] will a., 66

if everyone a., 292

aim, men only hit what a. at, 281
those who a. low hit target, 281

aircraft, meal aboard a., 121

all's well that ends well, 256

alone, man who goes a., 282

alternate, pursue a. objectives, 161

alternatives, absence of a. clears mind, 153
nations behave wisely once exhausted all a., 94
two a., one intelligent, one stupid, 243

anniversary, good idea to remember a., 106

answer, not every question deserves a., 227
a. not separate from problem, 218
if know a., don't know question, 199

answers, know all a., 283

ant, not a sluggard, 5

anticipate, what we a., 87

appearances, satisfied with a., 116

appears, what a. to be happening, 257

apple, fairest a. on highest bough, 237

approval, [to] meet everybody's a., 60

argument in simple sentence, 178

attack, do not renew a. in same manner, 161

auction for a book, 66

avoid, a. fried meats, 207
a. running, 207

away, anybody who gets a. with something, 252

B

bad, ain't as b. as you think, 224
   b. money drive out good, 118
   b. news drives good news out, 118
   b. words drive out good, 30
   things go from b. to worse, 193
ball, smaller the b., better the book 222
bar, less teeth the better the b., 128
barrenness is incurable, 230
beauty in eye of beholder, 140
bed, early to b., 108
bedfellows, strange b., 257
beggars must be no choosers, 26
behave as would wish friends to b., 68
believe, mean readily b. what want to b., 51
   never b. what client says, 85
   what we desire we readily b., 51
best-laid schemes o'mice & men, 44
bet, do not b., 245
   never b. more than have, 106
   never b. with 'One-Iron', 9
bigger they come, 105
bird in hand, 36
bitch, Mother Nature a b., 193
blame, how you place b., 235
   someone he can b., 152
blind, in country of b., 303
blockhead, member of crowd a b., 252
bluff, if going to b., 259
body in state of rest or uniform motion, 259
bonds, [traders] buy bonds because, 26
book, ask [author] to read manuscript of b., 290
   dispose of b. & need to refer to it, 231

never loan b., 231
   if forced to read b., 305
   some men have only one b. in them, 260
books, collections of b., 231
   b. over five hundred pages, 37
   some b. to be tasted, 21
   tell [author] have read one of his b., 290
   tell [author] have read all of his b., 290
bookshelf space never enough, 231
bore, one out of three hundred & twelve Americans a b., 293
box office, 250
bottle, keep cap on b., 124
brain, when ait hits b., 296
brave from safe distance, 10
bread, buttered b. on carpet, 216
   which side of b. to butter, 195
break, will b. when need most, 193
   play long enough & will b., 193, 316
brevity soul of wit, 256
broke, if it ain't b., 156
brothels, keep foot out of b., 9
buck stops here, 288
buggers can't be choosers, 26
build it & they will come, 251
bunk, avoid b., 203
bureaucracy, argument within b., 178
   effort by b. defending error, 198
   organisation of b., 141
bureaucrat, no fury like b. scorned, 70
bureaucrats, guidelines for b., 39
bus, don't run for b., 42
business, do b. of day in day, 303
   everybody's b., 298
   nobody should be in b. after fifty, 278

C

drivel, pure d. tends to drive
ordinary d. off TV, 118
drunk, not d. if can lie on floor
without holding on, 174
duck, if walks like a d., 234
dunces in confederacy, 275
duty, do d. nearest thee, 53
moral d. to impose your will,
286
never go into danger unless your
d., 54

E

early to rise, e. to bed, 283
easier, e. to do, harder to change,
10
e. to do many things, 230
e. to get into enemy's toils than
out again, 10
e. to get into than out of, 10
e. to take apart than put back
together, 10
eat, e. fruit, 42
e. to live, not live to e., 61
eating, e. cards & women, 8
e., poker & buying cars, 9
eats, e. first, morals after, 41
man is what he e., 103
economists, if all e. laid end to
end, 257
efficiency, no economy where no
e., 88
ego & your position, 224
elected, get e., 86
electrical current & voltage, 201
end, adjust e. to means, 161
e. cannot justify means, 225
e. crowns work, 257
e. must justify means, 225
invisible hand to promote e.,
266
ends, all's well that e., 256
enemies, e. accumulate, 146

careful in choice of e., 308
enemy of my e. is my friend, 148
all that is advantageous to e.,
295
to make an e., do favour, 178
we have met e. & it is us, 223
worst e. you can have, 148
energy required to change, 114
error, delay preferable to e., 143
bureaucracy defending e., 198
no one will see e., 104
only e. to be exposed, 180
only fool persists in e., 61
errors in writing, 101
events controlled me, 132
everything, e. that goes up, 58
cannot dust e., 71
e. funny as long as happens to
someone else, 238
e. takes longer, 192
e. takes longer except sex, 192
evidence, absence of e. not e. of
absence, 208
circumstantial e. strong, 282
evil, e. action has e. consequences,
197
e. & stupidity randomly
distributed, 269
e. easy & has infinite forms, 213
he who accepts e., 116
he who is bent on doing e., 226
only thing necessary for triumph
of e., 43
evils, between two e., 202
of two e. choose the less, 202
of two e. choose to be least, 202
when a choice of two e., 202
exception, e. disproves the rule, 46
e. proves the rule, 45
e. to rule, 45
excess, not drinking to be blamed
but e., 254
nothing succeeds like e., 91
executive, those who rise to e.

intelligent tinkering, 160

intentions, with best of i., 175
  road to hell paved with good i., 175

interferences, impractical to worry about i., 111

introduced, be i. by someone you've appointed to high office, 65
  never be i. at sporting event, 203

investment, return on i., 86

invisible hand, 266

it, i. ain't getting i. that hurts, 271
  if everybody doesn't want i., 225
  if got i., flaunt i., 42
  i. can be done, 224

I think therefore I am, 85

J

job, if more than one way to do j., 190

jobs, people become less competent for j., 216

joke, to get j. into Scottish understanding, 260

judge, no one should j. own case, 227

justice is truth in action, 88

K

keep, k. it simple stupid, 201
  k. juices flowing, 207

kind, be k., 224

kindness, no act of k. wasted, 168

kitchen, if can't stand heat, get out of k., 288

know, better ignorant than half k., 227
  better k. nothing than half-know many things, 37
  better k. nothing than what ain't so, 37

k. more than think you do, 268
  k. so much that isn't so, 37
  k. where you are going, 34

knowledge, desire of k. increases, 271
  k. is power, 20

known, nothing so firmly believed as what least k., 187
  of that which nothing k., nothing can be said, 311

knows, no one k. what can do, 227
  person who k. 'how', 231

L

lanes, other l. move, 99

language, enemy of clear l., 204
  limits of my l., 311

late, better l. than before invited, 36
  gets l. early, 33
  he that riseth l., 108
  if tell boss you were l., 53
  things you're l. for, 55

later than you think, 254

laugh & world laughs with you, 307

laughs, he l. best who l. last, 294
  he who l. last probably didn't get joke, 294

law, contempt for l., 40
  if l. on your side, 182
  if must break l., 51
  if there isn't a l., 101
  ignorance of l. no excuse, 253
  l. at most rigorous often injustice at worst, 279
  l. in policeman's nightstick, 309
  l. of culture, 53
  l. of majority, 281
  l. universal, 147
  no l. more binding than custom, 54

N

O

inanimate o. divided into three categories, 22

never let inanimate o. know you are in hurry, 252

never let inanimate o. know you are losing temper, 252

observe by watching, 34

occur, all things which can o., 79

offensive, do not throw weight into o., 161

officer, if need o. in hurry, 194

most dangerous thing is o. with map, 194

omelet, can't make o. without breaking eggs, 269

opera ain't over, 33

operation, only minor o. is one someone else is doing, 296

operations set policies, 113

opinion, fact o. widely held no evidence not absurd, 245

optimism, perpetual o. a force multiplier, 224

optimist knows how bad world can be, 203

o. proclaims we live in best of possible worlds, 203

o. thinks this best of possible worlds, 203

order, any o. that can be misunderstood, 194

over, ain't o. until o., 32

overlook, knowing what to o., 96

overlooked, anytime things appear to be going better, have o. something, 60

if everything seems going well, you've o. something, 192

P

paper, volume of p. expands, 213

parking, guy you beat out of prime p. space, 237

part, accessibility of dropped p., 13

pass away, this shall p. a., 284

passes, boys don't make p. at female smartasses, 210

past, more distant the p., better it looks, 105

p. a bucket of ashes, 250

those unable to learn from p. meetings, 250

those who cannot remember p. condemned to repeat it, 249

those who study p. will find other ways to err, 249

unless remember p., can't repeat at box office, 250

patient, if p. isn't dead, can make worse if try hard, 296

one look at p. better than a thousand phone calls, 296

operating on wrong p. makes bad day, 296

patsy, if don't know who p. is, 259

peace, who desires p. should prepare for war, 295

peacock, one day you're a p., 165

penny saved, a p. to squander, 36

people, p. become progressively less competent, 216

about one-fifth of people against everything, 150

p. will do anything, 132

some p. have bad luck all their lives, 236

two classes of p., 15

when p. free to do as please, 134

perform, ability to p. task decreases in proportion to number watching, 103

personal, when someone tells you it's not p., 66

pessimist, optimist thinks this best of worlds & p. knows it is, 203

Q

Y

Other books by Hugh Rawson

Rawson's Dictionary of Euphemisms and Other Doubletalk

Devious Derivations

Wicked Words

The Oxford Dictionary of American Quotations
(with Margaret Miner)

The New International Dictionary of Quotations
(with Margaret Miner)

A Dictionary of Quotations from Shakespeare
(with Margaret Miner)

A Dictionary of Quotations from the Bible
(with Margaret Miner)

An Investment in Knowledge
(with Hiller Krieghbaum)

Life's unwritten laws - online!

If you have enjoyed this book, you may like to visit the accompanying website where you can:

- read more about the historical background to the laws;
- comment on the laws, and add your own refinements;
- discuss the laws with other people;
- submit new laws of your own;
- buy merchandise with your favourite law printed on it.

www.lawsoflife.co.uk